Engaging with Living Religion

Understanding living religion requires students to experience everyday religious practice in diverse environments and communities. This guide provides the ideal introduction to fieldwork and the study of religion outside the lecture theatre. Covering theoretical and practical dimensions of research, the book helps students learn to 'read' religious sites and communities, and to develop their understanding of planning, interaction, observation, participation and interviews. Students are encouraged to explore their own expectations and sensitivities, and to develop a good understanding of ethical issues, group learning and individual research. The chapters contain student testimonies, examples of student work and student-led questions.

Stephen E. Gregg is Senior Lecturer in Religious Studies at the University of Wolverhampton, where he specialises in Contemporary Religion and Method and Theory in the Study of Religion. He is a member of the Executive Committee of the British Association for the Study of Religions, and has conducted research and led student study tours and study visits throughout the UK, Europe, Asia, North America, Australia and the Middle East.

Lynne Scholefield is Senior Research Fellow in Theology and Religious Studies at St Mary's University, Twickenham, where she specialises in Religion in Modern Britain and Interfaith Dialogue. She has conducted research and led study tours and study visits throughout the UK, Europe, Asia, North America and the Middle East.

Engaging with Living Religion
A Guide to Fieldwork in the Study of Religion

Stephen E. Gregg and Lynne Scholefield

Routledge
Taylor & Francis Group

LONDON AND NEW YORK

First published 2015
by Routledge
2 Park Square, Milton Park, Abingdon, Oxon, OX14 4RN

and by Routledge
711 Third Avenue, New York, NY 10017

Routledge is an imprint of the Taylor & Francis Group, an informa business

© 2015 Stephen E. Gregg and Lynne Scholefield

British Library Cataloguing in Publication Data
A catalogue record for this book is available from the British Library

Library of Congress Cataloging in Publication Data
Gregg, Stephen E.
Engaging with living religion : a guide to fieldwork in the study of religion /
Stephen E. Gregg
and Lynne Scholefield. -- 1st ed.
pages cm
Includes bibliographical references and index.
1. Religion--Methodology. 2. Religion--Fieldwork. I. Title.
BL41.G74 2015
200.72'3--dc23
2014039191

ISBN: 978-0-415-53447-5 (hbk)
ISBN: 978-0-415-53448-2 (pbk)
ISBN: 978-1-315-71667-1 (ebk)

Typeset in Sabon
by Taylor & Francis Books

Anyone who is not a complete idiot can do fieldwork, and if the people he is working among have not been studied before he cannot help making an original contribution to knowledge. But will it be to theoretical, or just to factual knowledge? Anyone can produce a new fact; the thing is to produce a new idea.

(E.E. Evans-Pritchard, 1973)

Contents

Acknowledgements

This book is the product of a shared experience with organisations, institutions, scholars, students and religious practitioners. We have been privileged to work with gifted and inspiring friends and colleagues whilst preparing this manuscript.

The idea for a book project came from work undertaken for the UK Higher Education Academy on a grant-funded project co-coordinated by the authors titled *Fieldwork in Religious Studies: Examining Practicalities and Possibilities*. The project brought colleagues from across the UK together to identify, highlight and share 'best practice' in pedagogy with regard to undergraduate student experience of fieldwork – often undergraduates engaging with religious communities through the media of day visits and tutor-led study tours. Earlier revisions of some sections of chapter 7 have previously appeared in the HEA Subject Centre for Philosophical and Religious Studies journal *Discourse* (Gregg and Scholefield, 2011), and we thank the Subject Centre staff for their support prior to the recent restructuring of the HEA. Throughout the project work, a consensus of opinion grew that the commonality of approach between the diverse tutors, programmes and institutions represented in the project was a need to structure and value the learning experience of students when they encountered religion off campus. The project group came up with the phrase 'learning outside the lecture theatre', and we have taken that phrase and extended discussion on it in this work. Particular thanks are due to Denise Cush and Catherine Robinson (Bath Spa University), Dominic Corrywright and Tom Cosgrove (Oxford Brookes University), Greg Barker and Amjad Hussain (Trinity College Carmarthen), Lynn Foulston and Nick Swann (University of Wales, Newport), and Deirdre Burke (University of Wolverhampton).

Thanks are also due to colleagues from the British Association for the Study of Religions (particularly those working on and with the Teaching and Learning Committee) and, in an earlier phase of our work, colleagues from the Shap Working Party on World Religions in Education. In addition, fruitful conversations have been had with Graham Harvey (Open University, UK), George Chryssides (Birmingham University, UK), Elena Procario-Foley (Iona College, New York, USA) and Carole Cusack (Sydney University, Australia).

At our own institutions, present and recent, we would like to thank colleagues for their ongoing conversations regarding curricula, assessments, pedagogy and the place of student fieldwork in evolving departments of Religious Studies/ Theology/Philosophy at a time of great change within the UK Higher Education sector. In particular, we would like to thank Peter McGrail, Andrew Cheatle and Elizabeth Harris at Liverpool Hope University, Opinderjit Kaur Takhar at Wolverhampton University, and Paul Rowan, Peter Tyler and Kathleen O'Gorman at St. Mary's University, Twickenham.

Special thanks must also go to our students, who have observed, studied and *engaged* with religious communities in so many different social, political and geographic contexts. Their individual work has often inspired us, and their group work, usually in our company, continues to energise and invigorate us. We are especially grateful to the students who have taken on leadership roles in many of our international study tours – in particular Mandy Jillings and Steph Modak.

Most importantly, however, we give sincere thanks to the religious individuals and communities with whom we have had the privilege to spend time in over fifty countries. They have welcomed us and challenged us, engaged us and changed us. From Unification Church members in New York, Scientologists in Birmingham, Buddhists in the Punjab, Hindus in Wales, Christians in New Mexico, Pagans in London, Jews in St Petersburg, Muslims in Iran and Sikhs in Southampton, to the multitude of complex and evolving religious identities that sit between and amongst peoples and communities in every place we have visited and every group we have shared experiences with, we are grateful for the opportunity to engage with real lives, real people and lived religion.

Bibliography

Evans-Pritchard, E.E. 1973, 'Some Reminiscences and Reflection on Fieldwork' in *Journal of the Anthropological Society of Oxford*, (4), 1–12. Accessible at: www.anthro.ox.ac.uk/fileadmin/ISCA/JASO/JASO_Archive_pdfs/1973_JASO_04.pdf

Gregg, S.E. and Scholefield, L. 2011, 'The Student Learning Experience in Religious Studies Field Visits and Study Tours: Managing Expectations and Outcomes' in *Discourse*, 10(3).

1 Why study religion off campus?

I am a Hindu because of sculptured cones of red kumkum powder and baskets of yellow turmeric nuggets, because of garlands of flowers and pieces of broken coconut, because of the clanging of bells to announce one's arrival to God, because of the whine of the reedy nadaswaram and the beating of drums, because of the patter of bare feet against stone floors down dark corridors pierced by shafts of sunlight, because of the arati lamps circling in the darkness, because of bhajans being sweetly sung, because of elephants standing around to bless, because of colourful murals telling colourful stories ...

(Yann Martel, *Life of Pi*, 2002, 67)

I think that it is most important to have an understanding of religion through the eyes of its followers – it helps us learn why they follow a particular tradition, and how they live their lives.

(First-year undergraduate Religious Studies student)

Actually hearing the call to prayer in Istanbul, seeing how regular people responded to it as a part of daily routine, and then visiting the Blue Mosque, really brought Islam alive for me.

(Third-year undergraduate Religious Studies student)

Why we are writing this book

Religion isn't lived in textbooks; it is performed, experienced and developed by living individuals and communities. Religions are not static, but evolving, creative and dynamic subjects of study.

Engagement with religious practitioners, communities and institutions saturates our approach to the study of religion. In nearly fifty countries across seven continents, we have had the fortune to talk, walk, eat and share with people from a staggering array of traditions and cultures. Sometimes this has been within formal meetings, guided events or carefully stage-managed receptions by religious communities. More often, it has been accidental, informal or responsive engagement with people expressing the norms and ideals of their everyday existence. The latter is often more enlightening. In our travels, both in a physical sense and in a sense of understanding, we have encountered religion in everyday life, in the open and in secret, in public discourse and private practice, in serenity and in dark and dangerous places (sometimes with very real physical danger), in clearly identifiable communities and in the spaces between and within interrelated identities. We have also encountered religion and religious practice when we were not expecting it.

In so doing, we have encountered forms of religion which often defy textbook description, or which do not easily fit into the neat categories that scholars often use to describe seemingly essential aspects of religions and religious identities. This means that much of the discussion in this book questions boundaries between religions and within religious communities. We will still refer to commonly used names for major religious traditions, as these are so embedded within modern university courses on religion, but every time we use these terms, you should think of them as plurals – no such thing as Christianity exists (is it really meaningful to use a singular noun to describe people and communities as diverse as Robert Mugabe and Desmond Tutu, Unitarians and Flagellants?) but it is perfectly sensible, in our opinion, to talk of Christianities, likewise it is better to think of Hinduisms instead of Hinduism and so on. As Harvey has stated:

> when we say what Christians or Buddhists, or practitioners of Chinese, Japanese, or Korean religions do, we are not saying this is all they do, or that all such people do all these things ... [we should therefore ask] ... whether what we talk about as happening in the United States, South Africa or Korea bears any resemblance to what happens in India, Britain or Saudi Arabia.
>
> (2009, 5)

So, there is always historical and geographical diversity within religions; they change over time and they are different in different places. For example, there are three major divisions of Christianity: Eastern Orthodox, Roman Catholic and Protestant. In fact, there are plenty of churches which don't fit neatly into this categorisation such as the Anglican Church or the Coptic Church based in Egypt. Judaism changed dramatically when the Temple in Jerusalem was destroyed. London, for example, has the most culturally diverse group of Muslims anywhere in the world, and their languages, traditions and ways of understanding Islam differ enormously.

As soon as we are studying religion in the field, we become aware of many more aspects of complexity. For example, many religious groups will claim historical continuity. In the cathedral in Toledo one can still attend a Mozarabic Christian rite that goes back to the seventh century when Muslims ruled Spain. On the banks of the Ganges there are rites of *arti* going back three or more thousand years. There are also claims of continuity across geographical space. There are many religious diasporas, that is people who are living outside the place where their religious tradition began or was established. It is interesting that these diaspora communities are sometimes very traditional; their identity is partly still anchored to their country of origin at the time when they left. Those in the 'home' country have moved on but the migrants' religious traditions are both affected by the new culture in which they are living and also, perhaps, stuck in their imagined past.

Whenever we visit places, we engage with the past to contextualise the present. Engaging with living religion offers the opportunity to engage with the lived past. In this regard, what is true for a believer is not always what is historically accurate. The narratives of religious belonging such as modern Wicca and the Goddess movement, for example, inform lived religion now by creating an idealised reception and inheritance of lived tradition. Places also create links to identity and the lived past – sitting around a fire at Avebury on a summer solstice morning is very different from sitting around a fire in one's own garden. Ruins and places of worship also provide a connection between the claimed past and the projection of this in the lived present.

Particular diasporic communities can also serve as good examples of this patchwork of diverse religious traditions that are sometimes cut from the same cloth, but are often related in complicated and diverse ways. Afe Adogame (2009) has written recently upon the place of African Traditional Religion both within Western Africa, and also within modern cities such as New York. Bettina Schmidt (2008) has written upon Caribbean diasporic identities, including Haitian Vodou, also in New York. Their engagement with living religious traditions, based on fieldwork and a deep involvement with real people and communities, highlights an interesting issue in the study of religions for, although they are examining traditions that share a 'source' in West African Traditional Religion, the contemporary manifestations of these are culturally, socially and linguistically removed, and thus changed, by the complexity and diversity of everyday lived religious practices and realities. This, for us, serves as a good example of how we must not essentialise religious traditions, or accept textbook descriptions about 'what Indigenous practitioners do' or 'what Muslims believe', but instead preference reflective and experiential writing about contemporary religious communities.

Not only is there inevitably change and diversity within religions but what we understand as religion also changes. In the history of religion what religion 'is' in different cultures and geographic areas, and what 'counts' as religion, has changed (Smith, 1998). Our understanding of religion will also shift depending on whether we focus more on affiliation and organisational aspects or on individuals and what they consider to be their religious experience and expression. These may or may not correspond to what is regarded as normative within a particular tradition. It is also the case that recently in Britain and elsewhere people have begun to talk and write more about spirituality and this is often compared favourably with religion (Heelas and Woodhead, 2004).

In this book we will focus not on institutions (although in fieldwork we must often come into contact with hierarchy and structure within the communities we are working) but on the individuals who make up these institutions. In doing this, we need to attempt to understand religions and religious life with the self-identity of religious practitioners as our starting point, not bringing in value judgements about what religion 'should or shouldn't be'. When we suggest that you respect religion in its many and various forms, we are asking you to take the time and effort to 'look again' at something, including what actually may be considered as religion or religious. This is what the word 'respect' means. Don't jump to conclusions *before* you have had a good look. We engage with recent scholarship to move the discussion on 'what religion is' away from essentialising and limiting categorical definitions to a newer understanding of religion as it is performed in everyday life. In chapter 2, we will explore this in some depth but here we just want to note that fieldwork is very important in this newly emerging approach to religion. As the 'World Religions' paradigm for teaching and research is increasingly critiqued, we need to replace notions of texts, founders and doctrines with examinations of everyday life and communities. By focusing on lived religion in our research, we privilege the 'everyday' and agree with Harvey when he suggests that "real life and lived religion ... might turn out to be the same thing" (2013, 9).

Of course, it is not new to suggest that students and scholars should spend time outside the lecture theatre engaging with religious communities. In the history of the study of religion, there are plenty of examples of fieldwork which have helped to develop our discipline – from early pioneers such as Bronilsaw Malinowski (1922) who lived amongst the people of the Andaman Islands in the early twentieth century to contemporary scholars examining newly emergent religious communities such as Susan Palmer (2010) and the Nuwaubian Nation of Moors. Much can be learned from reading about their experiences, but undergraduate students of religion are not going to carry out this kind of extensive research and that, more than anything, is the motivation for this book. The overwhelming number of students of religion will instead engage with religious communities and individuals as a part of a short-term research project, perhaps a final-year research dissertation, or even more likely in group visits run by their course tutors. In writing this book, therefore, we are not trying to rewrite a full-blown account of how to perform deep anthropological ethnography whilst living with remote communities for prolonged periods of time, but instead aim to provide students with the key skills to analyse and reflect upon their experiences in engaging with living religion in a variety of forms when it is found 'outside the lecture theatre'. In so doing, we want to encourage and allow students to operate as *neophyte researchers* in ways which value local and everyday interactions with religion.

Being a neophyte researcher

We like the term 'neophyte researcher' for someone beginning their study of living religion in the field because some definitions of the word 'neophyte' come from religious contexts. As you can see from this extract from the *Oxford English Dictionary*, the word has several meanings:

1 a new convert, esp. to a religious faith.
2 Roman Catholic Church – (a) a novice of a religious order (b) a newly ordained priest.
3 a beginner; a novice [NT Gk *neophutus* newly planted].

Of course we do not presume that you are, or should be, religious, but we do want to persuade (convert) you to do fieldwork. And we hope that this engagement with living religion that you are beginning to undertake will make a real difference to you and your understanding as it has for us.

To help explain why we wrote this book, we hope it may be useful to provide some background about the authors so that you know why we are interested in studying living religion, how we have used the field with students and ways in which we have learned from studying religion in the field. We have put this in the first person, speaking about 'I' because as will become clear throughout this book, when we engage with living religion we do so as the people we are. We must be reflexive about the impact of this engagement on ourselves, and the ways in which we impact upon the people we are meeting.

Approaches to writing this book

Stephen: I studied Religion as an undergraduate at a Theology and Religious Studies Department in a UK university. Although my degree was labelled Theology, a modular system allowed me to take a wide range of modules from Religious Studies, and I quickly realised the important differences between the disciplines – something which, as an 18 year old going to university, I had not appreciated. After my undergraduate degree, I registered for a PhD in Religious Studies and have remained in this area ever since (in fact, I prefer the term 'study of religion' to religious studies, but more on that below ...). As a lecturer, I have always preferenced tangible experiences for students in their learning which they can relate to their everyday experiences – not just the field visits and study tours which underpin much of this book, but also in working with students to appreciate contemporary media on religion, the relationship between religion and popular culture and the everyday realities of performing religious practices. Often, I seek to ensure that students are taken outside their 'comfort zone', both intellectually and emotionally. This often means playing the *advocatus diaboli* with them, perhaps with regard to 'what religion is', but it also means exploring troubling acts that are carried out in the name of religion, or seeking to understand views which run counter to majority cultural values – not only do I feel that this is an important way of helping students to learn, I would argue that not to do this is to do a disservice to the concept or category of religion in all its multiplicity and complexity. This approach means that I often take students outside of the lecture theatre to critique and 'test' what the textbooks tell them about religions and religious practitioners. Many of these experiences are referred to in this book, so I will not go into details now, but a recurring theme for me is to seek out what may be described as 'dislocated religion' or 'religion at the edges' – by seeking out religious acts and religious people in places that are beyond the obvious, we may better understand religion as an everyday lived reality.

Lynne: I have always been fascinated by what might be called 'the spiritual'. I studied Divinity at university, became a religious education high school teacher and then a university lecturer. I have been taking students to visit places of worship and meet with religious people and communities in the locality and further afield for the last forty years because that brings the learning alive and makes the experiences of religious people real. I recently met up with some students whom I taught in the early 1980s who still talk about the impact on them of visiting places of worship in Birmingham nearly thirty years ago. I have thought a lot about how students could be helped to gain more from these kinds of experiences, particularly by paying attention to the experiential nature of the learning, and that is why I wanted to write this book.

My own understanding of a religion such as Judaism, for example, developed through attending a Shabbat meal and Passover Seder, going to synagogue, meeting and talking with Jews, studying biblical and other texts with Jews, visiting Jewish museums and going to Israel as well as through reading and lectures. Travel to different places, in my own country and abroad, enables me to experience and understand what I could never do if I stayed at home – as long as I am open to the possibilities. It is very exciting to now take university students abroad to study as well as supervising their independent fieldwork study of religion. At the end of this chapter there is a question about where *you* would choose to go, if you could, to study religion. At the time of writing this I have just visited Vietnam and Cambodia, and will soon be going to Togo and Benin in West Africa. One place I would love to explore but which isn't possible at the moment is the Yemen – maybe one day!

One final point about what I have learned from being in the field. This wasn't expected, but has influenced me a lot. In Namibia there is a group called the Himba, and I was lucky enough to visit and talk with some of them. I was fascinated by the way in which they view time. For the Himba the past is in front of us where we can see it and the future is behind. That shift of perception has made me think differently about time ever since so I was intrigued to read in Graham Harvey's recent book, *Food, Sex & Strangers*, that he was told the same thing by indigenous people from opposite sides of the Pacific Ocean, in Aotearoa (New Zealand) and Chile (2013, 15).

Although both of the authors of this book teach at universities within the UK, the experience which underpins our work is based on collaborative scholarship and shared experiences with scholars and religious communities across the globe – we thank many of these people in our acknowledgements at the start of the book. This is important to note as, when we give examples from the UK, we are highlighting the importance of 'the local' as a key aspect in studying religion, and this method can be replicated wherever you are studying. The UK context does, however, strongly inform the approach we take to religious studies.

Formulating 'Lived Religion'

In our research and teaching to date, we have found it useful to categorise the ways in which we encounter religion under three headings. It is important to note straight away that these are not strictly separate or exclusive categories, and much of the content of the following chapters will bear this out, but in this introductory chapter, we want to introduce these key terms. They will form the framework on which we build our particular approach to supporting you as students and neophyte researchers to learn about religion 'outside the lecture theatre' and 'off campus'.

To understand the differences between ways of encountering religion, we will use three different terms. These are *reported* religion, *represented* religion and *living* religion. By *reported* religion, we mean traditional textbook commentaries on religious traditions, which for a long time have formed the basis of much standard lecture theatre teaching. Also within this category, we include mainstream news media and new media sources, which impact hugely on people's perceptions of religious groups. By *represented* religion, we mean the ways in which religious people and organisations present themselves and their traditions. This may be in a talk, in publications or in the ways in which they engage with visitors to their communities. By *living* religion, we mean what people actually believe and do. This is real, particular and often messy – a far cry from safe or neat accounts contained in textbooks.

Engaging with *reported* religion

You can find religion in textbooks, in newspaper articles and images, on radio and television and, of course, on the Internet. Chapter 6 explores virtual media in depth because they offer fascinating resources for studying religion, but much online information is still really textbook stuff delivered in a different, perhaps more glamorised form. The key thing about reported religion is that it is neatly packaged. For example, a textbook or a news broadcast might present Hinduism and Sikhism as two separate and distinct religions. In fact, the boundaries are not as clear cut as this, and (moving swiftly away from reported religion to represented and lived religion) there are some temples in India and elsewhere in the world which combine elements of both traditions. The Valmiki temple, for example, in Southall, London, might appear to be Sikh and many Valmikis see themselves as Sikhs. But Valmiki, whose large statue dominates the prayer hall in the Southall temple, is traditionally known as the author of the Hindu scripture the *Ramayana* and the walls are painted with this story. Valmikis are Dalits, that is untouchables within the South Asian caste system, and partly due to negative attitudes towards them from others from the Punjab, some Valmikis see themselves as neither Hindu nor Sikh (Takhar, 2011).

Many similar, seemingly helpful statements from textbooks explaining 'what Christians believe' or 'what Muslims do' need to be carefully critiqued – for every reported fact of religious belief or behaviour, there will be numerous examples of religious people or communities believing or acting differently. Even when hierarchical religious organisations promote an official teaching, the reality of how this teaching is received and enacted by religious communities in different places and times may differ radically.

Although journalists are often reporting on particular situations, they are not experts in religion and often rely for their understanding on limited sources. Whilst few will intend to misinform, caution must be exercised when interpreting media accounts of religion, whether it be populist misunderstandings of Tom Cruise's beliefs as a Scientologist or, perhaps far more seriously, the misrepresentation of Islam in much of the media due to the violent actions of some Muslims. It might be worth adding here that negative attitudes to Islam were deeply embedded in some Christian history, and that concern over media misrepresentation, particularly of new religious movements led to the setting up of 'Inform' – see website list at the end of the chapter.

Whilst it is the case that we must move beyond textbook understandings of religion, it does not mean that we should negate the historical, textual or doctrinal markers of religion which are explained in textbooks – indeed, by engaging with living religion in the field, students are able to see and comprehend the ways in which ritual, ceremony and performance are carried on as living traditions – the very embodiment of religious community identity proclaimed in reported religion, but realised in living and represented religion.

Engaging with *represented* religion

This happens a lot in the field so it is very important to be alert to what is happening. A lot of represented religion is what you hear or read. Of course, this takes various forms, such as literature produced by religious communities, including their own websites and new/social media, and statements and press releases from appointed individuals from within religious organisations. When someone is interviewed, by you, on TV or radio, or for a newspaper, then that person represents his or her religion, usually in the best light possible, and sometimes in a fairly simplified form. We will deal with some nuances to this at the end of the chapter, but basically, represented religion is how individuals and communities project their sense of identity. What they write or say tells us about their worldview, and about the reflective self-understanding of the people involved.

A lot of fieldwork will be engaging with represented religion. You might meet people on the street such as Hare Krishna devotees who will give you literature and maybe invite you to join them in some chanting. You can ask them questions and you may, sometimes, feel as though you are getting answers that are rather rehearsed. You are getting represented religion. A member of a particular tradition is telling you about what is involved, what is important, and maybe a bit about what it means for them.

Visits to places of worship often involve listening to someone talk. Hopefully they will explain things very clearly and answer questions so that you learn things you didn't know before. But pay attention to *how* they are telling you – what style or approach do they use? For example, they may tell a lot of stories, or tell you a lot of history, or discuss what is happening in the country where the religion began, or make comparisons between their religion and the wider religious tradition of the country which they may assume is your tradition, and so on. Each of these is a different way of representing the religion. It is important, as we will be discussing in detail later in the book, that you don't ignore what you see, feel, hear, smell, taste and touch – the living religion – and concentrate only on what someone tells you. Another example, although not technically off campus, is if you have a visitor or visitors to a class. Maybe someone is invited to give a talk or you are able to interview a number of people in small groups. Again, this is a great opportunity to hear at 'first hand' from religious people, but remember that what they say isn't the whole truth about their tradition. So, whilst you are listening think about what might be influencing what they say or what they are not saying.

Activity or action can be a form of represented religion too. Christians, for example, involved in the 'Drop the Debt campaign' not only are trying to influence public opinion and political decisions but also are embodying and representing a particular version of what it means for them to be a Christian. Other Christians might oppose them, arguing that 'Christians should keep out of politics'. The actual name, the 'Jubilee Debt Campaign', makes explicit reference to the biblical idea of the jubilee as the time for social justice (Leviticus 25:8–13), which carries religious meaning for both Jews and Christians. Of course, not everyone involved in the campaign is religious, but in the UK it is also a multi-faith expression or representation of religious identity.

Engaging with *living* religion

Consider the following short description:

> On a cold winter evening we arrived at a Devon farm, a long way from the main road. We met Mary and Dennis James, the couple who owned the farm, and they took us into a barn and up the wooden stairs into what might have been a hayloft. Facing us was a shaven-headed and fully robed Buddhist monk, sitting on a cushion on a raised platform. As soon as he spoke, it was obvious he was an American. I still vividly remember him explaining that the reason there were flowers on the shrine was that they died fairly quickly and so reminded people that everything passes. We talked for a long time.

This is an example of an encounter with living religion, of an American monk in a Thai Theravada order in a rural part of England that happened in the early 1980s. Over the years the community that was established there has grown, developing within its specific cultural context relative to the people and places that make up its community. Engaging in this way with religion in the field can lead to new understandings of what religion means to people, how they express this, and how it affects their identity and lives, beyond simplistic understandings of 'what Buddhists believe' or 'what Buddhists do' as if these descriptions could be used for all Buddhists in all places at all times.

This book is encouraging you to explore living religion in the field. This is where you experience and reflect on your experiences of religion. You can engage with individuals or groups from religious communities who are performing, living or acting in ways required of, or inspired by, their given religious community and identity. You might attend an occasion of worship such as a Sabbath morning service in a Conservative synagogue in New York, be watching a pagan procession in Glastonbury or be interviewing someone who identifies herself as a practising Roman Catholic who also uses pagan rituals on her home altar. Living religion is always going to be particular – the specific rather than the general, or typical. It may well not be systematic belief or practice; it may not be at all 'coherent'. It is what Primiano (1995), in an early article about living religion, calls 'vernacular religion'.

However, it may already be obvious that the lines between represented and lived religion are not always clear, and much of this book is a discussion about the ways in which religious people and communities represent their lived reality to others, and how we can study this. Idealised, textbook versions of religion interweave too with the more personal and particular. We split the discussion in this introduction into categories to begin to analyse the complex and messy relationships between these different aspects or forms of religion which make up the 'fuzzy frontiers' of religious identity (Scholefield, 2004). We will end this chapter with another example of this complexity:

During a study tour to Jerusalem, students have a talk from Ruth, an Israeli Jew, who grew up in New York but has lived in Jerusalem for several decades. A fluent Hebrew speaker, Ruth is a member of a modern Orthodox synagogue and describes herself as a Zionist. She talks about the demography of world Jewry, the political and religious diversity of Jews in Israel, and her own involvement in interfaith work with Christians and Muslims in Israel/Palestine. She talks about the importance of rain for all those living in this land, the sense of victimhood that both Israelis and Palestinians have, and her hopes for an end to the Israeli occupation of the West Bank as part of a political two-state solution.

In many ways we could categorise this as represented religion – Ruth is presenting views in an open and reflective way, which she hopes will help us to understand and have sympathy with a Jewish Israeli perspective on things. She knows that we have been to visit Bethlehem, walking through the checkpoint, and have seen and heard about some of the harsh realities of life for Palestinians under Israeli occupation. I have a hunch that if we had been a visiting group of Jewish students she would have spoken differently. But the main point to make here is that what Ruth has done, and we have experienced, is also living religion. We have seen what it means, for one person at least, to be a Zionist Jew in contemporary Israel. It means education and dialogue. Education is very important because right at the heart of Judaism is study, and study and moral activity go together. As Goldberg writes:

> In Hebrew, the word Torah means 'teaching' and it stems from a root which means direction ... If there is any overall instruction or command coming out of the Exodus master story it is that we Jews are to *become the story*. Jews are not simply enjoined to study Torah but to be Torah.
>
> (Goldberg, 1995, 102)

Ruth might not talk in these terms to us, who are not Jews, but we might interpret the way she entered into dialogue with us as she did, as living the Jewish story.

Chapter summary

This chapter has introduced the authors, the importance to us of fieldwork study of religion and examples of the kinds of encounters and experiences that this involves. We hope we have whetted your appetite to study religion in this way. We analysed three different ways of categorising religion – reported, represented and lived religion – and we stressed that they are not definitive, exclusive or unrelated categories. Often, reported religion will underpin or inform represented religion. Often, lived religion is acted out as represented religion to reinforce religious identities in a relational multireligious world.

Further reading

We want to get you excited about studying religion off campus and able to see the potential of such work. In each chapter we recommend both a book and an article for you to read next.

The book is called *Religions in Focus* (Harvey, 2009) and has chapters about lots of different religious groups and focuses on the 'lived reality of living religions'. Reading this will introduce you not only to lots of examples of living religion but also to some of the approaches and issues of studying religion in this way which are discussed in the next chapter.

An example of an interesting recent article which you can easily access online is 'Dismantling Religious Boundaries by Sharing the *Baraka* through Pilgrimages in Lebanon' by Nour Farra-Haddad. She discusses how many of the devotional practices observed at holy sites in the Lebanon are actually shared between Christians and Muslims. See: http://basr.ac.uk/diskus_old/diskus15/Diskus%2015%20Farra-Haddad.pdf

Questions for consideration

1 What has informed your understanding of religion? Who have you met, what have you experienced, what have you become aware of, which has helped your understanding of what religion is and what religious people do? In your reflection, try to give specific examples.

2 If you could travel to one place to explore an aspect of religion, where would you choose to go, and why?

3 What are your greatest strengths that will help you be a good 'neophyte researcher'? What might be the biggest difficulties for you in this approach?

Bibliography

This list includes all the texts referred to in the chapter and other recommended reading.

Adogame, A. 2009, 'Practitioners of Indigenous Religions of Africa and the African Diaspora' in Harvey, G. (ed.), *Religions in Focus*, London: Equinox, 75–100.
Goldberg, M. 1995, *Why Should Jews Survive?* Oxford: Oxford University Press.
Harvey, G. 2013, *Food, Sex & Strangers: Understanding Religion as Everyday Life*, Durham: Acumen.
——(ed.) 2009, *Religions in Focus*, London: Equinox.
Heelas, P. and Woodhead, L. 2004, *The Spiritual Revolution*, Oxford: Wiley-Blackwell.

Malinowski, B. 1922, *Argonauts of the Western Pacific: An Account of Native Enterprise and Adventure in the Archipelagos of Melanesian New Guinea*, London: Routledge & Kegan Paul.

Martel, Y. 2002, *The Life of Pi*, Edinburgh: Canongate.

Palmer, S.J. 2010, *The Nuwaubian Nation*, Farnham, Surrey: Ashgate.

Primiano, L.N. 1995, 'Vernacular Religion and the Search for Method in Religious Folklife' in *Western Folklore*, 54(1), 37–56.

Schmidt, B. 2008, *Caribbean Diaspora in the USA: Diversity of Caribbean Religions in New York City*, Aldershot, Hampshire: Ashgate.

Scholefield, L. 2004, 'Bagels, Schnitzel and McDonald's: "Fuzzy Frontiers" of Jewish Identity in an English Jewish Secondary School' in *British Journal of Religious Education*, 26(3), 237–48.

Smith, J.Z. 1998, 'Religion, Religions, Religious' in Taylor, M. (ed.) *Critical Terms in Religious Studies*, Chicago: Chicago University Press, 269–84.

Takhar, O.K. 2011, 'The Valmiki, Ravidasi, and Namdhari Communities in Britain: Self-representations and Transmissions of Tradition' in Jacobson, K.A. and Myrvold, K. (eds) *Sikhs in Europe: Migration, Identities and Representations*, Farnham, Surrey: Ashgate, 279–304.

Websites

This annotated list includes all the online sources we have referred to in the chapter as well as some recommended sites. We have given the URLs (web addresses) accessed on 31.10.14, but these do change so for ease of use we have listed them by the name of the organisation in alphabetical order.

DISKUS. This is the journal of the British Association for the Study of Religion (BASR). It is online and peer reviewed. There are articles about the theoretical aspects of the study of religions and examples of work done in the field. http://basr.ac.uk/

Inform – The Information Network on Religious Movements. Inform is an independent charity that was founded in 1988 by Professor Eileen Barker with the support of the British Home Office and the mainstream Churches. It is based at the London School of Economics. The primary aim of Inform is to help people by providing them with information that is as accurate, balanced and up to date as possible about alternative religious, spiritual and esoteric movements. www.inform.ac/

Jubilee Debt Campaign is an example of social and political activity on a global scale which for some people is an expression of the meaning of their religious commitment. See, for example, http://multifaith.jubileedebt.org.uk/

2 Ways of studying religion off campus

Academic approaches and issues

Introduction

The academic study of religion within modern universities continues an evolving and ever-shifting method of seeking to understand a huge variety of human phenomena that we label 'religion'. The way in which this is done, and the very concept or category that we are meaning when we use the word 'religion', is hotly contested between the different disciplines that have informed current studies.

For centuries, theological discourse dominated approaches, and of course this is still important in many universities, but in recent years, religious studies has sought to distance itself from its nineteenth-century roots within comparative religion, encased as this was in a Protestant theological academic heritage. Now is not the place to discuss this relationship at length (others have done this recently from a variety of viewpoints, including McCutcheon (2003) and Oliver and Warrier (2008)) but we raise it again, as we believe that a focus on living religion is perhaps the best way to advance the study of religion. Indeed, by re-examining religion as performed in everyday lives, we may perhaps avoid the essentialising mistakes of the past, which led to a concentration on texts, founders, 'core beliefs' and other round holes into which generations of scholars have sought to plug the square pegs of a great diversity of religious traditions. Suzanne Owen (2011), in her important article 'The World Religions Paradigm: Time for a Change', argues that the World Religions paradigm, which was produced by this narrow academic inheritance, approaches religious traditions outside of their very specific and particular contexts, thus failing to do justice to the very things we are studying. Sutcliffe and Gilhus concur when they argue that "the pioneers of the study of religion largely ignored local phenomena in their own backyards and projected their theories onto 'others', elsewhere" (Sutcliffe and Gilhus, 2013, 2). Stringer also notes the influence of Protestant Christianity upon the study of 'other' religious traditions when he wryly comments that (to scholars operating within this outdated model) "Buddhism is good. Hinduism is suspect, except in its intellectual traditions. The work of theologians is good. The so-called 'superstitious' practices of ordinary believers are generally not worthy of our attention." (Stringer, 2011, 2)

In recent scholarship which seeks to redress this balance, Harvey has coined the phrase 'elsewhering' religion. By this, he means that we should not approach the focus of our study – this 'thing' called 'religion' – through the largely Christian inheritance of Western academia, but seek to approach religion, both as a concept and as a lived reality, through a diversity of approaches which privilege embodied performative everyday action rather than 'belief'. Harvey argues that by doing this, we understand religions, including Christianity, better. We can explore religion as we find it, rather than mould it to meet the cultural essentialisms of what we expect to find. An important part of this approach is to understand that if we start with embodied, localised under-standings of religion, we are already, even as neophyte researchers, helping to develop the discipline. As Harvey notes, "In every lived religion the processes of change and exchange that follow from encountering others and alternatives are everyday" (Harvey, 2013, 177), that is, change and complexity, played out by individuals and communities, is normative of religion, and it is this everyday process of what may be called 'living with meaning' that we should be studying. We should not accept static 'reported' essentialisms of what 'religion' is or 'religions' are – and so by engaging with the everyday, we not only understand religion on a deeper level, we see, and are a part of, this very process of living change; part of the dynamism of living religion.

Recent scholarship on religion has also furthered our understanding of religion as a 'bottom-up' everyday lived reality, rather than a reified, essentialised 'top-down' phenomenon. In *Everyday Religion: Observing Modern Religious Lives*, Ammerman (2007) collects together a series of studies which examine, amongst other phenomena, 'unsynagogued Jews' (Davidman, 2007), religious meaning in the lives of pro-life campaigners (Munson, 2007) and the role of religion in civic ceremonies (Lichterman, 2007). The common theme throughout the collected essays is that we must approach religion *as it is lived* rather than as we expect to find it. Likewise, the separation of religious phenomena into 'World Religions', 'New Religions' or 'Indigenous Religions' should be avoided. As Harvey (2009, 7) has argued, the antiquity of traditions categorised as 'World Religions' rarely affects how people engage with (and within) such communities, 'New Religions' are often contextualised within much older cultural continuities, and 'Indigenous Religions' are today likely to be performed in London, Tokyo or New York.

Much of this recent work on living religion can trace a path back to Primiano (1995), who argued that we should use the term 'vernacular religion' to mean the everyday lived reality of religious individuals and communities, rather than the essentialised elite construction of textbook religion previously focused upon by Western academia. Crucially, however, Primiano did not suggest that this everyday vernacular religion sat in opposition to an elite form of religion in reality, but that *all* religion was vernacular religion. This is important, as it means that whether we study congregations or archbishops, devotees or swamis, we are studying vernacular religions – the ways in which people seek meaning in their lives and perform this worldview in their individual and communal daily actions (see Bowman, 2012).

Approaches to fieldwork in the study of religion

Encountering religion in the field is not a modern phenomenon. However, the theory of engagement with people, places and communities, and the importance of fieldwork within the study of religion, has developed apace in recent decades. The related disciplines of anthropology and sociology, about which we will talk in this chapter, have provided a century of inherited learning methodologies and practices, and it is on these shoulders that current scholarship in fieldwork stands. There is, however, a need to understand an approach to fieldwork specific to the academic study of religion, with all of the cultural and academic provenance that this brings, which draws from related disciplines and earlier teachers, but stands as a distinct methodology of approaching the study of religion from a religious studies perspective.

In the social scientific study of religion there are two major differing approaches to research, often called the *quantitative* and *qualitative* methodologies. Quantitative methods use surveys, polls and questionnaires to generate data that is usually presented in figures or graphs – they quantify trends and patterns in religious life. For example, based on quite small samples – sometimes fewer than 1,000 responses – a researcher can generalise about patterns in church attendance and, by comparing the latest results with earlier data, can generalise about changes in practice. For good examples of this sort of data, see the text box below on Social Trends and Religion. These methods produce lots of interesting and valuable material, but fieldwork usually draws more heavily on qualitative methods.

These qualitative approaches, which we shall be concerned with in this chapter, explore the particular details of a specific religious individual or group. This provides lots of rich descriptive detail, and enables the researcher to explore the meanings of religious belief and practice for that person or community. In other words, qualitative research can help us to understand how people make sense of their religion and their world; we get the perspectives of insiders. It is an interpretive approach, more concerned with 'how' and 'why' than 'how many' or 'how much'. Or, to quote one of the foremost anthropologists whom we will explore in more detail below, these fieldwork methods studying a particular group of people are about figuring out "what the devil they think they are up to" (Geertz, 1983, 58). There are lots of different ways of studying religion in the field in this way, and both theory and practice have changed and developed over time.

Qualitative research in the study of religion – recommended sources

There are lots of different handbooks covering the various philosophies and methodologies that make up qualitative research. For example, it would be worth looking at *The Oxford Handbook of Qualitative Research* (Leavy, 2014) or *Emergent Methods in Social Research* (Hesse-Biber and

Leavy, 2006). These books have chapters dealing with all the different approaches which researchers can take, but they are not focused on the study of religion.

The Routledge Handbook of Research Methods in the Study of Religion (Stausberg and Engler, 2011) takes many of the same theoretical issues and practical approaches, such as epistemology, ethics, grounded theory, discourse analysis or participant observation, and discusses them in the context of the study of religion.

Also of real interest for students beginning to study living religion in the field is the online training resource at the University of Kent: *Research Methods for the Study of Religion*. This has been developed by leading scholars to cover a range of topics, including conceptualising religion, comparative research, ethnography, and politics and ethics. Each topic page has a downloadable discussion paper or structured exercise which introduces key issues. The topic pages also provide additional resources, including sample studies, bibliographies or links to other relevant websites. There are also additional general resources such as journals, blog sites or research centres.

An early example of this approach was that of Bronislaw Malinowski, a Polish-born, London-based academic who is often regarded as the pioneer of modern anthropology, and in particular the school of anthropology called *functional* anthropology. Operating in the early decades of the twentieth century, Malinowski rejected the 'armchair' anthropology of the Victorian era – a period when early academics such as E.B. Tylor (1871) and J.G. Frazer (1894) wrote epic works based on cultures that they had either hardly interacted with, or not visited at all. In his most famous work, Malinowski lived alongside inhabitants of the Trobriand Islands, just off Papua New Guinea. With an enforced stay of several years due to the outbreak of World War I, Malinowski (1922) developed what has become known as *participant observation*, where the researcher seeks to understand the viewpoint of a culture other than his or her own by living, speaking, engaging and performing daily acts with and within their host community. Such an approach was revolutionary, and prioritised daily interaction with individuals and communities, although it is important to note that Malinowski's (1967) legacy is rather complicated by subsequent discoveries of his diaries, published posthumously in the 1960s, which are underpinned by a strict sense of 'otherness' towards his host communities and often bordered on prejudice and racism. Of course, it is too easy to project back contemporary attitudes to past generations, and some recent anthropologists have found the diaries helpful as they are examples of brutally honest reflective anthropology, but they again highlight the difficulties often faced by academics when writing reflectively about the complex and nuanced interpersonal relationships which sit at the heart of the study of everyday religion.

Following just a few years after Malinowski was E.E. Evans-Pritchard, an English anthropologist who undertook extensive fieldwork with the Azande and Nuer communities in Central Africa. Importantly, Evans-Pritchard approached the communities in which he studied as being *different* from his own cultural norms, but not *primitive*. By living amongst practitioners of witchcraft, Evans-Pritchard wrote about such religious practices, not from the viewpoint of a judgemental outsider, but from the viewpoint of one who has shared in and experienced the reality of what witchcraft practices meant to Azande people. In his famous work *Witchcraft, Magic and Oracles among the Azande*, Evans-Pritchard (1937) argues that the religious system, beliefs and practices which embodied the beliefs of the Azande people were perfectly logical when understood within an Azande worldview. This was of fundamental importance in the development of fieldwork as it was an important step in breaking down false binaries of us/them, advanced/primitive, true/false that were so prevalent in the writings of earlier Victorian scholars. As Evans-Pritchard wrote:

> In my own culture, in the climate of thought I was born into and brought up in and have been conditioned by, I rejected, and reject, Zande notions of witchcraft. In their culture, in the set of ideas I then lived in, I accepted them; in a kind of way I believed them ... You cannot have a remunerative, even intelligent, conversation with people about something they take as self-evident if you give them the impression that you regard their belief as an illusion or a delusion ... If one must act as though one believed, one ends in believing, or half-believing as one acts.
>
> (Evans-Pritchard, 1973, 4)

Put simply, by engaging with religious practices on a lived daily basis, Evans-Pritchard was able to go beyond the projected essentialisms of normative Western-inherited views of religion, and begin to ask questions about differing religious phenomena *in context*. It is also hugely significant that Evans-Pritchard linked belief with performative action – a theme we will pick up on later.

In the last decades of the twentieth century, Clifford Geertz stands as arguably the most influential exponent of anthropological approaches to the study of religion, and is most associated with the development of *symbolic* anthropology. Having undertaken extensive fieldwork in Java, Bali, Sumatra and Morocco, Geertz (1968, vi) understood religion as a system of symbols which uniquely enable and influence specific thoughts and actions within a community. Crucially, this meant that religion had to be understood within a *social context*. Geertz importantly noted that religion is a product of "collectively evolved, socially transmitted, and culturally objectified patterns of meaning – myths, rites, doctrines [and] fetishes ... whatever God may or may not be ... religion is a social institution, worship a social activity, and faith a social force" (1968, 19). For Geertz (1973), this meant that serious, deep, ethnography must be carried out in order to understand a religious system or worldview, and this led to his coining of the phrase 'thick description'. A 'thick description' is one which seeks not just to observe and describe a 'foreign' phenomenon, but to realise why such a phenomenon is taking place so as to understand its meaning within a specific social context, and thus make the action understandable to outsiders to that context. This term has become influential in many academic disciplines, and none more so than the contemporary study of religion for, if we are to understand living religion for, say, Hindus in New York or Mormons in Wales, we must understand the very specific and localised social histories and structures which underpin these modern communities.

Such giants of scholarship as Malinowski, Evans-Pritchard and Geertz are examples of the crucial importance of the anthropological method to the development of the modern study of religion, which seeks to answer questions of interaction and relationship with religious communities through a multi-methodological discipline, drawing from different academic inheritances. In addition to the anthropologists, it is also necessary to acknowledge the contribution of several leading sociologists of religion, who continue to influence studies to this day, and from whom we can draw important approaches to the study of religion as a *lived* reality.

Emile Durkheim (1858–1917) became the first professor of sociology in the 1890s after he had founded France's first university department dedicated to the subject. He was consistently interested in religion – his important early work *On Suicide* (Durkheim, 1897) focused on how suicide could be categorised by its multiple manifestations in different cultures, and specifically contrasted cases of suicide within Catholic and Protestant societies. His magnum opus, *The Elementary Forms of Religious Life* (1912), introduced the powerful, and lastingly influential, concepts of the 'sacred' and the 'profane' and built upon his previous work which argued that society was made up of something he called *solidarity*, which was understood to act as a conduit for the values, customs and beliefs of a social group. This inextricably linked religion to society and, for Durkheim, allowed religion to be explained without recourse to the supernatural.

He argued that humans made God in their own image as, firstly, our sense of moral responsibility comes from an understanding of the needs of our society, and this in turn leads to the creation of a 'God' figure who is seen as the source of this moral imperative, but which is in reality only a reflection of society's absolute claim over its members. Whilst much modern scholarship rejects Durkheim's view that the sacred and the profane are distinct categories, he retains a huge influence in the ways in which religion is studied in universities. He is particularly interesting for our current study as, through his work on the social roots of religious worldviews, he affirms the necessity of examining religion in very specific social contexts, reminding us to pay attention to the cultural milieu in which religious adherents and communities exist.

Max Weber (1864–1920) was, along with Durkheim, a founding father of sociology as an academic discipline. Specifically interested in the development of societies, and the place of religion as a dynamic in this development, Weber's (2011) most famous work was *The Protestant Ethic and the Spirit of Capitalism* (1905, translated into English by Talcott Parsons in 1930) which linked the 'success' of capitalist Western nations, over and above other non-capitalist, 'non-Western', 'non-Christian' nations, to Protestant ideologies of hard work, self-reliance and self-improvement. Whilst this evolutionary and rather colonial view must be seen within the political period in which Weber was writing, it highlights how he saw religion as a progressive element of society which could lead to social change. Weber understood religion and society to be so intertwined that he believed that when a functioning capitalist society was created, it meant that the Protestant ethic would have run its course, and the world would become 'disenchanted'. Again, as with Durkheim's central arguments, much recent scholarship does not accept Weber as having been completely correct – particularly with regard to his views on disenchantment, which is challenged by new understandings of what religion is, far removed from narrow views of Protestantism – but he remains important for one particularly relevant approach to the study of religion, which continues to be influential to this day.

Weber, unlike Durkheim, did not look from the social system down onto the individual, but started his investigation of people and communities with the individual and looked up to the society in which they operated. He believed that exploring how people behaved was crucial to understanding our social structures. To do this, he used the phrase *ich verstehe* (I understand). For example, if a person perpetrates a mugging, it is not enough to know that they have committed a crime – we need to understand the personal backstory which explains *why* they did it. In so doing, Weber was not seeking to excuse such actions, but to explain them in a specific social context. Of course, the example does not need to be a negative one linked with crime: a religious act, undertaken by a community which may not be a part of the majority culture in which they live, may at first seem strange, confusing or just plain silly to a scholar who does not share their beliefs and practices, but if we take the time to understand – *verstehen* – we can comprehend rituals, actions and viewpoints within the social and cosmological worldviews of the community in question and, in so doing, we do greater justice to the people and communities involved.

One example of a contemporary sociologist who has done exactly this is Eileen Barker, Emeritus Professor of the Sociology of Religion at the London School of Economics and founder of Inform, about which we talk later. Barker's most famous work is her 1984 text *The Making of a Moonie*, which utilised many of the research techniques we discuss in chapters 4 and 5 to learn about the lives of converts into the Unification Church. Barker was conducting her research at a time of great controversy for the movement, and the late 1970s and early 1980s saw numerous high-profile media stories where families claimed that their relatives were somehow brainwashed or hoodwinked into joining Moonie religious communities. Amidst an onslaught of negativity from media and legislators across both sides of the Atlantic, Barker asked a series of simple questions: Why did people join the organisation? How many stayed for any period of time? What did new converts do within the movement? In so doing, Barker concluded that Moonies were not brainwashed, but normal people performing normal activities, they just happened to be activities within social structures and theologies outside of the mainstream 'norm'.

Barker's work marks an interesting point between the giants of the past and the recent focus upon lived religion. Whilst she highlights the importance of *verstehen* (Barker, 1984, 20) and thus sits within an inheritance of classical sociological scholarship, she has applied this concept to radically alter scholarship on contemporary and newly emergent religious movements. As exemplified in *The Making of a Moonie*, Barker's focus on the everyday lived realities of converts to a new religious movement ensured that findings were based upon reflective analysis of lived realities rather than any attempt to fit the religious participants and movement into a predetermined category or framework, as the 'brainwashing' advocates had sought to do. This approach not only fundamentally changed the discipline of the study of new religious movements, but also acts as an example of how starting from a 'bottom-up' approach within the wider study of religion may be the best way to avoid essentialist misrepresentations of the religious 'other'. It is important, however, to note that it is not just minority traditions that are being approached in this way: Davies and Guest's (2007) text *Bishops, Wives and Children: Spiritual Capital Across the Generations* examines how religious traditions are transmitted by Anglican bishops, not through the medium of their rank and hierarchical Church office, but by examining their spiritual relationship with their families. Similarly, with regard to a Hindu movement, the anthropologist Maya Warrier has extensively researched the global, transnational and cross-cultural Mata Amritanandamayi Mission, not with a focus on the institutional operation of the movement, but by seeking to understand those "narrative[s] ... shaped by ... devotees' experiences of their lived realities" (Warrier, 2009, 2). These are important studies which are not concerned with institutional structures or metanarratives concerning the place of religion in society, but with real people living everyday lives.

The Religious Studies Project

One important resource that brings classic scholarship up to date – by using it, challenging it and developing it – is The Religious Studies Project website. Founded by David Robertson and Christopher Cotter and funded by the British Association for the Study of Religions, the project is an international collaboration of established and emergent scholars which aims to create a lasting repository of cutting-edge debate and a free resource archive for students.

The most helpful section of the project for students is the growing collection of podcasts, featuring interviews, discussions and debates with the world's leading academics of religion. At the time of writing there are over 100 podcasts uploaded, with more added every week, covering topics as diverse as Religion, Spirituality and Health, Religious Education, Fieldwork, Methodology in the Study of Religion and many more.

Sociological, anthropological, psychological and phenomenological approaches to the study of religion are all encompassed within this vast repository.

The podcasts can be accessed here: www.religiousstudiesproject.com/podcast/

Issues of knowledge

All approaches to knowledge operate with a particular *ontology, epistemology* and *methodology*. Ontology raises questions about the basic nature of reality, of what *is*, of what reality is like. It is obvious that debates about the existence of God, for example, are ontological. Epistemology is concerned with what there is that can be known, what it means to *know* something and about the relationship between the knower, or would-be knower, and what can be known. Methodology is about the *how* of knowing, the practicalities of getting the knowledge we believe to be there to be discovered. This section focuses on epistemology, and sets out some of the issues involved in thinking about knowing. Approaches to knowledge have changed a lot in the last few centuries but we particularly like a Latin phrase from the medieval theologian Thomas Aquinas to sum up the approach we are arguing for here. In Latin it is '*Quidquid recipitur ad modum recipientis recipitur*' which means, 'What is received is received according to the manner of the receiver'. Perhaps Evans-Pritchard said this best when he stated:

> one may say that since what we study are human beings the study involves the whole personality, heart as well as mind; and therefore what has shaped that personality, and not just academic background: sex, age, class, nationality, family and home, school, church, companions – one could enumerate any number of such influences. All I want to emphasise is that what one brings out of a field-study largely depends on what one brings to it.
>
> (Evans-Pritchard, 1973, 2)

In other words, what I know depends on who I am and how I understand knowing, as well as what might be there to be known. See 'Changing the "Subject" in Religious Studies' (Gregg and Scholefield, 2013) for some extended discussion of these issues.

'Caretaker' vs 'Karma-Yogin'

Of course, when you visit a religious community, it is not just your own perceptions and approaches that will affect the outcome and experience of your research, but also the perceptions and approaches of your host or guide. This person, often a member of the community in question, plays a vital role in how religion is represented to visitors, and what learning opportunities may arise. This does not refer to the simple fact that some people are better communicators than others, but addresses the methodological approach that is taken by these guides, often unconsciously, which affects their approach to their, often voluntary, duties in helping and guiding students. We label this factor as 'Caretaker' vs 'Karma-Yogin'.

It is apparent that the intimacy generated between visitors and a sacred site or religious community is deepened when the guide is personally undertaking a religious action in engaging with outsiders. The term 'Karma-Yogin' is borrowed from Hindu traditions, where it refers to a devotee who performs a religious duty with no desire for reward. This elevates the individual's role beyond that of a mere guide or caretaker, and means that there is a process of religious action occurring in the interaction with the students. Put simply, the very act of guiding and educating you becomes a religious act for the individual. For example, a swami acting as a guide at a Hindu ashram who talks to you about the practicalities of taking vows of chastity, poverty and obedience in a very human way is an excellent guide. Beyond this, however, the learning experience offered to you is deepened tremendously by the fact that the swami is not performing the role of a sacred tour guide, but is actually performing part of his *dharma*, or religious duty, by undertaking *seva*, or service to humanity, as a practical example of his duty as a karma-yogin. Such action means that you are not just being informed about a religion (simple *reported* or *represented* religion), but are part of the meaning of religious service and identity in the life of the host and guide – a wonderful example of engaging with *living* religious actions.

When you go and visit a religious community or meet and talk with religious people, YOU go. This means that your body, your expectations, your perceptions, your beliefs and ideas, your memories, your emotions, your imagination and your experiences are all involved in what you learn. The Spanish artist Antoni Muntadas, in his powerful work on the various ways in which we can interact with objects and spaces, says, "Warning! Perception Requires Involvement" (Muntadas, 2011, 183). The epistemological approach we take here could be described as *experiential knowledge*. For more on this see *Embodied Enquiry* (Todres, 2007). As Frances, a second-year undergraduate put it, more simply, in her evaluation of a study visit to Jerusalem: 'Fieldwork is amazing. It doesn't just get you thinking but touches your heart.'

This book will help you to get as much as possible out of the fieldwork that you do, to learn as much as possible, to understand how to reflect on what you have experienced and to communicate what you have learned. The questions at the end of the chapters, for example, are designed not only to aid comprehension of key ideas, but also to provide opportunities to reflect on your experiences and to discuss the issues raised when you engage with living religious people and communities.

Modernist, Enlightenment, empirical approaches to knowing separated the knowing subject, usually male, Western, white and Protestant, from an inanimate object of knowledge. This approach enabled huge progress in science and technology, but it also came to be seen as the only way of knowing. In the twentieth century these limits began to be questioned in many different academic fields, including the social sciences, and epistemology and methodology developed in different ways. Here we will briefly discuss some of the insights of feminist epistemology, which are interesting for fieldwork in the study of religion because they argue for ways of knowing which are relevant to qualitative research – both the planning and work in the field, and the writing up of the data. They also challenge the traditional patriarchal power structures which have distorted the study of religion. We discuss these power issues more fully later in the chapter.

Whilst feminism generally is about affirming the full humanity of all people, the key idea of feminist epistemology is about 'situated knowing'. This means that there is no neutral, objective, impartial perspective on the world; no one can be above all that is happening, just looking on. Everyone sees things from their own situation, or to put it another way, "every view is a view from somewhere and every act of speaking a speaking from somewhere" (Abu-Lughod, 2006, 155). The men of the Enlightenment treated their views as if they were actually a full, universal and absolute view of reality. But really, this was a very partial view of things which treated as normative, what was actually limited in time and space, and by the perspectives of those claiming to 'know'. As Donna Haraway put it, the problem is:

> how to have *simultaneously* an account of radical historical contingency for all knowledge claims and knowing subjects, a critical practice for recognising our own 'semiotic technologies' for making meaning, *and* a no-nonsense commitment to faithful accounts of a 'real world', one that can be partially shared and friendly to earth-wide projects of finite freedom, adequate material abundance, modest meaning in suffering, and limited happiness.
>
> (Haraway, 1991, 187)

In feminist epistemology, it is important to start with the knower, the one who is generating knowledge, and to recognise that everyone has strengths and limitations, a personal and social story, and approaches a situation, an event, an idea or a place with a number of agendas. Reflexivity is the art of developing a growing awareness and understanding of one's own situation, and responses to what happens in the field. It requires imagination, too, to attempt to understand the 'other', the people and places we are studying. There is also an awareness in some feminist thinking that things are connected, boundaries between self and other can become unsettled in the field, and that relationships are more important than individual self-determination and freedom of choice. This understanding chimes with many traditional religious views but is in contrast to the late modern Western idea of the autonomous, rational self. In this view religious phenomena will be understood as objects, but feminist approaches, amongst others, encourage a subject-subject, embodied relation with sacred objects, as well as people. Fieldwork, then, is a means of "incarnating subject matter" (Harris, 1991, 41). As Gordon Lynch writes:

> The sedimentation of religious narratives and discourses around particular sacred subjects means that adherents learn to encounter these subjects with the expectation that the sacred other will relate to them in certain ways – as a source of healing, moral challenge, forgiveness, power, hope, blessing and so on.
>
> (Lynch, 2010, 50)

It is also possible that a 'sacred subject', studied in the field, might have 'gifts' for students whether or not they are adherents of a particular faith; they might be opportunities for what one religious studies tutor called 'blessing'.

Although feminist writing, in theology and religious studies or anthropology, began by focusing on the experiences of women in a particular situation, attention soon shifted to *gender* as a category of analysis – see the website 'Feminism and Religion'. Part of this involves trying to understand how the body connects with various forces in religious and spiritual cultures. A more recent development in thinking about ways to interpret the world is Queer Theory, which problematises more traditional understandings of sex and gender, introduces ideas about identity as performance, and is interested in the transgression of boundaries – see *Gender Trouble* (Judith Butler, 1990) for an influential introduction to this field, especially her discussion about the performative nature of identity. These ideas are all relevant to theory and theorising about religion in the field. If identity is formed and reformed through performance, this gives us an interesting way of exploring ritual, and participation in various religious and spiritual activities – see, for example, *Dancing Theology in Fetish Boots* (Isherwood and Jordan, 2010). In fact, Queer Theory is becoming a very important part of the contemporary study of religion, as it helps us to change the way in which we approach the very subject we study. As Nynäs and Yip have noted, critiquing accepted notions of 'what religion is' by Queering our object(s) of study is vital as it changes "how we approach religion, what we highlight, include and exclude ... the private and the public, and the sacred and the secular" (Nynäs and Yip, 2012, 5).

Ritual

Ritual is a phenomenon that is frequently written about by scholars of religion, and there are many theoretical ways of understanding its meaning. Ritual can be seen as 'acting out' and symbolically expressing stories and ideas about the way the world began, what it means to be human and other major aspects of understanding reality. You can also consider rituals to be more about establishing and reinforcing particular social relations. Another way to approach rituals is as performance, a kind of theatre. This raises the issue which this whole book is addressing in different ways: how to understand the experiences and role of whoever is observing the ritual. The term 'participant observer' is used to indicate that there is a tension or a continuum between being a participant in ritual and being an observer. Studying religion in the field inevitably involves one in this process. For example, Tibetan monks perform a dance called Cham in a theatre in London, watched by a range of people, few, if any, of whom are Buddhists. However, this is not simply a piece of theatre, because, according to the beliefs of the dancing monks, just seeing the dance means that the audience will never be reborn in the hell realms, and so, the dance is partly performed for the audience's existential benefit. Having observed the dance, things are no longer the same because the ritual has both symbolised and actualised the change of status.

Observing religion in the field is a real reminder that *belief* is not a sufficient category to characterise religion. As David Morgan writes about the more complex range of practices which need to be considered:

> Their embodied forms of practice such as prayer, liturgy, and pilgrimage, their sensations of sound in corporate worship, their visual articulations of sacred writ, their creation of spaces that sculpt sound and shape living architectures of human bodies – all these vastly exceed the narrow idea of a religion as the profession of creeds or catechetical formulae singularly understood to represent an inner state of volition.
>
> (Morgan, 2010a, 2–3)

To put this another way, we are encouraging you not to think in dualistic terms of separate mind and body. Researchers need to bring their whole self to the fieldwork and to be aware of the mind/body forms of how people express their religion. A well-known example of this is the amazing statue *The Ecstasy of St Teresa of Avila* by Bernini, which is in a chapel in the Santa Maria della Vittoria church in Rome. Teresa wrote about her experiences in words that also express the inseparable nature of body and soul or mind. Or to put it another way, beliefs do not just exist in some dislocated mental space. Beliefs also have a social location (Day, 2011, 193).

Social trends and religion

There are numerous websites which are helpful for students in analysing and evaluating social trends in religion, and religion's place in society.

Here are some sites, which each give valuable contextualising information with regards to how religion operates in contemporary societies in specific social and political contexts:

PewResearch – this research centre focuses on religion within North American society, as well as large-scale, global-trend research projects. Particularly helpful for membership and attendance statistics, together with summaries of religious adherents' views on moral and ethical debates.

Religion and Society Project – the outcome of the UK's largest ever collaborative research project on religion within contemporary society, and the portal to access over seventy university-led projects from a £13 million initiative, this site provides access to research on topics as wide ranging as religious discrimination and Muslim-inspired modest fashion trends. The project is also linked to the Westminster Faith Debates, which are useful public forums on religious issues debated by politicians and public thinkers.

British Religion in Numbers – this portal has a searchable database which utilises government data, opinion polls, and faith community directories to provide an easy-access source of information for students asking quantitative questions regarding religious communities within the UK.

The Pluralism Project – Harvard University's ongoing research project (founded in 1991) seeks to map the changing landscape of American religious identity and community, and their website contains a rich variety of data and scholarship easily accessible for students.

Institute for Jewish Policy Research – Sometimes, it is useful to access tradition-specific data repositories, of which this is a good example. This institute publishes the results of major quantitative research into British Jewry.

In addition to the above, national census websites are invaluable sources of information on changing social trends in religious identity. Here are some relevant sources of information:

Australia: www.abs.gov.au/census
Canada: www12.statcan.gc.ca/census-recensement/index-eng.cfm
New Zealand: www.stats.govt.nz/Census.aspx
United Kingdom: www.ons.gov.uk/ons/guide-method/census/2011/uk-census/index.html

NB The census of the United States has not included a religion question since the 1950s, but the government has conducted some separate research. This can be found here: www.census.gov/compendia/statab/cats/population/religion.html

Relational issues

One of the major methodological issues within the study of religion(s) is the relationship between the researchers and the subject they are researching. Questions such as 'Do Catholics have insights into Catholic communities that a non-Catholic couldn't have?' or 'Do agnostics approach religions more even-handedly than atheists?' may have been asked in a previous generation of scholar-ship. Traditionally within the study of religion, insider/outsider discourse, as this subject has become known, has focused on the seemingly dualistic notion that one is either a member, or not a member, of a given worldview or religious community, and that questions can be asked about the approaches of people who fit on either side of this divide. Indeed, so powerful has this model been within the discipline that perhaps the most influential approach to the study of religion in the twentieth century, phenomenology, has often been applied at undergraduate level in a way which may be seen to support binary notions of 'inside' and 'outside' – namely, Ninian Smart's famous challenge not to judge someone "until you have walked a mile in their moccasins" (Smart, 1998, 11). Importantly, we say 'may' here as a reflective approach to Smart's practical suggestion leaves important room for an understanding of our relationality and connection. By asking you to walk in the steps of someone else, you are being challenged to deliberately empathise with another human being – as a subject, not an object. This approach may well be helpful as a way of breaking down insider/outsider binaries, as it highlights the view that the more one understands of oneself, the more one is able to begin to understand another, without reverting to simple prejudging. Cox, in his exposition of phenomenology, outlines the importance of this practice – technically referred to as 'epoché' – arguing that this sympathetic approach allows us to understand what we are studying from the viewpoint of our subjects (Cox, 2010, 48–72).

Such developments in our understanding of the imagined boundaries between identities and worldviews are supported by Arvind Sharma, who has contested simplistic conceptions of belonging, particularly with regard to Hindu identity, arguing that dualistic conceptions of religion, where one is either 'inside' or 'outside', are unhelpful as it makes religion a unilateral category of participa-tion, which is seen as separate from understandings of culture (2008, 23). This is a powerful argument, which applies to different traditions, not just Hindu traditions – contemporary phenomena about merged religious identities have given rise to JuBus (Jewish Buddhists), JeWitches (Jewish Witches), Qagans (Quaker Pagans), HinJews (Hindus and Jews) and many other relational religious identities.

Similarly, contemporary political developments in Europe have led to interesting examples of communities challenging monolithic categories of religious belong-ing, even if the laws of the countries involved may not have caught up yet. One example, from the time of writing this book, is a protest by hundreds of Icelandic liberals who have applied to become members of Iceland's national Muslim Association. Their actions are intended as a display of solidarity with the small number of other Muslim citizens, of whom there are only 770 registered at present, and were triggered by the recent denial of planning permission for a mosque to be built in the capital city, Reykjavik. This is more than a simple act of online protest such as putting one's name to a petition, however, as Icelandic law only allows a person to register as a member of one religious group at a time – in other words, someone's religious identity can only fit into the narrow categories of Icelandic legislation. Of course, what is particularly interesting about this case is that the individuals involved almost certainly have not incorporated ritualistic aspects of Muslim living, or contemplated divine will or the revelation of the Qur'an, but have acted upon core values of liberalism, multiculturalism, individual rights and freedom of religion, which underpin their everyday lives, to find common ground with fellow Icelanders who happen to be defined as belonging to a different religion – their relational identity has great areas of overlap which are not sufficiently explained by describing someone as 'Muslim' or 'not Muslim'. Such an example serves to show us that people's relational identities within, and between, the labels applied by the scholarship of generations past – and the laws based upon such labels – are not sufficiently nuanced for our contemporary networked inter-relational world; identities should be thought of as overlapping Venn diagrams, not boxed-off or separable categories.

When we approach living religion, then, it is clear that binary models of belonging – where one is either a thing or not a thing, a member or not a member, a believer or not a believer – are no longer fit for purpose. Instead, we need to understand that there is a continuum of belonging, often complicated and messy, but which can do greater service to the models of religious identity which real people enact within their daily lives. Of course, this also applies to the relationship between neophyte researchers and their host community, as well as religious participants themselves, and such a continuum must take into account numerous factors.

No individual is ever a complete outsider to a worldview, but has a relational understanding of convergent concepts, categories, practices and thought systems. As Cohen (1985) has argued, a sense of identity is symbolically constructed *in relation* to other symbolic constructions of identity by third parties. Issues such as gender, sexual orientation, language, class, philosophical worldview, political views and moral standpoints will all hugely impact upon an individual's relational identity with a diversity of religious traditions, all of which critiques notions of 'insideness' or 'outsideness'. For example, it is perfectly sensible to label members of the Church of Jesus Christ of Latter-Day Saints (LDS Church), commonly known as Mormons, as Christians. They self-identify as such, focus on the person of Christ in their theology and use the Bible, as well as the Book of Mormon, as the basis of their teachings and communal identity. However, the World Council of Churches – a transnational Christian ecumenical organisation – has consistently rejected Mormon applications to join. The situation is equally complicated for the scholar approaching Mormonism – if you are Christian, does this mean you are an 'insider' to a wider community and sense of commitment to Jesus Christ which means that you would find it easier to speak with LDS Church members, or would the fact that your theologies diverge make it even more difficult for you? Similarly, perhaps someone who believes in a god – perhaps a Jew – may have more empathy for another person who also believes in a monotheistic deity – perhaps a Muslim – even if they have major differences of opinion on other matters, than they would have for an atheist, polytheist or animist. Likewise, perhaps left-wing Catholics have more in common with left-wing Buddhists than they do with right-wing fellow Catholics when it comes to issues of social justice which affect how they negotiate their daily lives.

Such examples highlight how simple inside or outside labels are increasingly unhelpful – we suggest that in any reflective work you write on religious communities, an important part of that work is to position yourself in relation to the community in question, to help to contextualise your approach, and we will develop this theme in chapters 4 and 5.

Issues of power

Despite the protestations of our elected politicians, there can be no doubt that we still live in a world full of colonialism. Global music is predominantly influenced by America, fashion has its 'capitals' in London, Paris and New York, 'Western' sports such as football (soccer) and cricket are played more widely across the globe than any other sports, English is the international language of air travel, Arab states are modelling their schools, colleges and universities (and the inspection regimes that help them to develop) on European models, and if you turn on MTV in New Delhi, you will be met with smiling pale-faced Indians, dressed in 'Western' clothes who are hardly representative of their Dravidian heritage brother and sister South Indians. Perhaps the major economic powers of the world may be post-empire, but we hardly live in a post-colonial world. These are examples of how power, and the discourse of power, is a crucial factor in our understanding of contemporary social phenomena. This is particularly the case when it comes to studying religion.

The most obvious way in which this power dynamic has played out in the study of religion is in the preferential treatment that Christianity has received within the Academy. Whilst there may be theological reasons for this heritage, the problem arises that religious traditions and activities have often been (mis)understood through a lens of Christianity. Or more precisely, traditions have been (mis)understood against an essentialised vision of 'normative' Christianity. This is important, as this bad old 'comparative' religion – which uses a yardstick against which to compare, contrast and analyse a variety of religious phenomena – is as equally unhelpful for exploring living Christianity as it is for exploring other religious systems and experiences. For this reason, whenever we teach students about different religious traditions, we always insist that they use terminology and examples from the traditions in question – for example, we do not encourage students to translate *dharma*, a Sanskrit word often *mis*translated as 'duty' (it means so much more, including concepts of individual responsibility, social justice and cosmic balance). Instead, use the term *dharma* and understand it within specific Indian contexts – which for a full understanding of the term needs to incorporate personal, social and cosmological nuances of the concept. Likewise, when you engage with living religions, do not compartmentalise them into neat comparable categories; such neat academic boxes are often more misleading than helpful. Despite this, the history of our discipline is littered with examples of power dynamics affecting our approach to religion, which in turn has affected how people have approached religious communities and even the concept of religion itself.

Perhaps the most problematic issue has been the preference that has been given to texts, and their role in the history of our discipline. In the nineteenth century, the rise of biblical criticism in British, French and German universities introduced new ways of looking at 'sacred scriptures' – they were opportunities to engage with the records of human communities' religious experiences, and/or the relationship between the divine and the human. The rise of archaeology, geology, biology and other associated sciences and methodologies challenged and tested received notions of scriptural inerrancy, but this process of change must be understood in a post-Reformation landscape.

The Reformation had reorientated Christian worship across large parts of Europe to a concentration on the Bible as 'the Word' of God. Pulpits, used for reading and preaching from the Bible, became central to churches, as 'the Word', physically and purposefully, became the focus of attention and the defining point of Christian identity and practice. The inheritance of these historical shifts can still be seen. For example, the removal of church decorations, some often violently, is clearly visible on the outside of the western facade of Wells Cathedral, one of the masterpieces of European medieval architecture. The carved stone statues at the bottom of the facade have all been smashed or decapitated. The higher ones survived as the attackers must have simply destroyed what they could reach. Similarly, the scriptural literalism, often highlighted most popularly by the media when it comes to the 'Young Earth Creationist' Christians of the Southern States of the USA, only makes sense in a post-Reformation understanding of scripture and would have made little sense to earlier communities of Christians in medieval Europe.

The academic inheritance of this is that when universities in the nineteenth century began to examine religions other than Christianity, they first looked at texts, bringing with them the assumption that texts were central to all religious knowledge and identity as they believed they were for Christianity. This led to a concentration on, for example the Vedas for Hinduism and the Pali Canon for Buddhism, rather than the actual lived experience of Hindus and Buddhists. The texts of all religious traditions came to be seen as normative for that tradition, whereas they actually represent the recorded religious expression of a tiny minority of an elite class of men (almost always men). In addition, the texts are often in languages that are no longer spoken by ordinary members of the tradition, creating a further 'gap' between the reception of the text and the everyday realities, experience and knowledge of communities.

Within the development of the study of religion, much of this has been related to the discussion on 'Orientalism'. Put simply, this has been the process whereby 'foreign' or 'strange' cultural systems were 'othered' by the people studying them, thus seeing them as 'not normal' or 'strange' when compared to the scholars' own cultural systems. Perhaps confusingly, this problem can also occur even when scholars are seeking to be positive about cultures and traditions; we will explore this below, but it is important to note that the issue here isn't in being critical, any more than it is in being praising, but in *mis*representing what we are studying. An example here is what has happened in the post-war Christian rediscovery of the Jewish roots of Christianity. Biblical scholars always used to talk and write about the Old Testament, but wanting to recognise that both Jews and Christians see these books as revealed scripture, scholars have taken to referring to them as the 'Hebrew Scriptures' because they were originally written in Hebrew. They were trying to find a neutral term that did not make exclusively Christian claims for these texts. However, a result of this has been the suggestion (misunderstanding) that there is no difference between the Jewish and Christian texts, and that is deeply mistaken. The order of the books is different, which affects the meaning and understanding of the whole, and the ways in which the texts are interpreted are completely different. They are not experienced in the same way in worship or in study. Becoming aware of the ways in which these texts are used in the living religions needs to be part of the way in which they are studied at universities.

A scholar who has worked extensively in this area is Richard King (1999), whose important text *Orientalism and Religion* provides an often damning critique of how scholarship in 'Western' universities from the nineteenth century onwards has essentialised religion in the 'East' by utilising post-Enlightenment models of religion which do not culturally transfer beyond a European context. It is important to remember, however, that approaches such as King's, a complex and deep text, which seek to map a critical historical narrative on the history of the study of religions, are supported by numerous examples that students will come across in their normal studies. Flood, in his highly accessible *An Introduction to Hinduism*, notes that the great Hindu 'reformers' such as Rammohan Roy, who in the nineteenth century sought to change popular Hindu ritual away from *murti* (image) worship, were representing a form of Hinduism that was far removed from the popular practices of village-based Hinduism (Flood, 1996, 254). However, this elite form of Hinduism, which sees a direct chain of influence from Rammohan Roy, Debendranath Tagore, Keshub Chunder Sen, Vivekananda, Gandhi and late into the twentieth century with Sarvepalli Radhakrishnan, was prioritised by Western scholars who saw their form(s) of Neo-Vedanta as the form of Hinduism *par excellence*. This perpetuated misleading narratives concerning contemporary realities of how Hindu traditions are lived and performed.

Much recent scholarship has sought to redress such imbalances, and one helpful approach is Lynn Foulston's (1999) *At the Feet of the Goddess*, which is an ethnographic study of two goddess communities in India that analyses both the ritual and practice of devotees, and also explores origin myths with links to textual traditions. What is particularly helpful about this approach is that it does not start with the elite source of texts, but does not discount them either – it understands the use and interpretation of texts in everyday practice in specific and localised communities. This is an important example of starting from a bottom-up approach to how religion is performed as an everyday reality. Similarly, with regard to Islam, Carl Ernst (2004) has traced the Protestant Orientalist projection of what he calls the 'scripturalist fallacy' approach to religion in his *Following Muhammad: Rethinking Islam in the Contemporary World*. There is now a growing literature based around everyday religious experiences of Islam, including Zine's (2008) work on religious identity in Muslim schools which uses interviews with female pupils as its starting point, as opposed to the 'official' line of the patriarchal hierarchies of school management.

Such de-essentialising approaches are vital to the development of the study of religion in very specific contexts, which helps to avoid oversimplification or misrepresentation of often very diverse traditions. More than this, however, understanding that religion must be approached within a social context also means taking into account the power dynamics that affect assumptions that often lie behind these social and political contexts. This is important as it can change the very subject that underpins everything scholars of religion study – that is, the very definition of 'what religion is'. Harvey (2013) has recently used the example of the Church of the Flying Spaghetti Monster (FSM) to critique received definitions and categories of religion in the contemporary West. FSM has been defined by Cusack as a protest religion akin to other third-millennium invented religions such as Jediism and Matrixism (Cusack, 2010, 113–40), and has its origins in a satirical protest letter written by Bobby Henderson to the Kansas School Board which objected to the teaching of evolution without the 'balancing' narrative of the intelligent design creationism of the Church of the Flying Spaghetti Monster, which he argued was his deity of choice. Of course, this was a protest aimed at American Young Earth Creationists, who Henderson (2006) was worried were harming scientific learning in the class-room, but the movement has taken off as a religious organisation with a priesthood, holy text, complex mythological history, holiday calendar and ethical framework, including public pronouncements on high-profile moral issues such as same-sex marriage (www.venganza.org).

Cusack argues that FSM has become, even if it was not Henderson's original intention, an "aggressive culture-jamming ... rebellion against the materialist, spectaculist culture of the late modern West ... [a] religion of resistance ... [which] upholds Enlightenment rationality and scientific objectivity on the one hand, while making possible the instantiation of the FSM as the deity ... on the other" (Cusack, 2010, 140). However, as fascinating as the development of FSM has been, it is the shape of this development which is of most relevance to our current discussion. Indeed, Harvey has noted that the FSM only makes sense as a protest, satirical or rebellious religion if we accept Protestant theological definitions of what 'religions are', stating that the whole FSM project "reveals common assumptions about how religion might be defined: religions are popularly supposed to have transcendent but self-revealing deities, texts, cosmologies, rituals, hierarchies, and probably a degree of hypocrisy" (Harvey, 2013, 62). For Harvey, therefore, FSM is a protest religion by numbers – a construction of a religious phenomenon within a tightly defined cultural assumption which is clear about what religions are, and how religions operate.

Such assumptions about 'what religion is', based on these culturally inherited power discourses which define or produce a standard against which 'other' traditions are judged, are not just an issue for invented or parody religions – issues as important as the very laws of countries and the human rights afforded to people within them are affected by such inherited assumptions. One such example is the current debate, particularly amongst Pentecostals and Anglicans, surrounding homosexuality and Christianity in Africa. Public rhetoric by anti-gay campaigners has often focused on an argument that homosexual relationships are 'un-African', as if it were somehow indigenous to an archaic and deeply embedded African worldview or culture to be intolerant to diverse adult sexualities. The problem with this position is that the current church teachings, and indeed the very laws which cover same-sex rights, which the campaigners have used and reified, are themselves products of nineteenth-century colonial church attitudes and legal changes, which were distinctly un-African in that they were imposed upon a colonised people by an external dominant colonial power – often the British. Caution of course must be noted so that the power dynamics at play in these historical, political and religious contexts are not oversimplified, but using this example serves to highlight that rigid definitions of 'what religion is' and 'how it operates in society' are complicated by local and historical factors which still create social problems in the twenty-first century.

A further example is the treatment of many new religious movements in northern Europe in recent years – particularly within a French context. Palmer has written extensively about the 'Secte panic' that gripped France in the early 1990s, outlawing and demonising many alternative religious communities. As she has stated: "France is remarkable for its unique and paradoxical form of intolerance toward religious minorities. France's constitutional guidelines clearly offer protection for freedom of religion ... [but] intolerant attitudes ... have been gradually institutionalized." (Palmer, 2011, 3) Importantly, Palmer goes on to say: "Since the lay [French] state does not recognize any religion, it is theoretically impossible, either legally or philosophically, for the state to distinguish 'real' religions from 'fake' ones, exactly what the state has been trying to do since 1995" (2011, 4). In our current discussion, it is perhaps more helpful to use the terms 'normative'/'non-normative' rather than 'real'/'fake', but Palmer makes a crucial point in her observation of the French government's treatment of religious minorities, highlighting that the large anti-cult movement has its origins in the Roman Catholic Church within France. Indeed, as Gregg (2012) has previously noted, the Roman Catholic Church is still the majority cultural identity driver for some major new religious movements in France, and it is not surprising that a nominally secular government still relates to Catholic-informed conceptions of religion, given the history of Catholicism in Western Europe. It is possible that small shifts are occurring with regard to conceptions of religion in court cases, however, and one interesting example comes from the UK concerning the Church of Scientology.

Scientology is a complicated movement which operates under a number of transnational organisations and structures, including the Religious Technology Center and the International Association of Scientologists, but which has radically different legal standing in different countries across the world, which leads to a huge diversity of lived experience for Scientologists in different contexts. Put simply, the lived religious experience of a Scientologist in Bavaria, Germany, will be far removed from the experience of a Scientologist in Florida, USA. Much of the diversity of approach towards Scientology is based on pre-existing cultural attitudes towards 'what religion is', which has affected subsequent court decisions regarding the legal status of the organisation.

Within the UK, Scientology was denied charitable status – and thus the social and financial benefits that come with this – in a Charity Commission (1999) ruling. The judgement was based upon the conclusion that the "core practices of Scientology, being auditing and training, do not constitute worship as they do not display the essential characteristic of reverence or veneration for a supreme being" (1999, 2a) and that "public benefit arising from the practice of Scientology and/or the purposes of [the Church of Scientology] had not been established" (1999, 2c). It should be clear that this judgement essentialises 'what religion is' within a very narrow Protestant theological definition, and does not respond to the lived realities of religion in contemporary society. Of course, it was always likely that such a challenge to Scientology's social legiti-macy would come, and this has indeed been the case. A direct consequence of this ruling on the everyday lives of Scientologists was that they could not be legally married in their churches, as they were not recognised as places of worship under English law.

In December 2013 a Supreme Court ruling was made in the case of a British Scientologist couple who sought to marry at a London Church of Scientology. In an important ruling for the place of religion in UK society, the Supreme Court found in the Scientologist's favour stating that "religion should not be confined to religions which recognise a supreme deity" (Supreme Court, 2013, 51) and that "Scientologists do believe in a supreme deity of a kind, but of an abstract and impersonal nature" (2013, 52) and that, due to these factors, Scientology churches should be recognised as places of worship. Interestingly, the ruling accepted that "there has never been a universal legal definition of religion in English law" (2013, 34) but focused upon conceptions of deity or ultimate reality and, crucially, delivered a verdict that clearly still understood 'religion' in the context of a "belief system" (2013, 57). Although it can be observed that the Supreme Court ruling helped to modernise understandings of religion in contemporary society – with particular impact upon understandings of some aspects of Hindu and Buddhist traditions – the power dynamics of inherited social capital and assumptions about religion emergent from England's religious past are still clearly visible in the decision.

So, if we are to explore religions in very localised contexts, appreciating the wider power dynamics that impact upon both their own development and identity and our relationship with them and our approach to studying them, how can we best manage the problems that this creates? One way for neophyte researchers to negotiate these power dynamics skilfully is to ensure that writing and reflection on religious communities does not revert to statements such as 'Hindus believe that … '. Not only is this an essentialising approach, it focuses on an abstract notion of belief, whereas it is so much more helpful to focus on how people act – acts which may well be informed by a notion of belief – rather than what they say they believe. Beliefs are useful to understand as con-textualising information on how such beliefs guide people to act – they cannot, in themselves, be studied. Malinowski, who we introduced earlier, acknowl-edged this important point when he differentiated between the 'norms' and 'activities' of a community. The 'norms' were the *expectations* of the group – how they publicly presented their social behaviours to outsiders. The 'activities' of a group, however, were of much more interest to the scholar, for these are the *actual* social behaviours that occurred in a social group. These may or may not live up to the expectations of the 'norms' (Parsons, 2002). In this book, we have introduced our concepts of 'represented religion' and 'lived religion' – these can be seen to build upon Malinowski's categories of 'norms' and 'activities' – and investigating the 'lived' realities of religious communities is the best way of understanding communities in everyday life – how they actually are, rather than how they are believed to be.

This focus upon lived, rather than represented, religion means that it is important to understand voices from within traditions from the ground up – congregants as well as archbishops, devotees as well as gurus. In so doing, we challenge accepted issues of 'authority' in religion and question whose voices we should be listening to. Sometimes such issues are codified within the identity of traditions – for example, within Orthodox Jewish communities, rabbis are expected to have authoritative voices concerning *halakhic* (religious law) mat-ters; within Sikhism, after 1699, the Khalsa movement has sought to 'speak for' Sikhism. However, in the modern world, such issues of authority are being challenged. Linda Woodhead's recent research on the ethical stance of Catholic congregations in the UK shows a massive difference between congregants – who are more liberal – and clergy and Church leaders – who are more conservative (Woodhead, 2013). When we speak of 'Catholic attitudes' towards a certain issue, what then are we really speaking of? In generations past, textbooks would invariably refer to Church teachings such as Council documents, papal encyclicals and other formal documents, but if such teachings are now in some ways removed from the lived realities of Catholics, how can they represent how

Catholics actually believe and act? Again, we return to the issue of everyday lived religious experience as an authoritative and authentic way of engaging with religion as a social phenomenon.

Finally, in this discussion about the different power dynamics that affect our approach to the study of religion, it is helpful to remember that these hierarchical influences are not just the stuff of history – they continue in the present. One simple example will suffice. Earlier in this section, we mentioned the problem of 'elite' languages creating a dissonance between everyday religious participants and the texts which have been, to date, preferenced as authoritative in much scholarship. It is essential to recognise, however, that this is not just an issue of early Bronze Age Indians not relating to Sanskrit, or medieval Catholics not understanding the spoken words of the Latin Mass. Contemporary religious texts and ceremonies are often written or performed in languages outside the use of everyday people; in contemporary Britain, Canada and Germany, for example, many Sikhs do not understand Punjabi beyond ritual use, and across the world, from Malaysia, Indonesia, India, Turkey and across Europe, America and Australasia, Muslims often do not use Arabic in everyday discourse. These are not value judgements, of course, but observations that if we highlight scholarly linguistic exegesis of the Guru Granth Sahib or the Qur'an as somehow being representative of what Sikhism or Islam are, then we fall into the essentialising traps of the past by failing to engage with how the texts are actually used by hundreds of millions of religious adherents within vibrant and diverse religious communities today.

Complicating issues

One of the things that anyone studying religion in the field has to consider is how to deal with aspects of religion that challenge you, surprise you, or perhaps even offend you. What do we really mean by 'respect' for others' belief and practice, and how do we respond to unexpected or challenging issues which complicate our experiences when engaging with individuals and communities?

"I don't believe in owt"

The research for a very interesting book on belief in Britain was stimulated by an interview with a 14-year-old boy:

> I began my interview with Jordan by asking him my first question to which he replied in Yorkshire dialect, using 'nowt' for 'nothing' and 'owt' for 'anything'.

ABBY: What do you believe in?
JORDAN: Nowt.
ABBY: Sorry?
JORDAN: I don't believe in owt. I don't believe in any religions.

ABBY: You don't believe in any religions.
JORDAN: No. I'm Christian but I don't believe in owt.

As a product of a certain historical era, and one raised in a church-attending family, it was initially difficult for me to account for Jordan and the many other 'anomalies' I was to meet in my research. It was sometimes my own emotional and cognitive response to interviews that showed me I had entered difficult, and therefore potentially fruitful, territory.

(Day, 2011, 29)

If we are to engage with living religion then we have to take people's beliefs and actions *seriously* whatever our immediate response to them is. There is no need to agree with, or to approve, in order to seek to understand others. What is important is to be aware of our responses, and these skills of reflexivity are much more fully discussed in chapter 5. When you go on a visit or meet with religious people you take your whole self with you, which includes critical as well as respectful aspects. This is often very hard to do if we encounter challenging worldviews that make us uncomfortable or that contradict our presuppositions or expectations.

One scholar that we have found very useful when approaching these issues is Susan Palmer. In her work with the Nuwaubian Nation of Moors (2011), she has faced the issue of being a white female academic investigating a black patriarchal religious movement. To overcome this seemingly huge obstacle, she uses the term 'overstanding', which is borrowed from Rastafari traditions, to describe the way in which scholars can best negotiate these difficulties. Put simply, to 'understand' something is to view something from your own position – looking up at your subject with the limited view that that offers. To 'overstand' something is to view something from the position of your host community, and this allows a much wider field of view and context. Such an approach builds on the relational role scholars have with their communities of study, and helps to engage with everyday lived realities. This is important, Martin Stringer reminds us, as "for most people, 'religion' is situational and often contradictory" (Stringer, 2011, 51).

An important element of this is aspects of religion that we find discomforting or personally challenging. Here is one example of such an occasion, which reflects upon an experience engaging with religion in the field:

Standing on a hill, at Pashupatinath, just outside Kathmandu in Nepal, we watched as families brought bodies to be burned and then cast the ashes into the Bagmati River, although actually it was only a stream at the time. It was a vivid reminder that we all die. It also posed some questions. Should we have been watching at all? This was an intimate occasion of grief, and would we like tourists coming to see the funeral of our loved ones? What about taking photographs? Was it okay to watch but not okay to take pictures even if they were going to be used for teaching? What about the photos and videos of such events already on the Internet? Did that make it acceptable to have our cameras? Why do so many tourists come here to view such rituals?

A few days later and we were waiting to go up the mountain to the Manakamana Temple. So were hundreds of other people, in their best clothes, excited to be making this important pilgrimage. We go up, six at a time, in a cable car – the only one in Nepal – and arrive just below the village with the temple. The views of the valley below are amazing. The main street is lined with stalls selling food, clothes, games, flags and souvenirs. The temple is dedicated to the Goddess Bhagwati, the wish-fulfilling deity, and many of the pilgrims have come to make a sacrifice; the goats and birds that came up the mountain cable car in separate containers are collected at the top and brought up the hill to the temple. There they will be killed, although as non-Hindus we can only watch from the square as the queues into the temple build up and the dead animals are brought out to various restaurants to be cooked and eaten. Some of our fellow travellers are indignant that animal sacrifice should be allowed. "It's cruel", "It's primitive", they say. Perhaps, but it is also powerful, uncomfortable, compelling, a ritual that very definitely changes something, that takes us, for a while, into another world. Going back down in the cable car, the Nepalese woman sitting opposite us is sick into a paper bag.

Such an experience is complicated and difficult to express in academic writing, but serves as a useful example of how researchers need to react to difficult situations, and reflect upon unexpected events to contextualise lived religious experience in specific contexts. One such context is the contested territory of the West Bank. The following text box gives two further examples of complicating issues which affected how we, and our students, engaged with religious communities and identities as they were represented to us on recent study tours, which included a visit to Bethlehem University.

Reflections on 'complicating issues' in Bethlehem

Lynne: We were visiting students and staff at Bethlehem University. After lunch they took us up onto the roof to look at the views, and they pointed out the Dheisheh refugee camp where some of the students live. We had visited there earlier in the day. I had been thinking about that experience and I quietly asked one of the staff whether it really needed to still exist, more than sixty years after Palestinians left their homes in what became Israel and fled to the territory then occupied by Jordan. The West Bank was taken over by Israel in 1967 and Bethlehem has been under the administration of the Palestine National Authority since 1995. This person agreed that really there was no practical reason to still have a camp. This isn't the place to explore the other reasons why it is there. What interests us here is the hunch that what he said to me isn't part of the usual discourse at the University about the camp. I am sure that if the question had been asked in a big group I would have got a different answer. I was staff and so, perhaps, did not need to get only the official line. Would he have talked in the same way to a student? I don't know, but it complicates things. Black and white issues become grey.

Stephen: On my first visit to the University, I was interested to know how the campus catered for its diversity of students. Although the University is a Catholic foundation, over 70 per cent of its students are Muslim. As such, after our initial campus tour, which centred on a welcome by the University Chaplain in the University Chapel, I asked one of our student guides if I could see the Muslim prayer room. This seemed rather straightforward to me, as I had just seen the worship space for Christian students, and so wanted to balance this experience with knowledge about facilities for the (majority) Muslim students. The response I got surprised me. The student, a mature man in his late twenties, looked aghast at my request saying, "You don't need to see it, it's just a plain room". I politely repeated that, nonetheless, I would be very interested to see the part of campus that Muslim students used for formal prayers. At this point, our guide spoke in hushed tones with his fellow students and again tried to talk me out of my request. Eventually, the student took me to a sports hall and said, "This is where they meet on Fridays." As I looked into the nondescript space, I am not sure who was more uncomfortable – me, or the group of covered Muslim female undergraduates who were sheepishly playing volleyball until we entered the room. As we left, the student told me that "we are a Christian University, we couldn't have something like a mosque here". The University is proud of its mixed student demographic, and is rightly lauded for much community work in a troubled part of the world. Such a stance was complicated for me, by my experience of the everyday realities of attitudes towards 'non-Christian' students.

Such issues highlight the importance of engagement with bottom-up religion; the lived realities of daily life for religious adherents, and the ways in which this informs the projection of religious identities. They also highlight one way of understanding how religious communities find and make meaning in their individual and communal lives by demonstrating the importance of etiquette in relational living – what is said, what is done, how it is said and done, and within what strict parameters. Recently, Harvey (2013, 111ff.) has linked this to Polynesian notions of *Tapu* – the relational aspect of negotiating meaning and conduct in our daily lives, which may well sit at the heart of a useful understanding of 'what religion is'. The negotiated and contested spaces, identities and discourses between different religious communities in Bethlehem demonstrate how the art of performing religious identities is played out within carefully constructed communal boundaries of what is or is not expected, what is or is not acceptable, within very specific and evolving limits.

To transfer this theory into practice when engaged with living religious communities, we need to understand the transformative role of personal relationships with our host communities, to appreciate we are doing more than just transferring knowledge when we engage with individuals, and to ensure that we always seek to understand (or, indeed, to 'overstand') people and societies with whom we are privileged to share time.

Issues of writing and reflection

In chapter 5, on doing independent fieldwork, there is a section on the more practical aspects of writing up fieldwork. What we do here is to discuss some developments in thinking about and in the practice of writing up the results of qualitative research. Since we are no longer thinking about objective knowledge produced by some neutral and anonymous researcher, but rather, understanding what we do as some form of subject-subject, embodied and reflective process, then it obviously makes sense to approach the writing part of the research differently too. We could go as far as saying that how we write is part of how we know.

When you are thinking about how to do fieldwork, it is helpful to use the ideas of the education writer Elliot Eisner. He uses two key terms, *connoisseurship* and *criticism* to explore ways of understanding something: "Connoisseurship is the art of appreciation. It can be displayed in any realm in which the character, import or value of objects, situations, performances is distributed and variable" (Eisner, 1998, 63). Someone who is a wine connoisseur can tell a great deal from the look, smell and taste of a glass of wine. The more one understands about wine, the more one can discern. Similarly, an art connoisseur, looking at a painting or sculpture, can 'read' a lot in the work of art; they have developed the ability to 'see' deeply. So, in doing fieldwork in the study of religion, you have to learn to be a connoisseur. You have to practise because the more, different places you visit, the better. You also have to research as much as possible both before and after a visit. Eisner's idea of connoisseurship is about being able to 'see', not just to 'look', just as we discussed in the section on issues of knowledge above. It involves:

> the ability to name and appreciate the different dimensions of situations and experiences, and the way they relate to one another. We have to be able to draw upon, and make use of, a wide array of information. We also have to be able to place our experiences and understanding in a wider con-text, and connect them with our values and commitments. Connoisseurship is something that needs to be worked at – but it is not a technical exercise. The bringing together of the different elements into a whole, involves artistry.

> (Smith, 2005)

If connoisseurship is about seeing as fully as possible, then criticism is about communicating what you see so that someone else can see it too. If you read an article by an art critic and look at the painting he or she is writing about, your perceptions should be enhanced, you should see more because of what you read; it should evoke insight and understanding and it should help shape your future perception of a work of art. You may not agree with the criticism but you ought to be able to see what it is getting at. This is the kind of writing we want to encourage you to produce – writing which evokes something of the qualities and nature of the living religion you have engaged with in the field and the understanding you have developed as a result of your experiences. So, begin to think about how you could write 'criticism' about your experiences in the field. The text box below gives an example of the kind of vivid and interesting writing which can be done.

Ghosts of Spain

Read the following extract from *Ghosts of Spain* (Tremlett, 2012, 362–68). It is a very good example of 'thick description' together with comments and wider connections made by the author. Notice the concrete, vivid language which brings the occasion alive so that the reader can imagine just what is happening and what it is like.

I met Manuel standing beside his coffin. The long, wooden box, lined with quilted, padded white viscose, was standing upright, leaning against the wall of the church at Santa Marta de Ribarteme (in Galicia, Spain). Manuel and four friends were standing beside it, quietly waiting for the moment when he would step in ... The coffin parade at Santa Marta de Ribarteme was, I had been assured, one of the supreme examples of those twin Galician characteristics of religiosity and superstition ... Inside the tiny, stone church, a queue of men and women was barging its way noisily forward towards a polychrome statue of Santa Marta – Lazarus's sister, who once served Jesus his supper. A man with a microphone and a weary expression was berating them. 'If you could hear yourselves,' he said, 'you would realise that this sounds like anything other than the house of God.' But still they pushed anxiously forward. They were sweating in the summer heat – a hot crush of frail bodies, frayed nerves and raised voices ... The sickly and the well reached out to wipe the statue, or its pedestal, with their handkerchiefs. Once the saint had been touched, the handkerchiefs were immediately passed over the owners' brow, neck or face ... A uniformed wind band struck up some doleful marching music as two statues, a smaller San Antonio leading out Santa Marta herself, lurched out of the church door balanced on the villagers' shoulders. Manuel and the others stepped into their coffins and were raised aloft by their pall-bearers ... Less than an hour later, after wandering through some woods, the procession arrived back at the church. Manuel entered in his coffin. He said his prayers, stepped out of his box, and having paid the priest 180 euros to borrow the coffin, handed it back. It was carried over to a stone shed where it joined a dozen others. Manuel, and his exhausted friends, headed back to Tuy ... Miracles are part of Roman Catholic belief. Hiring a coffin may be an extreme way of giving thanks, but then there are no more traditional Roman Catholics in Spain than the Galicians.

If writing up fieldwork is to enable the reader to 'see' what you saw then it is worth considering how best to do that. "Vision is a complex assemblage of seeing what is there, seeing by virtue of habit what one expects to see there, seeing what one desires to be there and seeing what one is told to see there" (Morgan, 2005, 74). Reflecting on our expectations and desires helps us to be aware of their influence on what we see and when we write we need to make this as clear as possible. We have used the idea of 'represented religion' to refer to what participants tell us we should be seeing and this is an important part of what is going on. It is useful to include the words that an informant actually uses when you write up fieldwork. In a way, by doing this, you are getting between represented religion and living religion. The connections between language and perception are complex and not only will your seeing in the field be enhanced by more sophisticated knowledge and understanding, but the language you use in the writing process will affect the reader's ability to see what you mean. Good writing will include rich description, reflection on experience, including how you know what you claim you know, and connections with wider reading. All of these contribute to the analysis and interpretation.

It is worth stressing here that, if you read other people's accounts of their fieldwork in religion, that will help you to develop your own writing skills. At the end of this chapter there are suggestions for further reading, and the article by Mary Jo Neitz would be a good place to start. Especially as neophyte researchers, it is important to remember that we can always learn from those who have gone into the field before us, and especially those who have perhaps spent time with communities you are unlikely to visit as a part of your studies. As Evans-Pritchard noted, when quoting Malinowski:

Everybody goes to [their host community] with preconceived ideas but, as Malinowski used to point out, whereas the layman's are uninformed, usually prejudiced, the anthropologist's are scientific, at any rate in the sense that they are based on a very considerable body of accumulated and sifted knowledge.

(1973, 2)

Pilgrim/tourist/student – distinctiveness and crossover

On the door of St Catherine's church in Bethlehem there is this sign: "We are hoping that: if you enter here as a tourist, you would exit as a pilgrim. If you enter here as a pilgrim you would leave a holier one." This sign assumes that there is a clear distinction between pilgrims and tourists. The idea would be that pilgrims travel as part of their religious or spiritual practice. They go to a place which has religious significance and their journey accumulates some kind of religious merit. On the other hand, tourists have mundane, secular motives and their journeys do not involve significant personal meaning. Our experience as both travellers and tutors leading fieldwork visits in the study of religion is that this binary opposition between pilgrims and tourists is false. One of our students wrote in an assignment, "I can't help but wonder what really is holy. Am I a tourist or a pilgrim? Every pilgrim is just a tourist in disguise."

This section explores some ideas about pilgrims, tourists and the study of living religion, and some of the crossovers between them. For example, Terry Slater, a geographer, describes how his visit to Bologna, mainly for an academic conference, was both historical, spatial and personal. He visited the site of the bombing at Bologna station where two of his ex-students had died and had an experience of what he names as 'the motherhood of God'. He calls this experience a pilgrimage although it was not to a recognised pilgrimage site, but became a pilgrimage with "the complex layering of time and space in the lived world of the individual" (Slater, 2004, 251).

There is a long history of religious tourism and many earlier pilgrimages had elements that can easily be compared to modern journeys to a particular place. We will be analysing some of the similarities and differences in these roles, but there is no way of knowing in advance of a visit what its impact will be. That is part of the excitement of fieldwork in the study of religion. It is also the case that the impact of a place differs between students and also from visit to visit. This is why it is important to keep in mind YOUR responses to a place, and the ways in which your own previous life, worldviews and values impact on your experience of this place and this time. Finally, it is important to note that you will be mainly studying religion in the field along with a group of other students and staff. In *The Canterbury Tales*, Chaucer describes the pilgrims as a 'company'. That word literally means 'with bread' and eating with people on a visit may be significant for your experience of the visit.

Traditional religious pilgrims are often also travellers exploring the world beyond their own villages, cities and regions, and they bring home souvenirs and reminders of what they have learned. In medieval European Christian pilgrimage, for example, there was definitely an element of what is called in Latin, *curiositas*, a desire to see and understand the world, which was sometimes criticised as detracting from more spiritual motivations. In their introduction to *Reframing Pilgrimage*, Coleman and Eade, the editors, note how Muslim travel can be constructed not only as *hajj* (pilgrimage to Mecca) but also as *hijra* (migration), *rihla* (travel for learning and other purposes), and *ziyara* (visits to shrines); motives can be mixed (2004, 8). In the nineteenth century, Thomas Cook, well known for his promotion of modern tourism, began by taking people to Palestine to explore the historical and devotional aspects of Christianity.

Many today who take part in traditional pilgrimage journeys do not do so out of explicitly religious motives. For example, the Camino de Santiago de Compostela is growing in popularity each year, with thousands of people walking or cycling part or all of the traditional routes. Some are observant Christians but for many others the motivations are less clear. This is a good example of 'religious tourism', where the lines between secular and sacred are very blurred.

The Way

There is a very good film about the Camino de Santiago de Compostela written and directed by Emilio Estevez called *The Way*. The blurb advertising the film has these words:

> *The Way* is a powerful and inspirational story about family, friends and the challenges we face whilst navigating this ever-changing and complicated world. Martin Sheen plays Tom, an irascible American doctor who comes to France to deal with the tragic loss of his son (played by Emilio Estevez). Rather than return home, Tom decides to embark on the historical pilgrimage 'The Way of St. James' to honour his son's desire to finish the journey. What Tom doesn't plan on is the profound impact this trip will have on him. Through unexpected and oftentimes amusing experiences along 'The Way', Tom discovers the difference between 'the life we live and the life we choose'.

It is interesting to view the film and look at the website – see the end of the chapter for details – to explore the different motivations of those on the journey.

Alex Norman has studied the Camino as a case study for what he calls 'spiritual tourism'. He writes:

> The way the Camino is portrayed as a pilgrimage activity contributes significantly to the way it is performed. In the accounts of pilgrims' journeys we find that not only has the Camino been depicted as a means to absolve one's sins, but it is also understood to comprise a somatic process whereby one 'works through' the problems of life, before returning home. ... The themes of discovery are also multifaceted and also means the journey becomes one of learning; whether about the self, about others, about 'life' in general. Generally it is the self that is the focus.
>
> (2011, 171)

The phrase 'somatic process' is interesting. It refers to the fact that the Camino is something that cannot just be seen on film or even visited. One must *do* the pilgrimage; it is a bodily engagement, a practice that one can only do for oneself, even if in the company of others.

This embodiment is also a characteristic, to some degree, of fieldwork in the study of religion. Studying religion in the field also involves travelling; it is an external journey but, as the pilgrims who spoke to Alex Norman often said, it could also be understood as part of a life journey. They hoped that the Camino would affect their lives positively in ways they could not necessarily anticipate. Engaging with living religion in the field may also do that.

Pilgrim or student of religion?

The following are two reflections from students about an extended study visit undertaken as a part of their studies – they highlight the radically different ways that students in the same group can approach engagement with religion in the field:

'I had my "theology student" cap on for most of the journey; however, when I walked into the garden I took that cap off. My first impressions were that it looked very small in comparison to my childhood imagery of it. Once I was in, I wanted to go off by myself for the first time on the trip and I sat quietly at a resting point by the side of the garden. Without any thought I began to cry ... I managed to enter into the world that I had read about since I was a child. It was surreal ... it gave me the confidence to find God "my way" again simply by giving myself the space I needed to do that.'

'As well as providing "vertical learning" – a direct transference of information, it also conveyed "horizontal learning" – giving breadth, diversity, nuances. It made me very aware that there was always another side/aspect to the information – consequences, details, etc. I learned not to take information at face value.'

Not only do religious tourists and students studying religion in the field potentially change as a result of their experiences, but, according to Stausberg, the tourism itself makes religions more mobile. He wrote:

Tourism puts religious people, objects and ideas on the move; it contributes to the cultural and religious traffic, provides points of entry into other rounds of meaning, uproots elements of religion, and immerses them in a horizontal flow that in turn takes them beyond the organizational control of religious groups.

(2011, 223)

Travel has probably always done this and continues to do so. For example, during a holiday to the Caucasus there were lots of visits to churches and monasteries at the top of fairly steep hills. As we will see in the next chapter, mountains often have religious significance. For example, Psalm 24: 3 says, "Who shall ascend the mountain of the Lord? And who shall stand in his holy place?" It was very interesting to notice that, in Georgia, several of the tourists who could not walk up a particularly steep climb to the church at the top, refused to take a taxi. It was as if, by not walking, they were not worthy to visit the church. They weren't on a pilgrimage, but they felt they couldn't make it easy.

Engaging with living religion, even on our doorstep, may make us pilgrim, student, tourist or all three at once.

Travel and religion

Studying religion in the field involves a journey, however short. Studying religion abroad requires a much longer journey. There are some very interesting examples of accounts of journeys related to religion, not all of them pilgrimages, made by people in the past. Reading about any of these would develop your understanding of aspects of the study of religion, as well as, hopefully, encouraging you to follow in their footsteps.

- Egeria, a late fourth-century woman who made a pilgrimage to the Holy Land. She wrote an account of her journey to women at home which was copied and some fragments remain (for a translation of the text, see www.ccel.org/m/mcclure/etheria/etheria.htm).
- Ibn Battutah, a fourteenth-century North African Muslim who travelled widely for thirty years in Africa, the Middle East and Asia (Mackintosh-Smith, 2002).
- Two nineteenth-century Scottish women who found and studied texts at St Catherine's Monastery in the Sinai desert (Martin Soskice, 2010).
- Marco Polo who travelled from Venice to China in the thirteenth century (Berggreen, 2007).
- Judah Halevi was a Jewish traveller from Spain to Palestine via Egypt. There are references to him, as well as a lot of other evidence of living religion, in the Cairo Geniza (Hoffman and Cole, 2012).
- Geoffrey Chaucer's *The Canterbury Tales*, although a work of fiction, gives a very vivid picture of medieval Christian pilgrimage (see Ackroyd, 2010, for a very good translation).
- John Bunyan, *The Pilgrim's Progress*, written in England in 1678 whilst Bunyan was in prison for preaching what were forbidden religious ideas, is not about an external, physical journey, but imagines living a devout Christian life as a journey (see Bunyan, 2008).

Chapter summary

This chapter has included a lot of examples of living religion and ways of thinking about what it means to study them in the field. We want to encourage you to engage with scholarship so that your understanding and interpretation of what you experience during fieldwork is as deep and rich as possible. What you have read here will provide a framework for this. In the next chapter we focus on the places where you will be studying living religion in the field.

Further reading

Mary Jo Neitz (2000) 'Queering the Dragonfest: Changing Sexualities in a Post-Patriarchal Religion'. This is a very interesting, mainly theoretical article that draws significantly on two case studies of Wiccan practice in America.

Fiona Bowie's (2006) introductory text *The Anthropology of Religion* will make you aware of much of the relevant story of the study of religion in the field and the kinds of issues that scholars of religion have debated. However, much of the material relates to societies that very few students are likely to visit.

Questions for consideration

1 How has recent scholarship critiqued the 'World Religions' approach to the study of religion?
2 Reflect on how you think fieldwork study can contribute to a better understanding of religion. If you have already done some fieldwork, make sure you use your experiences in the field to help form your ideas.
3 How might ethnographic methods contribute to the study of religion locally?
4 Draw a scattergraph of your relation to different religious traditions and worldviews. Reflect on how this might affect your study in the field.
5 Write a vivid paragraph of 'thick description' of a religious place you have visited.

Bibliography

This list includes all the texts referred to in the chapter and other recommended reading. All websites accessed on 31.10.14.

Abu-Lughod, L. 2006 [originally published in 1991], 'Writing against Culture' in Lewin, E. (ed.) *Feminist Anthropology: A Reader*, Oxford: Blackwell, 153–69.
Ackroyd, P. 2010, *The Canterbury Tales: A Retelling by Peter Ackroyd*, London: Penguin Classics.
Ammerman, N.T. 2007, *Everyday Religion: Observing Modern Religious Lives*, New York: Oxford University Press USA.
Barker, E. 1984, *The Making of a Moonie: Brainwashing or Choice?* Oxford: Basil Blackwell.

Bergreen, L. 2007, *Marco Polo: From Venice to Xanadu*, New York: Knopf.

Bowie, F. 2006 (2nd edn), *The Anthropology of Religion*, Oxford: Black.

Bowman, M. 2012, *Vernacular Religion in Everyday Life: Expressions of Belief*, Durham: Acumen Publishing Ltd.

Bunyan, J. 2008 (Pooley ed.), *The Pilgrim's Progress*, London: Penguin Classics.

Butler, J. 1990, *Gender Trouble: Feminism and the Subversion of Identity*, London: Routledge.

Charity Commission, 1999, *Decision of the Charity Commission for England and Wales made on 17th November 1999: Application for Registration as a Charity by the Church of Scientology (England and Wales)*. Accessible at: www.charitycommission.gov.uk/media/100909/cosfulldoc.pdf

Chryssides, G.D. and Zeller, B. 2014, *The Bloomsbury Companion to New Religious Movements*, London: Bloomsbury.

Cohen, A.P. (1985), *The Symbolic Construction of Community*, London: Routledge.

Coleman, S. and Eade, J. (eds) 2004, *Reframing Pilgrimage*, London: Routledge.

Cousineau, P. 1998, *The Art of Pilgrimage*, Boston, MA: Conari Press.

Cox, J.L. 2010, *An Introduction to the Phenomenology of Religion*, London: Continuum.

Cusack, C.M. 2010, *Invented Religions: Imagination, Fiction and Faith*, Farnham, Surrey: Ashgate.

Davidman, L. 2007, 'The New Voluntarism and the Case of Unsynagogued Jews' in Ammerman (ed.) *Everyday Religion: Observing Modern Religious Lives*, New York: Oxford University Press USA, 51–68.

Davies, D.J. and Guest, M. 2007, *Bishops, Wives and Children: Spiritual Capital Across the Generations*, Aldershot, Hampshire: Ashgate.

Dawn, M. 2011, *The Accidental Pilgrim*, London: Hodder & Stoughton.

Day, A. 2011, *Believing in Belonging*, Oxford: Oxford University Press.

Durkheim, E. 1912 [trans. J. Swain 1915], *The Elementary Forms of Religious Life*, London: George Allen & Unwin Ltd.

——1897 [trans. Robin Buss 2006], *On Suicide*, London: Penguin Classics.

Eisner, E. 1998, *The Enlightened Eye*, Upper Saddle River, NJ: Merrill.

——1985, *The Educational Imagination*, London: Collier Macmillan.

Ernst, C.W. 2004, *Following Muhammad: Rethinking Islam in the Contemporary World*, Chapel Hill, NC, and London: University of North Carolina Press.

Evans-Pritchard, E.E. 1973, 'Some Reminiscences and Reflection on Fieldwork' in *Journal of the Anthropological Society of Oxford*, (4), 1–12. Accessible at: www.anthro.ox.ac.uk/fileadmin/ISCA/JASO/JASO_Archive_pdfs/1973_JASO_04.pdf

——1937 (abridged edn 1976), *Witchcraft, Oracles and Magic among the Azande*, Oxford: Oxford University Press.

Flood, G. 1996, *An Introduction to Hinduism*, Cambridge: Cambridge University Press.

Foulston, L. 1999, *At the Feet of the Goddess: The Divine Feminine in Local Hindu Religion*, Sussex: Sussex University Press.

Frazer, J.G. 1894, *The Golden Bough: A Study in Comparative Religion*, New York and London: MacMillan & Co.

Geertz, C. 1983, *Local Knowledge: Further Essays in Interpretive Anthropology*, New York: Basic Books.

——1973, *The Interpretation of Cultures*, New York: Basic Books.

——1968, *Islam Observed: Religious Development in Morocco and Indonesia*, Chicago: University of Chicago Press.

Gregg, S.E. 2012, 'Poking Fun at the Pope: Anti-Catholic Dialogue, Performance and the "Symbolic Construction" of Identity in the International Raelian Movement' in *The International Journal for the Study of New Religions*, 3(1), 71–91.

Gregg, S.E. and Scholefield, L. 2013, 'Changing the "Subject" in Religious Studies: Reflections upon Teaching and Learning in Student Encounters with Religions' in *DISKUS*, 14, 70–81.

Haraway, D.J. 1991, 'Situated Knowledges: The Science Question in Feminism and the Privilege of Partial Perspective' in Haraway, D.J. *Simians, Cyborgs and Women*, London: Free Association Books, 183–201.

Harris, M. 1991, *Teaching and Religious Imagination*, San Francisco: HarperCollins.

Harvey, G. 2013, *Food, Sex & Strangers: Understanding Religion as Everyday Life*, Durham: Acumen.

——(ed.) 2009, *Religions in Focus*, London: Equinox.

Henderson, B. 2006, *The Gospel of the Flying Spaghetti Monster*, London: HarperCollins.

Hesse-Biber, S.N and Leavy, P.L. (eds) 2006, *Emergent Methods in Social Research*, Thousand Oaks, CA: Sage Publications.

Hoffman, A. and Cole, P. 2012, *Sacred Trash: the Lost and Found World of the Cairo Geniza*, New York: Schocken Books.

Isherwood, L. and Jordan, M.D. 2010, *Dancing Theology in Fetish Boots*, London: SCM Press.

Juschka, D. (ed.) 2001, *Feminism in the Study of Religion: A Reader*, London: Continuum.

King, R. 1999, *Orientalism and Religion*, London: Routledge.

Koepping, E. 2009, *Food, Friends and Funerals: On Lived Religion*, London: Lit Verlag.

Leavy, P. (ed.) 2014, *The Oxford Handbook of Qualitative Research*, Oxford: Oxford University Press.

Lichterman, P. 2007, 'A Place on the Map: Communicating Religious Presence in Civic Life' in Ammerman (ed.) *Everyday Religion: Observing Modern Religious Lives*, New York: Oxford University Press USA, 137–52.

Lynch, G. 2010, 'Object Theory: Toward an Intersubjective, Mediated, and Dynamic Theory of Religion' in Morgan, D. (ed.) *Religion and Material Culture*, London: Routledge, 40–54.

Mackintosh-Smith, T. 2002, *Travels with a Tangerine: A Journey in the Footsteps of Ibn Battutah*, London: Picador.

Malinowski, B. 1967, *A Diary in the Strict Sense of the Term*, Stanford: Stanford University Press.

——1922, *Argonauts of the Western Pacific: An Account of Native Enterprise and Adventure in the Archipelagos of Melanesian New Guinea*, London: Routledge & Kegan Paul.

Martin Soskice, J. 2010, *Sisters of Sinai*, London: Vintage Books.

McCutcheon, R.T. 2003, *The Discipline of Religion: Structure, Meaning, Rhetoric*, London: Routledge.

Morgan, D. 2010a, 'Introduction: The Matter of Belief' in Morgan, D. (ed.) *Religion and Material Culture*, London: Routledge, 1–17.

——(ed.) 2010b, *Religion and Material Culture*, London: Routledge.

——2005, *The Sacred Gaze*, Berkeley and Los Angeles: University of California Press.

Munson, Z. 2007, 'When a Funeral Isn't Just a Funeral: The Layered Meaning of Everyday Action' in Ammerman (ed.) *Everyday Religion: Observing Modern Religious Lives*, New York: Oxford University Press USA, 121–36.

Muntadas, A. 2011, *Entre/Between*, Madrid: Museo Nacional Centro de Arte, Reina Sofia.

Neitz, M.J. 2000, 'Queering the Dragonfest: Changing Sexualities in a Post-Patriarchal Religion' in *Sociology of Religion*, 61(4), 369–91.

Norman, A. 2011, *Spiritual Tourism: Travel and Religious Practice in Western Society*, London: Continuum.

Nynäs, P. and Yip, A.K-T. 2012, *Religion, Gender and Sexuality in Everyday Life*, Farnham, Surrey: Ashgate.

Oliver, S. and Warrier, M. (eds) (2008), *Theology and Religious Studies: An Exploration of Disciplinary Boundaries*, London: T&T Clark.

Owen, S. 2011, 'The World Religions Paradigm: Time for a Change' in *Arts and Humanities in Higher Education*, 10(3), 253–68.

Palmer, S.J. 2011, *The New Heretics of France: Minority Religion, La République, and the Government-Sponsored "War on Sects"*, New York: Oxford University Press.

——2010, *The Nuwaubian Nation*, Farnham, Surrey: Ashgate.

Parsons, T. 2002 [1957], 'Malinowski and the Theory of Social Systems' in Firth, R. (ed.) *Man and Culture: an Evaluation of the Work of Bronislaw Malinowski*, Abingdon: Routledge.

Primiano, L.N. 1995, 'Vernacular Religion and the Search for Method in Religious Folklife' in *Western Folklore*, 54(1), 37–56.

Sharma, A. 2008, 'The Hermeneutics of the Word "Religion" and Its Implications' in Sherma, R.D. and Sharma, A. (eds) *Hermeneutics and Hindu Thought: Toward a Fusion of Horizons*, London: Springer.

Slater, T. 2004, 'Encountering God: Personal Reflections on "Geographer as Pilgrim"' in *Area*, 36(3), 245–53.

Smart, N. 1998 (2nd edn), *The World's Religions*, Cambridge: Cambridge University Press.

Smith, M.K. 2005, 'Elliot W. Eisner, Connoisseurship, Criticism and the Art of Education' in *The Encyclopaedia of Informal Education* accessed online at www.infed.org/thinkers/eisner.htm

Stausberg, M. 2011, *Religion and Tourism*, London: Routledge.

Stausberg, M. and Engler, S. (eds) 2011, *The Routledge Handbook of Research Methods in the Study of Religion*, Abingdon: Routledge.

Stringer, M.D. 2011, *Contemporary Western Ethnography and the Definition of Religion*, London: Continuum.

Supreme Court, 2013, R v *Registrar General of Births, Deaths and Marriages*, Michaelmas Term UKSC77. Accessible at: http://supremecourt.uk/decided-cases/docs/UKSC_2013_0030_Judgment.pdf

Sutcliffe, S.J. and Gilhus, I.S. (eds) 2013, *New Age Spirituality: Rethinking Religion*, Durham: Acumen.

Todres, L. 2007, *Embodied Enquiry: Phenomenological Touchstones for Research, Psychotherapy and Spirituality*, London: Palgrave MacMillan.

Tremlett, G. 2012 (2nd edn), *Ghosts of Spain*, London: Faber & Faber.

Tylor, E.B. 1871, *Primitive Culture: Researches into the Development of Mythology, Philosophy, Religion, Art and Culture*, London: John Murray.

Warrier, M. 2009, *Hindu Selves in a Modern World: Guru Faith in the Mata Amritanandamayi Mission*, New York: Routledge.

Weber, K.E.M. 2011 [trans. Stephen Kalberg], *The Protestant Ethic and the Spirit of Capitalism*, Oxford: Oxford University Press.

Woodhead, L. 2013, 'Endangered Species' in *The Tablet*, 14 November, London: The Tablet Publishing Company.

Woodhead, L. and Catto, R. 2012, *Religion and Change in Modern Britain*, London: Routledge.

Woodhead, L., Kawanami, H. and Partridge, C. (eds) 2009 (2nd edn), *Religions in the Modern World: Traditions and Transformations*, London: Routledge.

Zine, J. 2008, 'Honour and Identity: An Ethnographic Account of Muslim Girls in a Canadian Islamic School' in *Topia: Canadian Journal of Cultural Studies*, 19, 35–61.

Websites

This annotated list includes all the online sources we have referred to in the chapter as well as some recommended sites. We have given the URLs (web addresses) accessed on 31.10.14, but these do change so for ease of use we have listed them by the name of the organisation in alphabetical order.

British Religion in Numbers. This major British resource has both data and written guides to understanding religious data. www.brin.ac.uk/

Feminism and Religion is a site which publishes serious articles on feminism and religion; there is a new one every day. There is a good search facility. http://feminismand-religion.com/

Institute for Jewish Policy Research. This organisation publishes the results of major quantitative research into British Jewry. www.jpr.org.uk/

PewResearch – Religion and Public Life Project has extensive data and analysis about many topics related to religion and society, including religious affiliation, and religious belief and practice in America. http://religions.pewforum.org/

The Pluralism Project at Harvard University has been running since 1991, charting the changing religious landscape of the United States within a global context. There are a number of case studies included as a means of teaching theology and religious studies. www.pluralism.org/

Religion and Society Project. The major UK-based project led by Prof. Linda Woodhead. www.religionandsociety.org.uk/

The Religious Studies Project (discussed in an earlier textbox) is a major resource from the British Association for the Study of Religions with a large podcast archive aimed at students. www.religiousstudiesproject.com/

Research Methods for the Study of Religion: University of Kent. This is probably the best website for excellent articles and select bibliographies about a whole range of different ways of studying living religion. www.kent.ac.uk/religionmethods/index.html

Teaching Across Religions of South Asia is a website aimed at staff, not students, but it is very accessible and will help you to explore the ways in which people practice, think about and identify with religious traditions in South Asia and the South Asian diaspora which frequently cut across established boundaries of what constitutes 'religion'. http://tarosaproject.wordpress.com/

The Way is a film about the pilgrimage to Santiago de Compostela. This site has interesting reflections on the meanings of the pilgrimage and the ideas in the film. www.theway-themovie.com/index.php

Westminster Faith Debates. An offshoot of the Religion and Society Project, which brings together politicians, religious leaders, academics and public intellectuals to speak on religion. http://faithdebates.org.uk/

3 Where to study religion off campus
Places of worship and beyond

Introduction

In an early draft of this chapter, we used a different title, which was 'Where to study religion off campus: it's not all about temples!'. As a part of the review process that is common to all academic publishing, an anonymous scholar who was reading the book proposal suggested that this could be construed as insensitive. Linking with Jewish discourse on Zionism and historical-political debates surrounding Israel and the Jewish diaspora, and also perhaps to the fact that some North American Jewish communities refer to their places of community and worship as 'temples', the reviewer suggested that perhaps the phrase should be avoided. As you can see from the title of this chapter, we followed this advice, but what we find interesting is that a huge assumption was made by the peer reviewer about the categorisation and understanding of a sacred space where religion can be studied. For this (American) reviewer, the term 'temple' needed to be protected against misunderstanding, when engaging with discourse on or about religion. What was particularly interesting for us was the simple fact that we were actually thinking of Hindu temples when we named the chapter. This (mis)understanding of the symbolism, meaning and function of discussion around a designated sacred space serves as a helpful example of how powerful and meaningful such places are within religious communities, their identities and our interaction with them.

We hope that this chapter will help to break down assumptions about what we mean by sacred spaces and places, how we talk about them and engage with them, and how we understand them as places of symbolism and importance for specific living religious communities, rather than idealised textbook notions or essentialisms regarding their meaning and function. In so doing, we hope that you will begin to break down assumptions about buildings as the main centres of religious community or power, and instead engage with religious people, activities and artefacts in a diversity of environments, some of which may not be immediately obvious. However, before we focus on less obvious ways of engaging with religious communities, we explore the relevance of buildings and the built environment, but with a particular focus upon their role in shaping living religion.

Religious buildings

Buildings themselves are not religious, but it is how they are understood, designed and used that makes them of religious importance. In fact, this relationship between physical buildings and their community use and function applies to many centres of society or community. One interesting example is the Palace of Westminster, better known as the British Houses of Parliament. In 1943 Winston Churchill made a speech including the following:

> On the night of May 10, 1941, with one of the last bombs of the last serious raid, our House of Commons was destroyed by the violence of the enemy, and we have now to consider whether we should build it up again, and how, and when. *We shape our buildings, and afterwards our buildings shape us.* Having dwelt and served for more than forty years in the late Chamber, and having derived very great pleasure and advantage therefrom, I, naturally, should like to see it restored in all essentials to its old form, convenience and dignity. (House of Commons meeting in the House of Lords)
>
> (Hansard, 1943)

The old House was rebuilt in 1950 in its old form, remaining insufficient to seat all its members. Buildings, monuments, sites and places all have particular designs and uses which are at the same time influenced by heritage, community and practice, and also inform notions of community, identity and ritual/performance. This can be seen in secular examples such as the House of Commons, although the origins of the UK parliament as St Stephen's Chapel should not be forgotten, but is especially the case in faith buildings and arenas.

For a rather different approach to religious buildings like churches have a look at Philip Larkin's poem 'Church Going' – you can hear it read on YouTube (see the website list at the end of the chapter for details). It is interesting for the range of perspectives on an old church that it suggests and you might reflect on what your responses to this place might be. As such, it is a helpful entry point into how we think about buildings and landscapes as places of community and practice.

Places of worship

Most students studying religion will visit at least one place of worship during their course. Often this will be part of a large group visit and will include listening to someone speak about the religion. This section includes ideas about places of worship to set some theoretical context for such a visit and suggestions about how to get the most out of visiting a place of worship. Practical information about the etiquette required in places of worship of different religious traditions, and what might be expected to be happening in them during a visit, is covered in the next chapter on group visits.

It is really interesting to note how much effort people put into their places of worship. They are often larger than any other buildings, more solidly built and more highly decorated. It is easy to see how, in England, the parish church would dominate the surrounding village, or the way in which, in a Middle Eastern town, the mosque might be the only complete and permanent-looking building. Throughout the world there are huge places of worship – temples, cathedrals, mosques and so on – which have been built using quite simple technologies and huge amounts of human ingenuity and effort. Where these buildings are situated is not a matter of chance. Richard Carp says this about visiting a Hindu temple:

> A temple should not be studied 'in itself', as if viewed in a photograph from which all surrounding buildings and activities have been censored. Its context matters – where it is and where it would not be allowed to be, what is and is not around it, who is there and who cannot be, and what they do (and when), as well as when and under what conditions certain activities take place, are all important clues to the temple's significance.
>
> (Carp, 2011, 480)

Imagine a group of school pupils coming back from visiting a church in a rural town, which is part of the United Reformed Church. Situated on Jesu Street, it is one of the oldest Nonconformist churches in England. When they are asked what the most memorable item in the church was, most of them say, 'the turquoise carpet'. That is what struck them most, but they missed the features of the church shaped by the Calvinist Protestant Christian theology that gives rise to, and is expressed by, the worship that takes place there. They also had difficulties making sense of the particular history of this church and community. They are known locally as 'the little door' people because in the seventeenth century their Nonconformist services were illegal, and if the person acting as a 'lookout' for any trouble sounded the alarm, the worshippers slipped through a small door into an adjoining building and then made their escape. It requires knowledge and imagination to understand that what is now a respected branch of the Christian Church was once a persecuted minority.

Making these kinds of connections and developing nuanced understanding should develop from the fieldwork you do on a degree course. Places of worship can open up religious beliefs and practices in the art and architecture, differing ways of understanding what is holy or mundane, and individual and community stories which relate to history, and also in many cases to migrations from other places. These actual places can also problematise neat textbook classifications of religion.

One of the rather strange things about an educational visit to a place of worship is that you may often encounter an empty building. The experience for worshippers would be very different. A speaker may be more interested in giving information about the religion than in evoking a sense of what happens in the building during worship. If that is the case, you will have to work quite hard during the visit to get a sense of how the specific details of the worship and the understanding of the nature of the worship have shaped the building, and how this particular building facilitates the religious activities that take place there. The priest of a Serbian Orthodox Church in Birmingham made this process much easier for students when he stood in front of them with his arms wide open, and said in a loud voice, "Welcome to Heaven". The church and the liturgy that takes place there offer, in Orthodox understanding, a taste of heaven.

Starting points

Here are some suggestions for what you can do during a visit:

- take notes, and photos, of the environment in which the place of worship is situated;
- identify the main focal points in the worship space and think about how they function;
- notice the public areas and those to which only some people are admitted;
- really look around at the objects in the space and the ways in which painting, sculpture, design and decoration, if there are any, have been used;
- sit or stand quietly where a worshipper would be and become aware of the atmosphere and the sense that you get of the place.

Specific techniques to deepen your engagement will be discussed in subsequent chapters.

Places of worship are not necessarily the first places that a religious community builds. In New York, Jews established a Jewish cemetery before they built a synagogue and in the mid nineteenth century, after the Roman Catholic Church was re-established in Britain, the Catholic hierarchy decided that it was more important to build Catholic schools than churches. Understanding the reasons for these decisions, for example, provides a wider context for making sense of the particulars of a place of worship. So would an awareness of the changing uses of a specific building you are visiting. For example, in Spitalfields, London, Brick Lane Jamme Masjid was once a synagogue and before that a Huguenot church; as the refugee communities in the area changed, so did the identity of the building. In Cordoba, Spain, the magnificent *Mezquita* (mosque) became the Cathedral of the Assumption of Our Lady during the *Reconquista*. It is interesting to note that recent attempts by Muslims in Spain to be allowed to pray in the building have been rejected, reflecting contested views of what constitutes Spanish history and identity. In Istanbul, Turkey, Hagia Sophia was once a Greek Orthodox basilica, then an imperial mosque and is now a museum. In Liverpool, England, Sikhs have created a gurdwara community centre in a deconsecrated Methodist church.

It is also worth reflecting that when a migrant group actually builds a place of worship, rather than using a converted house, for example, that it is something of a statement that the group is there to stay; they are well enough established, in a particular area, to successfully buy land, gain planning permission and raise the money for the build. Building a very large, grand structure carries further messages about a group's sense of their meaning and purpose. It is interesting to note that in London, Sikhs, Hindus and Ahmadiyya Muslims have all built imposing places of worship in the last couple of decades. The Shri Swaminarayan Mandir, popularly known as the 'Neasden Temple', claims to be Europe's 'first traditional Hindu temple'. The Gurdwara Sri Guru Singh Sabha, in Southall, is the 'largest Sikh temple in Europe'. The Baitul Futuh Mosque, in Morden, is billed as 'the largest mosque in Europe' on their website. This is a particularly interesting case since this group is not recognised as authentically Muslim by many Islamic authorities and they have suffered persecution in some countries. Study of a place of worship such as this has huge potential to develop a wider understanding of Islam and Muslim identity in many different ways.

Many places of worship also serve multiple functions, both for their own congregation and for other groups. The three mentioned in the last paragraph all have programmes for educating visitors about their religion, and organise major festival celebrations with members of their religious tradition attending from all over the UK and abroad. Many smaller places play a role in the wider local community, often involving voluntary charity work and hosting diverse groups and meetings, in addition to serving as places of refuge in the case of unrest or disaster in their area. This means that there is often no simple answer to the question of who these places of worship are for, but in some cases the boundaries may be more clearly drawn. One group of church organisers in Southampton refused to allow their building to be used for a yoga class because of the perceived connections of exercise yoga with spiritual yoga exercises from Hindu traditions.

Also of note is the fact that many places of worship or community centres are often in distinct social areas that have developed along national or ethnic lines as well as religious ones, and which leads to a concentration of shops, eateries and services that are linked to a specific demographic group. This phenomenon gives rise to areas such as Little India in London and China Town in Melbourne, and allows tour guides to conduct visits to 'Jewish' New York. Importantly, however, such concentrations of cultural identity often highlight the diversity which exists in these areas, rather than any sense of their homogenous natures. Exploring such areas brings the advantage that you will encounter a variety of different historical periods, where communities have developed and changed over time – you will notice that many different languages are spoken, that there are widely differing housing stocks and levels of economic well-being, and that there has been a huge variety of ethnic shifts across recent decades. One such example is Southall in London – known for a long time as a centre for Pakistani immigrants, but now dominated by Somalis, as second-generation British-Asians have become more affluent and so have migrated out to the suburbs; thus Hinduism, Islam (and to a lesser extent Sikhism) still predominate in the area, but *different types* of Hinduism, Islam and Sikhism from thirty years ago.

Ancient sites and the 'natural' landscape

'Are you mountain, desert or ocean?' That is a question often asked in travel magazines. All three are places which in varying religious traditions are seen as sacred – although perhaps rivers, wells, fountains, streams and islands have more obvious religious connections than the sea, and other natural phenomena such as trees, woods, caves, rocks and stones are also seen as 'sacred' or are valued within many religious traditions. Sometimes there are links with stories of creation because in this 'spiritual geography' there are deep connections between body, mind, spirit, the land, the cosmos, the divine and various levels of meaning. In this section we are beginning to discuss studying religion beyond buildings by exploring what might be meant by 'sacred space'. In his book *Spaces for the Sacred*, Philip Sheldrake links place, memory and human identity, saying that "place is space that has the capacity to be remembered and to evoke what is most precious" (2001, 1). He suggests thinking about places as texts, layered with meaning (2001, 17). Fieldwork study of such places is intended to enable us to experience and explore these meanings. Ucko says:

> At any particular moment such places are vested with identity, an identity which involves both the supernatural sphere and the power of social self-definition and personal self-identity. Sometimes the supernatural power of such localized sacred sites may become inter-cultural, even international.
>
> (Ucko, 1994, xviii)

We will explore all those elements in the section on Glastonbury towards the end of this chapter, but here we are focusing more on some aspects of the natural landscape and ancient sites.

Let's begin with some examples of stones. In Genesis 28:10–22 there is a story where Jacob dreams of a ladder between earth and heaven with angels descending and ascending on it. When he wakes he makes the pillar/stone where he slept an altar; he says, "How awesome is this place. It is none other than the house of God and this is the gate of heaven" (v.17). This site is identified in Jewish tradition as Mount Moriah, the place in which Abraham bound Isaac to offer him as a sacrifice to God (the *akedah*) and is also the place where the Temple would be built in Jerusalem. There is a story that the stone was brought to Ireland, and then may be the same stone known as the 'Stone of Scone' or 'Stone of Destiny' brought to Westminster Abbey from Scotland and placed inside the chair where British monarchs are crowned. Whatever the historical realities, stones such as this are deeply connected with ideas of sacred kingship in many cultures, and the Stone of Scone has appeared in numerous songs, films, novels and other creative works.

Stones also play an important part in the ancient (pre)history of religious traditions. Perhaps the most famous example in the world is the Neolithic complex of Stonehenge on Salisbury Plain in England. Here, a monumental building project started perhaps as early as 3000 BCE and reached its zenith in around 2500 BCE. The huge megaliths, erected as trilithons, or one smaller stone placed horizontally on two larger vertical stones, are the famous picture post-card view of the site, but recent archaeological work has put forward the theory that it is the much smaller bluestones in the centre of the complex which may have been of particular religious importance. The first thing that strikes a visitor to Stonehenge is how different the small bluestones are from the large grey megaliths of the outer circle, and this is because they were not locally quarried, but were brought in from outside Salisbury Plain. In fact, they were brought in from outside England, as a recent geological survey has located the precise quarry from where they would have been removed. The quarry is in the Preseli Hills in Pembrokeshire, West Wales – over 150 miles from Stone-henge, a staggering distance to transport such items nearly 5,000 years ago. From this starting point, archaeologists have sought to understand *why* people would have gone to so much effort to use these particular stones, and the latest theory, based on a multi-university research project called Stonehenge Riverside Project, argues that the bluestones were used as healing stones, and that Stonehenge itself was a sacred place to unify people from all across the British Isles and beyond. The mass of burials around the site, which is the largest collection of graves from this period in history yet to be discovered, supports this theory as many of the bodies show bone deformities, and skeletons have been DNA traced and include crippled individuals who had travelled from mainland Europe (see Parker Pearson, 2014).

The important recent academic developments at Stonehenge, which have notably focused on the use of the site and the living conditions of those who built it, rather than just on theories of construction which have previously dominated the archaeological debate, serve to remind us of the importance of religious life and physical landscape. As we outlined above in the section on buildings, many places of religious importance (for example Hagia Sophia in Istanbul) have effectively put up a sign saying 'under new management' and continue to be treated by different communities as meaningful. The same is often the case with the natural landscape. Across England, there are hundreds of pre-Christian sites, often in the form of sacred wells, trees or groves, which have simply been taken over by Christian traditions in the form of permanent churches or as places of natural landscape pilgrimage. Examples abound, par-ticularly in the Celtic fringes of the British Isles, and often centre on holy springs or wells, but one particular link is with the Christian archangel Saint Michael. All across pre-Christian England, high places were often used as places of pilgrimage, ritual and meaning-making, and when these sites were 'Christianised' they were very often dedicated to St Michael or St Michael and

All Angels. The reason for this is that, in the Book of Revelation, the last and apocalyptic book of the Bible, St Michael was the figure who defeated the dragon – a beast which was often used to symbolise non-Christian traditions by early Church leaders. It may not come as a surprise, therefore, to learn that there are over 800 churches in high places across England, all probably pre-Christian sites of religious meaning, which are dedicated to St Michael, including Brentor in Dartmoor, Devon, St Michael's Mount in Cornwall and St Michael's Tower in Glastonbury, of which we will discover more at the end of this chapter. Such examples demonstrate very clearly that it is not just the buildings relevant to certain traditions which hold meaning, but also the very landscape which they are built in, and built from.

Sacred space

There is something about all these places where the veil or membrane between heaven and earth, or the human world and the spirit world, is thin or the door propped ajar. They may also be described as *liminal*, that is places on the edge, not quite located in ordinary time and space. Some may be wild and isolated but they are also places which have drawn generations of people to them because they are understood as sacred. *Sacred* or *holy* often means 'set apart', 'special' or 'different'. A sacred place (or time or person) has particular significance and power, and there may well be rules that must be observed:

> The cave has power
> whirlwind dances
> on the valley floor
> Sometimes people
> come to watch
> not all of them can see.
> (Tauhindali quoted in Theodoratus and LaPena, 1994, 24)

In this poem the final line suggests that not everyone who is there will be able to apprehend the sacred, but there may also be aspects of places which a visitor is not allowed to actually see or enter – the 'secret sacred' sites (Ucko, 1994, xvff.), such as some aboriginal places in Australia. Uluru, the most famous of these sites, is also an example of a contested site – we discuss this notion of contestation fully at the end of the chapter. The Anangu, the local aboriginal people, do not climb it because of its great sacredness and they ask visitors not to. However, Uluru is currently leased to Australia as a national park and visitors are able to climb the rock, although it is not an easy walk. A well-known example of a place where outsiders cannot go is Mecca, the focus for Muslim prayer and pilgrimage; only Muslims may go there. It is also the case that, in many parts of the Muslim world, non-Muslims are not allowed to enter a mosque. So, as a student doing fieldwork there are places you can't go or you may only be able to go a certain way into a place. For example, in an Orthodox church you cannot go behind the *iconostasis* and see the altar and what happens there. During the service this heightens the mystery of the liturgy, and from time to time the doors open and a priest brings out the Book of the Gospels, or the consecrated bread and wine for Communion.

Sometimes, these 'closed off' or 'secret' places of religions are linked with knowledge as well as place. Within Scientology, for example, it is highly likely you as an individual or a class group will be welcomed at any Church of Scientology around the world, and will have easy access to clergy, Auditors (the Scientology name for religious counsellors) and parishioners. However, it is equally likely that you will only encounter a very limited aspect of the lived lives of Scientologists. Often this will include a demonstration of Auditing, the sharing of histories and hagiographies about Scientology's founder, L. Ron Hubbard, and information on religious courses run by the Church. However, some parts of Scientology, like many religions in history, are esoteric – that is, it has knowledge and training which can only be experienced by practitioners who follow a specific path of practice and understanding, called the Bridge to Total Freedom. This hierarchy of training separates levels of Scientologists with regard to status and rank within the organisation, but also separates people physically. Not all churches are allowed to offer the higher-level training courses, and the very highest levels are only allowed to be taken at the International Headquarters of the Church in Clearwater, Florida, or on the *Freewinds*, which is a large ocean-going cruise liner owned and operated by the Church. *Freewinds* is a particularly interesting example of the use of place and space in religious traditions as being on a ship necessarily distances a person from everyday life, from everyday distractions, and creates a contemplative space in which to focus on religious practice and thought. The process of separating out the places where higher levels of training can occur within Scientology is a good example of the creation of, and emphasis given to, sacred space in a recently founded religious tradition. For more information on this complex and interesting religious movement, see Lewis' edited book *Scientology* (Lewis, 2009).

So, in many religious places not everyone can go all the way into the most sacred part. This was the case for many early Christian and Byzantine churches where visitors or potential new members of the church could enter the *narthex* at the west end of the building, but could go no further; they could hear the services going on but could not fully see what was happening and could not participate. It is a transition space between the ordinary outside world and the inner sacred space of the church. It seems to us that 'narthical learning' is a good term for what we are doing in the study of religion when we visit sacred places. As part of the study of religion we go to a place of worship or other special place. We are not initiates, full members or even perhaps 'pilgrims' in a traditional sense, and so we can only ever go a little way in; we are always, to some extent, on the edge. And yet we are present, in a bodily and intimate engagement with the place and the people, "contemplative, open to surprises and taking the time to digest the experience quietly" (Roebben, 2009, 19). The narthex is a place of encounter and engagement; our presence changes things and we may be changed in the process.

Many people have certainly been changed by experience in the desert! For a good example of this see T.E. Lawrence (Lawrence of Arabia) who wrote a classic book about his experiences called *Seven Pillars of Wisdom* (2000, new edition). Judaism, Christianity and Islam all began in the desert. Mount Sinai, where, according to tradition, Moses received the commandments during the long journey of the Exodus from Egypt to the Promised Land, is in the Sinai desert. Jesus spent a formative period in the desert during the forty days at the beginning of his ministry; the desert is very close to Jerusalem. St Catherine's, the Christian monastery at the foot of Mount Sinai, and officially known as 'The Sacred Monastery of the God-Trodden Mount Sinai', for example, is a reminder that from the third century Christians went out into the desert to find a renewed spiritual life. They are known as the desert fathers (and mothers) and some Christian monastic groups still seek out the desert for its spiritual potential – see, for example, *Letters from the Desert* (Carretto, 1972). The Arabs, amongst whom Islam began, were desert people, with traditions still carried by some Bedouin in the Middle East.

Sometimes there are links between places which may be sacred, fieldwork in these places and understanding of religion. There are echoes of these things with the work of the artist Richard Long and this short discussion of his work takes us into the next section on museums and art galleries. One exhibition was called, very interestingly, 'Heaven and Earth' (Wallis, 2009). Long makes art mainly by walking and this interface between his body, walking and the earth is highly evocative of the dialogue between person and place (Serota, 2009, 29). One of the important things about fieldwork is to *walk* – in fact the word 'to saunter' has been linked to the French '*sainte terre*' or holy land or earth. Long's work marks 'being there' in different ways. He uses lists of names and places not unlike those at Yad Vashem, the Holocaust museum in Jerusalem. He uses photographs taken not as a record shot but as a "testament to his presence" and "an image that stands for the whole experience of the walk" (Serota, 2009, 28). He is also exploring alignment, how we select what to view, and where it should be seen from, how it should be framed (cf. Haldane, 2003). Dominic Rainsford (2003) explores the relationships between self and not-selves in Long's work and sees echoes in it of how we should act towards others whom we recognise as in some way not like us.

Museums and art galleries

Some of your study visits may be to museums and galleries, and you will certainly be encouraged by your lecturers to engage with such sites whenever possible. When you visit you may have a guide, instructions (often with an audio guide) to follow a set path, designated tasks to complete, or be left to wander by yourself. Each of these ways of interacting with the artefacts on display has its challenges and opportunities, but it is important to reflect upon how it affects your learning experience. Guides will often focus on the historical details of artefacts, perhaps more so than their use – religious paintings are a good example of this, where you will often see paintings which were once used as backdrops to altars in churches, but which are displayed in galleries or museums mainly for their aesthetic quality or provenance linked to a particularly important artist or school of artists. Of course, in their original setting, the pieces were not only designed to be beautiful, but were an integral part of the ritual life of the churches in question, often relating stories and theologies to premodern societies where literacy was not understood in the same way as today, and where visual representations of history, saints and eschatology were central to the performance of religious life. We must also remember that every guided visit is designed to highlight a selection of particular examples that are understandable within the narrative framework of the guide's stories and information. This is often very helpful, but to go beyond the 'textbook' accounts of many guides (human, audio or written) you must always consider the original context in which pieces or artefacts were used, and locate their importance to the religious communities in question.

There are some particular problems for the study of living religion in museums, caused because the full subjective nature of sacred material culture is often sealed behind glass – a 'do not touch' experience where the economic or political value of objects often means that they are reified, separated and encased for their 'protection'. This raises a key question: can one be touched by something one can't touch? Museums are full of images and objects that connect to religion, or at least, they did so in the past, but how do we connect to them?

When you are looking at objects in a museum, keep asking questions such as 'What touches me?', 'What surprises me?' and 'How am I connected with the people who made and used this?' This will help you to interpret them and see their possible significances, but in doing this, we are not suggesting that you necessarily seek 'spiritual' meaning from this exercise – indeed, the thing that makes museums and galleries such interesting places to study religion is that they contest and complicate what 'religious things' are and how we relate to them.

This relationship between religious objects in museums, their role(s) and our interactions with them is taken up by Crispin Paine in his book *Religious Objects in Museums: Private Lives and Public Duties* (2013). In this book, Paine outlines and critiques the relationship between objects, museum staff, religious communities and museum visitors, focusing on their dynamics of interaction. Particularly interesting in Paine's account is the shift in recent years from museums hoarding objects for public display in an act of de-sacralising where they were primarily displayed for artistic or aesthetic worth, to a much more engaged style of curatorship wherein religious objects are displayed and explained within their cultural context. In so doing, the role of religious objects in museums is moving from passive to active – perhaps once misrepresented objects are now being seen as meaning-making components of religious lives for individuals and communities.

Of course, an important part of this meaning-making is the relationship the viewer has with the artefact in question. In art galleries, one of the important dynamics that affects our viewing experience is the size and location of an artwork. The *Mona Lisa* in the Louvre in Paris is much smaller than many people imagine, whilst Picasso's *Guernica* in the Reina Sofia in Madrid is huge – and its impact comes, at least partly, from its size. Similarly, African Minkisi (objects of religious power that were linked to fetishism in previous generations of scholarship) come in all shapes and sizes – from the portable and individual to the cumbersome and public. Each of these elements affects not only the role of the items in their original cultural context, but also how curators can display them, and we can interact with, around, beneath or above them. In this sense, the *context* of the pieces needs to be thought about. Are we interacting with pieces simply because they have been set apart as special enough to be in a museum, or are we interacting with them to draw meaning that relates to contemporary religious communities, or religious communities active at the time the pieces were created? Perhaps we should always con-textualise what we view in a gallery or museum by remembering the actions of artist Marcel Duchamp who, in 1917, installed a male urinal in a New York gallery under the title *Fountain*. His logic was simple – by placing an everyday or ordinary object in an art gallery, he essentially categorised that object as 'art', with all the cultural, economic and aesthetic connotations that that category applies to an item.

In remembering Duchamp, we should understand that every item we view in a museum or gallery has been curated to create an emotion, effect or reaction from the viewers. This reaction can be very different in different contexts. Allen Roberts has explored the idea that images and artwork "not only permit but provoke re-signification" (2010, 132). Images travel and, as they do, they acquire new and different meanings. For example, St James, originally a disciple and contemporary of Jesus in Judea, and martyred there, 'travels' to Spain, where the church with his relics in Santiago de Compostela becomes a major centre for Christian pilgrimage. Then, in the medieval world, St James becomes 'the Moor slayer' who leads Christian armies in the reconquest of Spain, and kills Muslims. He also travels with the Spanish to the New World, as its patron saint, and then to Haiti, where the image of St James becomes known as Sen Jak, and is part of the Vodou practised there (2010, 120–22). In such examples, one core image or persona – James – is understood in entirely different roles in different historical contexts and geographical realms; a further reminder that each and every artefact in a gallery or museum must be contextualised not just within its curated reality but in its original cultural reality also.

In recent years the British Museum in London has had a number of special exhibitions of explicitly religious phenomena such as the *Hajj* (Porter, 2012), the Muslim pilgrimage to Mecca, or *Treasures of Heaven* (Bagnoli et al., 2011), about Christian saints, relics and devotion in medieval Europe. Similarly, the National Gallery in London has organised an exhibition of explicitly Christian religious art in *Seeing Salvation* (MacGregor and Langmuir, 2000). However, it is also important to engage with museums and exhibitions that are not explicitly about religion, but that have important links to religion. Your interaction with these sites will often take the form of the 'unexpected' encounters with religion that we have mentioned throughout this book.

Perhaps the most interesting sites that we have visited include museums of migration and economic history. Examples such as the Melbourne Immigration Museum and the Museum of Liverpool contain oral and written personal narratives of migrant and diaspora communities, together with the artefacts and material culture of a large range of religious and ethnic communities. In Melbourne, the large Chinese community is remembered and everyday objects such as clothes, cookware and posters advertising jobs and entertainment are displayed throughout the galleries. All of these objects are representative of individual and communal religious lives that are played out in relation to often highly oppressive colonial and post-colonial societies which have consciously 'othered' 'foreign' lifestyles, languages, religions and cultures. By engaging with the stories of migrants across religious and cultural divides, you can begin to understand the ways in which religion has been played out in everyday lives, not just in contemporary society, but at significant points in history. Textbooks are often focused upon the public rituals of major religious traditions within diaspora communities and the Chinese Dragon used at New Year's celebrations in Melbourne is proudly displayed in the museum. But we can also learn more about the everyday lives of migrant communities by examining economic pressures, living conditions, legal restrictions on employment and linguistic opportunities and challenges which all impact upon the performance of everyday religious lives and communities. Such opportunities to engage with religion can often be taken by 'reading between the lines' of museums and galleries that might not explicitly focus on the religious, but that provide enormously important and enriching context for the performance of everyday religious lives.

One particular issue regarding the relationship between museums and religions, religious items and religious communities is the issue of ethics regarding the custody, display and interaction with objects considered to be sacred or religious by specific religious communities. In many museums around the world there are now human remains such as skeletons or mummified bodies on display. The museum may be seeking to inform the visitor about the ethical and religious observances of archaic cultures, often relating this to death, burial and 'religious customs' in wider society and past societies. Importantly, however, there is often very careful negotiation regarding the etiquette of visitors around such displays. In the National Museum of Wales in Cardiff, there are signs on the doors of the archaeology gallery that forbid photography, explaining that there are human remains on display. Such boundaries of behaviour, usually carefully arrived at after consultation between curators and academics, can also involve religious communities, and tell us much about the projection of religious identity ('represented religion').

'Charlie'

One high-profile example in recent years was the case of 'Charlie', the skeleton of a 3-year-old child found during an archaeological dig at the Avebury World Heritage Site in South-West England. Probably dating from the early Neolithic period, 'Charlie' has been on public display since 1938 in a variety of local museums. In 2006, however, a group of Druids, who use the local stone circles as an important part of their annual summer and winter solstice celebrations, requested that the bones be handed over to them so that the child could be afforded a dignified burial. English Heritage, the charity which is responsible for the bones, conducted a public consultation (Cleal, 2008) and produced a report based on those public findings, in addition to legal and academic judgements, which argued that the bones should remain on public display and in public ownership as "there is no clear evidence for genetic, cultural or religious continuity of a kind that would justify preferential status to be given to the beliefs of the group which requested reburial" (Kerton, 2010). Whilst this was a reasonably straightforward decision from the viewpoint of English Heritage (over 90 per cent of respondents had agreed that the bones should remain on public display), it is an important example of a religious group taking actions that are compelled (perhaps even impelled) by their core worldview.

Harvey has stated that "Paganism is a new religion that is evolving within the modernist West, drawing on older repertoires to engage with contemporary concerns" (Harvey, 2013, 171). The Avebury case is a strong example of this – whilst the 'scientific' response of English Heritage is perhaps hard to argue with, a deeper examination of the case can see the necessity of the Druids' actions as a performative understanding of their communal religious identity, informed by the past (or perhaps more accurately their interpretation of the past) and projected into contemporary lived religion.

Similar cases have been conducted around the world, often with different results. In the USA, the Native American Graves Protection and Repatriation Act, usually shortened to NAGPRA, has ensured that over 38,000 bodies have been repatriated from museum collections to Native American communities. In these cases, it is necessary under US law to demonstrate "a relationship of shared group identity which can be reasonably traced historically or prehistorically between a present day Indian tribe or Native Hawaiian organization and an identifiable earlier group" (see website list below). Of course, this is what was missing from the Druids' claim at Avebury, but, as scholars of religion, we can understand that religious communities constantly make and remake their identities, which are not fixed, but evolve and react to continual reinterpretations of history, myth, ritual and identity. To 'locate' religion within an unbroken ethnic or cultural continuity, as the NAGPRA legislation does, is just one way to approach the religious identities of living religious communities – the Druid case of Avebury helps us to contest and complicate legal or institutional approaches to religion(s) as religious groups continue to renegotiate their lived and performative traditions.

Maps

Exploring religion through fieldwork takes us to places and so it is very interesting to also study maps – not to help us find our way physically to a place, but because maps tell us how places are understood, what they mean. They are a kind of visual narrative which can be read. One specific example of this can be seen in a museum attached to one of England's great medieval cathedrals: Hereford. This thirteenth-century Mappa Mundi, the largest surviving medieval world map, shows the world as understood by Western European society; it is an object which at the same time creates and reflects an entire Christian worldview. Jerusalem is in the centre, both the navel of the world and the meeting point of heaven and earth, and the map contrasts "divine timelessness and infinity with the transience and limitations of human time" (Barber, 2005, 60). There was a larger medieval map than this, known as the Ebstorf world map, which was destroyed in a bombing raid during World War II. It had been photographed and has been reconstructed from this. Grayson Perry, who we discuss next, made a 'Map of Nowhere' in response to this.

An earlier Christian map, the Madaba Map, made in mosaic in a church in Madaba, Jordan, and still on view, originally covered the entire width of the nave. It shows the way ideas about the 'Holy Land' were forming in the sixth century and Jerusalem is portrayed in a way which still helps to make sense of the Old City.

A Jain example from the eighteenth century is a cosmological map which shows not only the visible world but also the invisible world of heavens and hells. It too is a form of 'sacred geography' which not only depicts an area corresponding to India occupied by 'civilised men' and other areas where 'barbarians dwell', but also indicates how it is only through birth somewhere in these human realms that a soul can obtain *moksha*, release from transmigration.

Inextricably linked with modern museums and art galleries is the ubiquitous merchandising stall or shop. Indeed, so entwined are the two acts of interacting with culture and buying representations or remembrances of these cultural items that the British graffiti artist Banksy named his critically acclaimed documentary on street art *Exit Through the Gift Shop* (Banksy, 2010). Gift shops are therefore rich places to view how people interact with everyday religious items that have everyday purposes. Material representations of religion, often in the form of pop culture artefacts, act as important ways into the study of religion in everyday life. Cheaply made plastic models of the Vatican (complete with '*il papa*' waving from a window), evil eye pendants from street stalls outside the Blue Mosque in Istanbul, or over-priced bottles containing water from the Ganges or the River Jordan may convey as much religious meaning or remembrance to a religious person as any valuable bronze sculpture of Shiva, or other 'high culture' religious art. Each of these everyday items provides an opportunity for religious individuals to take something of the sacred nature of the place and memory of their original experience with them, perhaps to their home where the item will act as a sacred-making object for future ritual or reflection. Their availability at gift shops and stalls linked with religious sites or museums and galleries is an important reminder that the seemingly mundane action of 'souvenir collecting' can be an important example of relating religion to everyday life and activity.

"Do not look for meaning here": Grayson Perry, art and religion

Turner Prize winning Grayson Perry is probably Britain's highest profile contemporary artist. Famous for his transvestism, which is often displayed through his alter ego Claire, who has a penchant for gingham dresses, Perry is fast becoming an establishment favourite and was selected to give the highly prestigious 2013 BBC Reith Lectures. In his career to date, Perry has consistently explored the relationship between religion, sacredness, imagined worlds and art. He is a fascinating example of how we can explore concepts about religion (even if what we are exploring is not trying to be *religious*) in unexpected places.

   Perry's highest profile exhibition to date has been his one-man takeover of the British Museum – the first time in the museum's history that the museum had been guest-curated by an artist, and which was titled *The Tomb of the Unknown Craftsman*. The exhibition was a fusion of Perry's artwork inspired by his own imaginary world, centred around his childhood teddy bear, Allen Measles, as a deity figure, and also Perry's homage and respect for the individual men and women who had crafted and created the many astonishing artefacts from human history that make up the British Museum's vast collection. The exhibition focused around the idea of art and religious ideas and actions, and included a huge tapestry by the artist showing many possible pilgrimage destinations and called the 'Map of Truths and Beliefs' (Perry, 2011, between 120 and 121). Another of his works is called 'Pilgrimage to the British Museum' (2011, 21) and, as an important part of his curation, Perry placed his own work alongside a rich range of artefacts from the Museum's collection under headings such as 'cultural conversations', 'shrines', 'magick', 'maps' and 'souvenirs of pilgrimage'. In this carefully created exhibition, Perry describes his role as similar to that of a shaman, someone who can connect this present material world with that of the (spirit) world of meanings and significance. He states:

Part of my role as an artist is similar to that of a shaman or witch doctor. I dress up, I tell stories, give things meaning and make them a bit more significant. Like religion this is not a rational process, I use my intuition. Sometimes our very human desire for meaning can get in the way of having a good experience of the world. Some people call this irrational unconscious experience spirituality. I don't.

(Perry, 2011, 91)

Perry's work is in almost constant dialogue with conceptions of religion, and his six-tapestry work *The Vanity of Small Differences* demonstrates the influence of religious imagery upon art. *The Vanity of Small Differences* was a product of Perry's performance of a social-anthropological investigation into three social groups of British people who self-identified as working class, middle class and upper class. The tapestries are inspired by William Hogarth's *A Rake's Progress* series of paintings (1733), and update the motif to follow a working-class lad who marries a middle-class wife and sells his software business for millions before dying in a car accident. The tapestries take direct inspiration from previous religious artworks such as Mantegna's *The Adoration of the Shepherds* (c. 1450), Grünewald's *Isenheim Altarpiece* (1512–16) and Masaccio's *The Expulsion from the Garden of Eden* (c. 1425). The tapestries, which reflect the individuals Perry met in distinct communities across contemporary Britain, remind us of the intrinsic interrelation between concepts of class, society, economy and religion which underpin, and even dominate, the construction of our individual and communal identities.

Religion in the street

It is important to remember that religion 'happens' not just in separated and designated places or specially sanctified buildings, but also in shared spaces and public ways. Very often, engagement with living religion in these places will take on unexpected forms, and you may often come across religious life and religious performance and meaning even when you are not looking for it. Opposed to the often deliberately planned engagement with religion at sacred sites or organised visits, the spontaneous nature of chance encounters with religion on the street is an important way of understanding religious meaning being played out in particular and specific localised contexts.

Often, you will come across public performance of religion through forms of street evangelism – it is a familiar sight in airports across the world to be met by Hare Krishna devotees bearing books and flowers, and most major towns and cities have a local Kingdom Hall from which Jehovah's Witnesses will arrange door-to-door witnessing. Similarly, the Church of Jesus Christ and Latter-Day Saints (Mormons) requires many of its young adult members to perform active evangelism door-to-door and in public places, meaning meetings with these religious communities are often unplanned and spontaneous. In such situations, your response will almost certainly depend on whether or not you hold a religious view in agreement or disagreement with the message of the evangelists. However, whatever your own views, these scenarios are valuable opportunities to ask direct questions and seek personalised answers regarding these religious communities. In addition, we have always found that it is useful to collect as much literature as possible from these volunteers about their communities – which is often specific to your locale – as these primary sources will always be useful for your coursework at a later date.

Such opportunities to talk with members of communities also open up the possibility to visit and meet people and organisations that you might not otherwise have contact with – evangelists are often useful 'gatekeepers' to their communities. Sometimes, the public performance of evangelism will be by individuals in very public places, such as shopping centres, which often makes it slightly trickier to interact with them, but take the time to listen to their message, and reflect upon how their worldview is projected. In the case of a Christian evangelist, for example, you could reflect upon where you might position them in relation to 'mainstream' Christian churches, and analyse what themes and teachings they choose to focus upon. One particularly vibrant place to engage with such activities and performances (and they are often very entertaining performances) is Speakers' Corner in Hyde Park in London. A gathering place for proponents of free speech and self-appointed teachers and prophets, the site has been renowned for its public debates since the 1870s, and has inspired similar public speaking venues in parks across the world.

Public rituals are also very important examples of religion in the street. Although they are often planned by the participants, your interaction with them will often not be. It is quite likely that at some point you will happen across a public ritual that you did not anticipate – this has happened to us in countries as diverse as Malta, India and Israel – and even if you are aware of it in advance, you will not necessarily be able to stage-manage your observation and participation due to the nature of public events involving large crowds. Events such as Semana Santa (Holy Week) processions in Seville, Spain, the Festa Del Redontore (Festival of the Redeemer) in Venice, Italy, the Durbar (End of Eid al-Fitr) celebrations in Kano, Nigeria, and the Horn Dance in Abbots Bromley, England, are all examples of the many thousands of explicitly religious public ritual events that occur around the world each year.

Often, public performances such as these are understandable on two levels: religious acts of individuals and their communities, and commercial exercises to help an area's economy through tourist and visitor revenue. However, to see these two factors as unrelated is to misunderstand how religious acts play out in everyday religion; the specially arranged days such as the festivals mentioned above are always interlinked with trade and commerce, which is an important part of everyday living, and certainly this has not been any different in times past when the great temple complexes of South India, for example, had markets held within the temple walls.

Public performances of ritual are often at their most vocal when the gathering is to protest perceived injustices. During the Swaraj (self-rule) protests that eventually helped to lead India to independence from Britain, M.K. Gandhi organised the Salt March, a 240-mile march through the West Indian state of Gujarat in 1930 to protest at British taxation on salt which had led to terrible poverty and malnutrition amongst many Indians. Similarly, Rev. Dr Martin Luther King, Jr led many protest marches in the 1950s and 1960s in the USA, organised with the aid of well-established networks of church leaders and congregants such as the Southern Christian Leadership Conference.

Yet, such examples are not just resigned to history. Interesting recent examples of public rituals of protest that have included, and have often been organised by, religious groups include the Jubilee 2000 'Drop the Debt' campaign organised by a group of mainstream Christian churches to put pressure on political leaders to ease financial repayment burdens on countries which were former colonies. Then there were the 'Not in My Name' anti-Iraq War demonstrations of 2003 and the 'Occupy Wall Street' campaign of 2011 which spread to financial capitals all over the world and which, in London, included an occupation of St Paul's Cathedral and public speeches by protesters, including clergy. Similarly, public protests can often be *about* religion even if they are not performed by religious people. Recent high-profile examples include protests against the Catholic Church in Ireland and Australia concerning the child abuse crimes uncovered in the past few years. Such groups will include Catholics, ex-Catholics and other interested parties, but much can be learned from both the protest itself, and also any responses that are given by religious groups that are targeted. We can observe both the performed religious lives of the protesters and the projected religious identities of the responding churches, groups and institutions.

Markets – particularly clothing and food markets – are also fascinating arenas in which to engage with religious communities, and materials and cultural items that give their identities meaning. Sikh street food in the alleyways of Amritsar in the Punjab and the food and clothing markets hawking Jewish and Bangladeshi (amongst many other) items in Brick Lane in London enable one to smell, taste, hear and feel everyday living for diverse religious communities. Many such places, for example, the Manchester 'curry mile' area of Muslim, largely Bangladeshi, restaurants and Liverpool's Smithdown Road, serve as examples of how diasporic communities have used food – and particular cultural understandings of food – as a way of creating communities and generating income for these communities whilst integrating into wider society as migrant communities. An afternoon walking through Brick Lane in London, or China Town in New York, is an attack on the senses full of diverse religious and cultural source material to help bring to life the place of religion on the high street.

Whilst walking through such areas, you will undoubtedly notice the almost constant barrage of advertisements, commercial and political, that proliferate in modern towns and cities. Such adverts are a particularly interesting method for communities to project their religious or ethical identities into shared public spaces. In recent years within the UK, and globally with some of the examples that follow, religion has played a central part in contested and controversial debates surrounding adverts that have been played out in very public arenas.

Perhaps the highest profile recent advertising campaign surrounding religion was the Atheist Bus Campaign. Based on a 2008 Comment is Free (*Guardian* newspaper) blog by Ariane Sherine, the campaign was a direct response to evangelical Christian advertising on London underground trains, which offered the following message: "*When the son of man comes, will he find faith on the earth? (Luke 18:8)*". The advertisements then give a web address, which contained the following warning for anyone who does not "*accept the word of Jesus on the cross*": "*You will be condemned to everlasting separation from God and then you spend all eternity in torment in hell. Jesus spoke about this as a lake of fire which was prepared for the devil and all his angels (Mt. 25:41).*" (Sherine, 2009) Finding the advertisement and associated website offensive, Sherine rhetorically asked in her blog whether any atheists would come together to pay for some counter-adverts in London. The campaign originally intended to raise £5,500, sufficient to place advertising banners on thirty London buses for four weeks. Largely supported (although not financially) by the centre-left newspaper the *Guardian*, the campaign eventually raised over £153,000, including £83,000 in a two-day period, which was, at the time, a fund-raising record for justgiving.com, the largest charity administration website in the UK. The money was used to pay for atheist advertising on over 800 buses in twenty-seven cities throughout the UK, and subsequently grew internationally, with adverts running in Germany, Finland, the Netherlands, Canada, Switzerland, Croatia, Italy, Spain, Australia and the USA.

The wording of the advert is particularly interesting. "*There's probably no God. Now stop worrying and enjoy your life,*" was chosen as a direct response to very strict advertising laws within the UK, administered by the Advertising Standards Agency. The relevant laws ban any advertising which is deemed to be unprovable or lacking in empirical or statistical evidence (CAP, 2010). The atheist campaign therefore used the word 'probably', in much the same vein as the famous Carlsberg beer adverts which claim that their product is 'probably' the best beer in the world. As was to be expected, the campaign led to counter-adverts and criticisms by religious groups, although it is interesting to note that that none of the major UK Churches was involved. Indeed, the Methodist Church thanked the campaign for encouraging a "*continued interest in God*" (Butt, 2009), and the Church of England stated: "*We would defend the right of any group representing a religious or philosophical position to be able to promote that view through appropriate channels*" (BBC, 2009).

The campaigns that did arise were almost exclusively organised by fringe or minority Churches or organisations within the UK – that is, small movements or individuals, rather than 'institutions' – examples include the Christian Party, the Russian Orthodox Church and the Trinitarian Bible Society (Smithers, 2009). Crucially, however, the religious responses to the atheist campaign were not constrained by the same advertising boundaries that limited Sherine's adverts. The Christian Party slogan: *"There definitely is a God. So join the Christian party and enjoy your life,"* which adorned buses across the UK, was deemed by the Advertising Standards Agency to be a political opinion, and thus exempt from the need for evidential backing. This is noteworthy about the place of religion, as a category and as a lived reality, in contemporary Britain as, despite falling attendances at mainstream Christian churches, 'religious voices' are a constant part of public discourse.

One other advertisement, also linked with politics and religion, that caused a controversy in recent years was in March 2009, when the far-right, anti-immigration British Nationalist Party unveiled a new advertising billboard for the run-up to the European Parliament and Local Government elections to be held later that year. Quoting John 15:20, the advert asked the question *"What would Jesus do?"* relating biblical comments on persecution to the supposed plight of white Christians in the UK (Telegraph, 2009). The campaign was roundly condemned by all major UK Churches, who sought to realign biblical understandings of persecution and hospitality to foreigners through a series of press statements (Ekklesia, 2009). Whilst this is an extreme version of religious voices, it is important to note that it is essential to engage with a spectrum of religious views, however distasteful we may find some of them, and to engage with any counterviews, so that we do service to the complexity of the ways in which different religious groups project their identities in everyday life, and in very public places. Indeed, these debates never go away. At the time of writing this, there is a legal challenge to the London Mayoral Office concerning a series of advertisements linked to 'gay-cure' theology, which had been previously banned from London public transport, but which may be allowed to return, post-appeal (Bingham, 2014).

You will also encounter much religion 'happening' in public places during ceremonies which are not explicitly religious in nature, but that retain or emulate religious elements. All of these are great ways to engage with religion in different social situations. Examples abound and are as diverse as the hymn 'Abide with Me' being sung at the English FA Cup Final each year since 1927, or the 'Welcome to Country' ceremony held in various Australian Universities to recognise the rights of indigenous people prior to the start of academic conferences. Often, such public ceremonies and rituals take on a very personal nature, even though they are performed and materialised in public places. One such example is the rise in popularity of temporary memorials to the dead, often at the places where road traffic accidents have occurred, and which often take the form of written messages and flowers tied to lamp posts, railings or other street furniture. These very personal, but publicly projected, memorials could be seen as linked to the tradition across much of the Mediterranean world which sees roadside shrines, often to Mary, on mountainside roads and particularly dangerous road junctions.

Whilst the examples given above will help you to 'notice' religious identities and religious acts when they occur in unexpected places, this element of the experience can often manifest in ways which make the researcher uncomfortable.

In the next section, we explore how this can affect your engagement with different religious communities and places.

Visiting 'dark' or 'contested' places

We have discussed some aspects of 'nasty' religion in the last chapter. Here the focus is on issues which arise when visiting 'dark' places or 'places of conflict'. They often involve engaging with human suffering, sometimes in the very recent past. For some of us, if the cruelty, violence and pain are in our living memory, or happened near to us, then this affects us more. Some people will react differently to Ground Zero in New York than to Jallianwala Bagh in Amritsar, even though similar numbers of innocent people died at each location; one tragedy was recent and the other a century ago, one is in America and the other in India. Whilst each individual human life should be treated with respect and dignity, the emotional responses and the kind of meanings associated with a particular 'dark' place will not be the same for every visit or for every visitor, whether pilgrim, tourist or researcher.

This is important because it reminds us that (some) places are powerful and their meaning is not fixed. As we argue throughout this book, what someone will get out of fieldwork depends, partly, on what they bring and how open they are to the impact of a place on them. Sometimes, having a guide to explain things – the *represented* meaning – may get in the way of this more direct experience of the living site and the people there, but it will provide a particular perspective on a place and what happened there. It is not always clear what draws people to visit these sites of suffering, but issues of memory, memorialisation and witness are important. The places sharply raise profound questions of human meaning and purpose, of good and evil, of despair and hope, and force us to face ourselves. Religions grapple with all these issues and, so, part of exploring living religion may include a visit to a 'dark' place (see *Dark Tourism* (Lennon and Foley, 2010) for further discussion).

Student voices

A third-year student wrote this response to a visit to the Holocaust museum in Jerusalem:

> This was the second time I had wound my way through the Yad Vashem museum, and just as before I struggled to feel connected to any of it. Just as before, I felt guilty that I could be so detached.
>
> But on this visit I walked out to the edge of the site to 'The Valley of the Communities' memorial. The monument resembles a maze of ruins. Walls and columns carved down into the hillside, excavated out of the ground, and the names of destroyed Jewish communities carved over the rock faces in remembrance. As you walk deeper into the Valley only the distant crunch of gravel underfoot alerts you that

someone else is nearby, out of sight. I felt a faint shiver of panic that I might never find my way out.

Tracing the names of the communities chiselled into the rock, fingers grazing the smooth sweep of the 'B' of 'BERLIN' and the sharp angle of the 'L', I think there is something deeply significant about remembering *communities* as much as individuals, something that speaks of human interconnectedness, the threading together of lives.

As I turned another corner I saw a man knelt alone on the ground sobbing. He must have heard me approaching because after a moment he straightened up and walked on. I wish I knew who he was crying for. I wanted to put my hands against his stiff shoulder blades. Instead I kept my palm firmly against the cold stone wall.

As with all fieldwork, it is important to have purposes in mind as well as an openness to what you find. Preparation should involve gaining some awareness of the context, events and possible issues. To understand the individuals and communities involved in 'dark' places will also mean hearing their stories and observing what they do. For a very interesting reflection on visiting the slave market and cells in Zanzibar, off the east coast of Africa, read African-American Muslim feminist scholar Amina Wadud (2014).

'Dark' places

The following are examples of 'dark' places which might be worth visiting as part of the study of living religion. Where you cannot visit in person, you might consider visiting online. See the website list at the end of the chapter for the details.

- battle or massacre sites such as Wounded Knee, South Dakota, USA, or Jallianwala Bagh, Amritsar, India
- museums related to the Nazi Holocaust such as Yad Vashem, Jerusalem, Israel; the United States Holocaust Memorial Museum in Washington, D.C., USA; the Anne Frank Museum in Amsterdam, the Netherlands; or Beth Shalom, The Holocaust Centre near Nottingham, England
- Nazi concentration and extermination camps such as Auschwitz/Birkenau, Poland
- Jewish ghettos such as in Prague, Czech Republic, or Rome, Italy
- museums such as the Armenian Genocide Museum-Institute in Yerevan, Armenia; Tuol Sleng in Phnom Penh, Cambodia, and the Killing Fields just outside the city; and Nyamata Genocide Memorial, Rwanda
- slave markets in Africa or museums related to slavery such as the International Slavery Museum in Liverpool, England, or The President's House, Philadelphia, USA

- Hiroshima and Nagasaki in Japan where the atom bombs were dropped at the end of World War II
- World War I and II Graveyards in Europe, Turkey and elsewhere, and Arlington National Cemetery, Virginia, USA
- Ground Zero in Manhattan, New York, USA, marking the September 11 attack

For further discussion see Sharpley and Stone (2009), White and Frew (2013).

There are also many places, sometimes places of pilgrimage, which have tombs, relics or memorials of martyrs, that is people who have been killed, sometimes horribly, in a way that is understood to be 'for their faith'. There may be grisly human remains on show, some gurdwaras have gruesome pictures of the torture and death of some of the Gurus and many churches and cathedrals have images of the Crucifixion of Jesus of Nazareth which graphically portray the pain of this agonising form of Roman execution.

There are two things to consider which might help you to explore these aspects of living religion more reflectively, but not necessarily more comfortably. The first is that the terrible reality of suffering, and ways of responding to it, often feature in religious teaching. This is perhaps most clear in Buddhism and Christianity. Asking a speaker in any of these 'dark' places about the meaning of suffering might be a useful way to begin to engage with this issue and the specific site being explored. The second aspect to reflect on is that religious practitioners say that they find inspiration from visiting these places and hearing the stories that lie behind them. Some devotees will also ritually participate in the pain and suffering. Catholic pilgrims climb on their knees up marble steps, the Scala Sancta, in Rome, especially during Lent and on Good Friday, elsewhere they carry very heavy images of Christ through the streets during Holy Week; and in the Philippines some devotees may whip themselves and even have themselves nailed to a cross. In a similar way some Shiite Muslims, at Ashura, mark the suffering and death of Imam Hussein at Karbala with mass self-flagellation ceremonies. In Tibet, pilgrims may travel for weeks or even months towards Lhasa, prostrating themselves at every step. In India, and amongst some Native American Indians, hooks are inserted into the body which is then suspended so it is hanging from the hooks.

Living in the twenty-first century, we probably have very different experiences of physical pain from all the generations who have lived before us because we see almost all pain as bad and as benefitting from analgesics – painkillers. In the past, physical pain would have been a much more familiar bodily experience, and many religions have used pain as a spiritual discipline and seen suffering as redemptive. Our attitudes now might well be different. It would be useful to reflect on what you might consider 'good pain'. This is a difficult topic and visiting any of these 'dark' places, in the flesh or online, will also be hard. So, you need to look after yourself emotionally, and find the ways that are right for you to respond. As Shunryo Suzuki, the Soto Zen teacher said, "If you can't do anything except bow, you should do it" (2011, 29), and in the words of an old (possibly Jewish) saying, "it is better to light one candle than to curse the darkness".

Contested spaces may be more problematic for the participants than for the student doing fieldwork, but it is important to be aware that battles – both literal and figurative – are and have been fought over these places. Even where conflict is a long time in the past, the scars will still be there. Jerusalem is a good example of a place which is understood to be holy in three religions and which has been a fairly continuous site of bloody conflict. It is still being fought over in religious, political and sometimes violent ways. No study of the city should ignore this conflict and it is important not to prejudge the situation. There are many different narratives and views and making judgements that one group is right and another wrong is not the role of the study of religion; neither is indifference to the lived realities of different groups. In studying a contested space 'on the ground', you should aim to understand more fully the different views and experiences, and analyse and interpret their significance.

A closer look at Glastonbury

Perhaps one of the most interesting places to study religion in the modern world is the ancient English town of Glastonbury, in the South-West of England. A settlement dating back to at least the Neolithic era, the area was for centuries a series of raised plateaus in a complex of inland river systems only navigable by boat, and is now home to around 9,000 residents. The area is rich in archaeology, has one of Europe's first major roadways, only recently discovered and dating from around 4000 BCE, and has a rich and complex religious story within recorded history. As such, we think it is the perfect example to demonstrate how you can engage with all of the different aspects of living religion which we are discussing in this chapter.

Glastonbury claims to be the first site of Christian worship in England, a claim that rests on the story of the teenage Jesus visiting Glastonbury with his uncle, Joseph of Arimathea, as a consequence of Joseph's tin metal trading with South-West England. Further stories tell of Joseph returning to Glastonbury after the Crucifixion carrying with him the blood of Christ in a vessel that would dominate medieval mythology, and some recent popular fiction books, as the Holy Grail. Legend has it that Joseph planted his staff into the ground, and from this sprung a tree, subsequently known as the Glastonbury Thorn, that flowers every Christmas. This foundational myth of English identity is remembered in the unofficial national song of England, based on William Blake's early nineteenth-century poem 'And did those feet in ancient time' later set to music by Hubert Parry and popularly known as 'Jerusalem', which begins with the words:

And did those feet in ancient time,
Walk upon England's mountains green:
And was the holy Lamb of God
On England's pleasant pastures seen!

Intriguingly, Blake did not make statements about Jesus actually having visited Glastonbury, but tantalisingly asks the question of whether he did or not, and if it was the case, then perhaps it meant that a brief period of 'heaven on earth' occurred which Blake contrasted with the inhuman treatment of workers and destruction of the natural landscape that was happening as a consequence of the Industrial Revolution at the time he was writing, and which Blake famously described as 'these dark Satanic Mills'. This linking of sacred and secular history is also apparent in the town's relationship with Britain's most famous mythic figure of all: King Arthur. Linked in local lore with Avalon, from the Old Welsh for 'Isle of Apples', Glastonbury is a legendary burial place of Arthur and Guinevere, and the town is referred to as Avalon in much contemporary literature. With regard to the fabric of the town, the landscape is dominated by two structures: the Tower of St Michael on the iconic Glastonbury Tor, and the ruins of Glastonbury Abbey, once one of the richest religious houses in England. The parish churches of St Benedict and St John the Baptist sit at the heart of the town, and on the outskirts of town by the foot of the Tor is the peaceful Chalice Well Gardens – so called as the water that comes from the red spring in the grounds tastes of blood due to the high levels of iron minerals from the surrounding hills. Public performance of religion is also a part of the town's religious life – every year just prior to Christmas the vicar of St John's Church performs a ceremony with the local mayor and a pupil from the local school to take a cutting from the Holy Thorn which is then sent on to the Queen, to be placed on her table for Christmas morning. In addition, there are two annual Christian pilgrimages/processions through the town, representing Catholic and Anglican traditions that go back at least to the early twentieth century. As well as the major 'Western' Christian denominations, there is a Celtic Orthodox Church, which has its origins in England, France and America and which traces its foundation to Joseph of Arimathea in Glastonbury in 37 CE (2011).

Another Glastonbury

And yet there is another story to Glastonbury. In fact, a plethora of entwining, convergent and contesting stories. If you take a walk up the High Street of modern Glastonbury, you will be faced with a barrage of colour, smell and noise. Indian incense will waft past fat bronzes of Ganesha; street performers will assault your senses and, with humour, your pockets; the sun will reflect off hanging healing crystals in shop windows; signs advertising aura photography and karmic healing sessions will block your path on the pavement; Green Man figures watch as you pass by; and Native American dreamcatchers and tools of the Wicca craft sit on shelves alongside books on local folk history and faery lore. Stepping off the High Street, you enter courtyards containing Europe's first legally dedicated Goddess Temple and the Isle of Avalon Foundation. At the Temple, you can undertake training courses to become a priestess (or priest) of Avalon, and at the Foundation, you can sign up for courses as diverse as Spiritual Counselling, Shamanic Craft Workshop and Faery Days.

Leaving the High Street and walking towards the Tor, you will pass Chalice Well Gardens where a red spring, associated with the blood of Christ by Christians, is remembered as the menstrual fluids of the Goddess in the landscape by local Goddess devotees and pagan communities. As you climb the Tor itself, you are walking up the left breast of the Goddess, looking down upon her reclined body as her outstretched legs follow the path of Wearyall Hill. The Abbey rests on the site of her vagina – heart of the birth Goddess. You may remember that the Abbey is dedicated to Mary, a female aspect of divinity. If you turn your eyes back to the tower of St Michael on the Tor, you will see a stone-carved frieze of St Brigit, patron saint of fertility and childbirth, and an early Christian inculturation of the Irish fertility Goddess, Brigid.

Each year, you can visit the Goddess Conference, an international gathering of Goddess devotees, indigenous peoples and craft practitioners who come together to celebrate the feminine divine. Such identities are publicly performed in the annual Goddess Procession, with banners depicting the feminine divine from, amongst others, European, Indian, American and Aboriginal traditions. Returning to the town centre, you can peruse bookshelves heavy with stories of UFO sightings and encounters within the local landscape, and purchase maps that take you on walking tours of the Glastonbury zodiac and local ley lines. Visiting Glastonbury, as an academic tourist or on an organised education visit, offers a wonderful opportunity to engage with living religion in unexpected ways. Shops, local papers, cafes, billboards and posters all project and perform a sometimes bewildering array of worldviews and contested religious narratives.

Glastonbury also complicates categories and terms used by scholars of religion. A young couple, recently married, entered the Goddess Temple, tentatively asking if they could speak to a priestess as they "were quite interested in New Age religion". The priestess, with one thought on the 30,000-year-old Venus of Willendorf, and with tongue half in her cheek, suggested "you may like to try the Catholic Church down the road ... they've only been here 2,000 years". On another occasion, whilst walking on top of the Tor, a woman of Asian heritage cast broken clay fragments of a small fertility Goddess statue to decompose into the fabric of the landscape. Whilst walking down the Tor together, holding on to each other for dear life whilst dangerously high winds sought to knock us off the perilous curving path, the Goddess devotee told the story of how she had spent a week on a course at the Glastonbury Goddess Temple and was about to return to her home in London. She volunteered her religious identity as Muslim.

Such remembrances – two of many based on previous visits to Glastonbury – serve as examples of how speaking with individuals is the best way of understanding how religious identities are created, contested and expressed. By doing this, we can begin to engage with the messy and fuzzy boundaries of lived religions rather than the falsely constructed boundaries of the textbook.

Chapter summary

This chapter has explored a number of links between religion and geography, the sacred and place, boundaries and belonging. It is worth noting that some places may be very challenging for some students because of a perceived conflict with their own beliefs and worldviews. For example, it may be the case that evangelical Christian students are challenged by a visit to a Scientology church. We discuss this issue further in the next chapter. It is worth remembering too that, as a student of religion, there are some religious places where you may not be allowed to enter at all.

Further reading

Although it was written some time ago, *Sacred Place* edited by Jean Holm and John Bowker (1994) is a really good introduction to ideas and examples of sacred space in eight different religious traditions. Written by leading scholars, it is very easy to read and understand.

Read an article about Glastonbury by Marion Bowman such as 'The Holy Thorn Ceremony: Revival, Rivalry and Civil Religion in Glastonbury' (2006).

Questions for consideration

1 Do you have a meaningful place in your life? Where is it? What is it like? Why would you consider it significant?
2 Lynn Davidman writes that "by becoming self-reflexive about my own 'sacred' spaces and practices, I was better able to see the many symbolic practices by which my respondents are comforted" (2002, 21). If you were to set up a shrine to express the things you hold as being of ultimate value, what would it be like? What would it include? How would you explain it to someone else?
3 Reflect on the different rooms and buildings where you have been a student – how did the spaces affect you, other people, how you learned, and how you were taught? What does that tell you about the influences of buildings and their impact on those who use them?

4 When you visited a place that worshippers understand to be 'holy', what was it that made this place holy for them? How did you reflect upon this 'holiness' or 'sacredness' after your visit – how did it make you feel, and did it affect your understanding of the place?

5 Think of a time you went to an art gallery or encountered an artistic performance which related to religion or used religious motifs. How did the art engage with religion? What was the context? How did you (and other people present) react to it? Did it challenge, reinforce or change your understanding of 'religion' or the place of 'religion' in everyday encounters?

6 When was the last occasion you 'encountered religion' when you weren't expecting to? How was religion portrayed, and for what reasons? Did the encounter affect how you understand the place of 'religion' in everyday lives?

Bibliography

This list includes all the texts referred to in the chapter and other recommended reading. All websites accessed on 31.10.14, unless otherwise specified.

Bagnoli, M., Klein, H.A., Griffith Mann, C. and Robinson, J. (eds) 2011, *Treasures of Heaven: Saints, Relics and Devotion in Medieval Europe*, London: The British Museum Press.

Banksy 2010, *Exit Through the Gift Shop*, US, UK and France: Revolver Entertainment.

Barber, P. (ed.) 2005, *The Map Book*, London: Weidenfeld & Nicholson.

BBC 2009, "Atheists Launch Bus Ad Campaign' accessed online at http://news.bbc.co.uk/1/hi/uk/7813812.stm

Bingham, J. 2014, 'Court to Investigate Whether Boris Johnson Banned "Gay Cure" Bus Ads for "Political Capital"' in *Telegraph* 27 January, accessed online at www.telegraph.co.uk/news/religion/10599302/Court-to-investigate-whether-Boris-Johnson-banned-gay-cure-bus-ads-for-political-capital.html

Bowman, M. 2006, 'The Holy Thorn Ceremony: Revival, Rivalry and Civil Religion in Glastonbury' in *Folklore*, 117(2), 123–40.

——2005, 'Ancient Avalon, New Jerusalem, Heart Chakra of Planet Earth: The Local and the Global in Glastonbury' in *Numen*, 52(2), 157–90.

——2004, 'Procession and Possession in Glastonbury: Continuity, Change and the Manipulation of Tradition' in *Folklore*, 115(3), 273–85.

Butt, R. 2009, 'Atheist Bus Campaign Spreads the Word of No God Nationwide' accessed online at www.theguardian.com/world/2009/jan/06/atheist-bus-campaign-nationwide (09/04/14)

Cameron, H., Richter, P., Davis, D. and Ward, F. (eds) 2005, *Studying Local Churches*, London: SCM Press.

CAP 2010, 'The UK Code of Non-broadcast Advertising, Sales Promotion and Direct Marketing' accessed online at www.cap.org.uk/Advertising-Codes/Non-broadcast-HTML/Prefaceof-the-non-broadcast-CAP-code.aspx (09/04/14)

Carmichael, D.L., Hubert, J., Reeves, B. and Schanche, A. (eds) 1994, *Sacred Sites, Sacred Places*, London: Routledge.

Carp, R. 2011, 'Material Culture' in Stausberg, M. and Engler, S. (eds) *The Routledge Handbook of Research Methods in the Study of Religion*, Abingdon: Routledge, 474–90.

Carretto, C. 1972, *Letters from the Desert*, London: Darton, Longman & Todd.

Celtic Orthodox Church 2011, 'Who We Are' accessed online at www.orthodoxie-celtique. net/who%20we%20are.html (accessed 09/04/14)

Cleal, R. 2008, 'Human Remains from Windmill Hill and West Kennet Avenue, Avebury Parish, Wiltshire, Held by the Alexander Keiller Museum'. Accessible at: www. english-heritage.org.uk/content/imported-docs/a-e/appendix4clealhumanremainsreport-corrected.pdf

Davidman, L. 2002, 'Truth, Subjectivity and Ethnographic Research' in Spickard, J.V., Landres, J.S. and McGuire, M.B. (eds) *Personal Knowledge and Beyond: Reshaping the Ethnography of Religion*, New York: New York University Press, 17–26.

Ekklesia 2009, 'Churches Dismiss BNP's Election Poster' accessed online at www.ekklesia. co.uk/node/9108

Haldane, J. 2003, 'Transforming Nature: Art and Landscape' in *The Art Book*, 10(3), 10–12.

Hansard 1943, 'House of Commons Rebuilding' 28 October, vol. 393, 403 accessed online at hansard.millbanksystems.com/commons/1943/oct/28/house-of-commons-rebuilding

Harvey, G. 2013, *Food, Sex & Strangers: Understanding Religion as Everyday Life*, Durham: Acumen.

Holm, J. and Bowker, J. (eds) 1994, *Sacred Place*, London: Pinter.

Kerton, N. 2010, 'Prehistoric Skeletons Will Remain at Avebury Museum Say Bosses' accessed online at www.gazetteandherald.co.uk/news/7986642.Prehistoric_skeletons_will_remain_at_Avebury_museum_say_bosses/

Knott, K. 2005, *The Location of Religion: A Spatial Analysis*, London and Oakville, CA: Equinox.

Lawrence, T.E. 2000 (new edition), *Seven Pillars of Wisdom*, London: Penguin Classics.

Lennon, J. and Foley, M. 2010, *Dark Tourism*, Andover, Hampshire: Cengage Learning.

Lewis, J.R. (ed.) 2009, *Scientology*, Oxford: Oxford University Press.

Long, R. 2009, *Heaven and Earth*, London: Tate.

MacGregor, N. and Langmuir, E. 2000, *Seeing Salvation: Images of Christ in Art*, London: BBC.

Paine, C. 2013, *Religious Objects in Museums: Private Lives and Public Duties*, London: Bloomsbury.

Parker Pearson, M. 2014, *Stonehenge: A New Understanding*, New York: Experiment.

Perry, G. 2011, *The Tomb of the Unknown Craftsman*, London: The British Museum Press.

Porter, V. (ed.) 2012, *Hajj: Journey to the Heart of Islam*, London: The British Museum Press.

Rainsford, D. 2003, 'Solitary Walkers, Encountering Blocks: Epistemology and Ethics in Romanticism and Land Art' in *European Journal of English Studies*, 7(2), 177–92.

Roberts, A. 2010, 'Tempering "the Tyranny of Already": Re-signification and the Migration of Images' in Morgan, D. (ed.) *Religion and Material Culture*, Oxford: Routledge, 115–34.

Roebben, B. 2009, 'Narthical Religious Learning; Redefining Religious Education in Terms of Pilgrimage' in *British Journal of Religious Education*, 31(1), 17–27.

Serota, N. 2009, 'Walking Abroad' in Wallis, C. (ed.) *Richard Long: Heaven and Earth*, London: Tate Publishing, 28–29.

Sharpley, R. and Stone, P.R. (eds) 2009, *The Darker Side of Travel: The Theory and Practice of Dark Tourism*, Bristol: Channel View Publications.

Sheldrake, P. 2001, *Spaces for the Sacred*, London: SCM Press.

Sherine, A. 2009, 'Atheists: Gimme Five' accessed online at www.guardian.co.uk/com mentisfree/2008/jun/20/transport.religion

Smithers, R. 2009, 'Christian Party Advert Draws More than 1,000 Complaints' accessed online at www.theguardian.com/media/2009/mar/11/god-advert-christian-complaints

Suzuki, S. 2011 (40th anniversary edition), *Zen Mind, Beginner's Mind*, Boston: Shambala.

Telegraph, 2009, 'BNP Uses Jesus in Advertising Campaign' accessed online at www. telegraph.co.uk/news/religion/5077988/BNP-uses-Jesus-in-advertising-campaign.html (accessed 09/04/14)

Theodoratus, D.J. and LaPena, F. 1994, 'Wintu Sacred Geography of Northern California' in Carmichael, D.J. et al. (eds) *Sacred Sites, Sacred Places*, London: Routledge, 20–31.

Ucko, P.J. 1994, 'Foreword' in Carmichael, D.J. et al. (eds) *Sacred Sites, Sacred Places*, London: Routledge, xi–xxiii.

Wadud, A. 2014, 'Freedom and Faith' in *Feminism and Religion* at http://feminismand religion.com/2014/03/06/freedom-and-faith-by-amina-wadud/

Wallis, C. (ed.) 2009, *Richard Long: Heaven and Earth*, London: Tate Publishing.

White, L. and Frew, E. (eds) 2013, *Dark Tourism and Place Identity: Managing and Interpreting Dark Places*, New York: Routledge.

Websites

This annotated list includes all the online sources we have referred to in the chapter as well as some recommended sites. We have given the URLs (web addresses) accessed on 31.10.14 but these do change so we have listed them by the name of the organisation in alphabetical order.

Auschwitz/Birkenau. In many ways Auschwitz has come to stand for the Holocaust. This is the official website – http://en.auschwitz.org/m/

Cemeteries are always interesting places to visit within the study of religion. There are good websites for Arlington National Cemetery – www.arlingtoncemetery.mil/ – and World War I and II – www.ww1cemeteries.com/

Christianity and Culture at York University provides both primary sources and a range of multimedia tools for exploring church buildings and pilgrimage traditions – both of these are relevant to this book. www.christianityandculture.org.uk/

Genocide museums. The Armenian Genocide Museum in Yerevan has excellent displays and resources about the first twentieth-century genocide – www.genocide-museum.am/eng/index.php. The genocide in Cambodia can be explored at the Killing Fields Museum – www.killingfieldsmuseum.com – and at Tuol Sleng Genocide Museum – www.phnompenh.gov.kh/phnom-penh-city-toul-sleng-genocide-museum-140.html. The Nyamata Genocide Memorial in Rwanda has its archives at www.genocidearchiver wanda.org.rw/index.php/Nyamata

Ghettos. The ghetto in Prague has a number of different synagogues which are now used as museums – www.jewishmuseum.cz/en/ainfo.htm. In the Rome ghetto the museum focuses on Jewish history in Rome – http://lnx.museoebraico.roma.it/w/?page_id_=+351&lang_=+en&lang=en

Glastonbury. The Abbey is an important site in English Christian history – www.glastonburyabbey.com/. Glastonbury Goddess Temple offers training courses for priestesses as well as organising processions and other rituals – www.goddesstemple.co.uk/. *Goddess in Glastonbury* is a free online book about the Goddess in Glastonbury – www.kathyjones.co.uk/index.php/all-books/16-the-goddess-in-glastonbury. The Isle of Avalon Foundation offers courses on spirituality, healing and personal growth and the website has articles and other resources – www.isleofavalonfoundation.com/

Holocaust museums. There is a very good website for the Anne Frank Museum in Amsterdam which also has a fascinating virtual tour of the secret annex – www.annefrank.org/en/.

Beth Shalom Holocaust Centre in Nottingham has some interesting survivor testimony – http://holocaustcentre.net/. The United States Holocaust Memorial Museum has material on genocide as well the Holocaust. Plenty of research material – www.ushmm.org/. Yad Vashem Holocaust museum in Jerusalem offers excellent materials for research – www.yadvashem.org/

Philip Larkin reads his poem 'Church Going'. www.youtube.com/watch?v=w5aKknj-q3o

Memorials. Jallianwala Bagh – for some background history about this massacre at Amritsar see www.jallianwalabagh.ca/pages.php?id=4. Hiroshima and Nagasaki are now memorialised by a peace museum – www.pcf.city.hiroshima.jp/index_e2.html. There is a museum at Ground Zero in New York – www.911memorial.org/

North American Graves Protection and Repatriation Act material can be found at www.cr.nps.gov/local-law/FHPL_NAGPRA.pdf

Religion in Museums. This is a blog about various ways in which people find the religious or spiritual in museums. There are regular postings about different exhibitions in various parts of the world which makes this an interesting source for seeing how someone encounters religion and communicates their experience. Good links to other websites. http://religioninmuseums.wordpress.com/

Sacred Destinations combines tourism with religious sites in a very interesting and, presumably, commercial way. It has a useful search facility and carries this quotation on its main page by Trappist monk Thomas Merton: "If we instinctively seek a paradisiacal and special place on earth, it is because we know in our inmost hearts that the earth was given to us in order that we might find meaning, order, truth and salvation in it." www.sacred-destinations.com/

Sacred Sites has some beautiful photos of places around the world and a very extensive bibliography although some of the ideas put forward by photographer Martin Gray are controversial. www.sacredsites.com/

Slave trade sites. There are a number of excellent museums related to the slave trade such as in Liverpool, England – www.liverpoolmuseums.org.uk/ism/ – and Philadelphia, USA – www.phila.gov/presidentshouse//index.html

The Sunday Assembly is, according to their website, "a godless congregation that celebrates life. Our motto: live better, help often, wonder more. Our mission: to help everyone find and fulfill [*sic*] their full potential. Our vision: a godless congregation in every town, city and village that wants one." These 'non-religious' gatherings have spread very quickly to many parts of the world. http://sundayassembly.com

4 Group fieldwork

Short field visits and residential study tours

Introduction

The next two chapters consider how you can get the best out of doing fieldwork. The information is aimed directly at you as a neophyte researcher engaging with religion off campus. This chapter focuses on group fieldwork, organised by a tutor, where you probably are not involved much in choosing the places or planning exactly what you do when you are there. The following one deals with all the differing aspects of doing independent fieldwork. Obviously there is overlap in the skills needed for any study in the field, so when you have read this chapter you might like to read the sections in chapter 5 that are relevant to your group fieldwork.

Types of group fieldwork

Short study visits

- often visits linked to students' familiar environment or locality;
- often focused on one venue or tradition;
- often linked to a particular module of study;
- may or may not be formally assessed for credit.

Longer study visits

- often one- or two-day visits;
- often taking place in one town or city within a few hours' travelling distance;
- often exploring more than one venue or tradition;
- may or may not be formally assessed for credit.

Study tours

- often residential;
- often linked to international destinations;
- often focused on multiple traditions or historical time periods;
- often a module in its own right with associated assessment/credit.

At the heart of this book is the idea that encountering *living* religion is a very important part of the study of religion. For many students this begins with group study visits and the local area is a good starting point. These short visits are often to places of worship although, as we have seen in chapter 3, there are lots of other sacred places which can be visited. Short visits are often within timetable time and are to perhaps one or two places. For example, an introductory module on the study of religion might involve a visit to local Hindu and Sikh temples. As we have seen, the terms 'Hindu' and 'Sikh' are not necessarily as clearly differentiated as might be imagined from textbook reported religion, and that is why they are a good example of the value of group fieldwork in developing an understanding of religion. There are some specific details about this in the next section.

Some universities are situated in places with rich, diverse religious populations, such as large multicultural cities, and then these short visits are very easy to manage. Obvious examples of such cities are London, Chicago, Sydney or New York. However there are many universities where it is necessary to travel further to encounter a range of places. In these cases a one- or two-day visit is valuable even for introductory courses. There are also places so rich in traditions that it is worth visiting them even if this requires quite a long journey. We discussed Glastonbury, in England, as one such example in the last chapter and we consider an interesting 'Hindu' ashram, Skanda Vale, in Wales, in the section below on 'tricky issues'. The further away from home, the easier it is for students when the visit is arranged for them and there is the added interest of a residential stay. Even short group visits build a sense of identity amongst the participants and enable staff and students to get to know one another better, and this is even more the case when everyone is travelling together, staying overnight and sharing meals.

Finally, there are study tours. These last several days and may involve an international dimension. On such a tour you might visit a particular city such as London, Rome, New York, Jerusalem or Istanbul, or you could cover wider areas such as Northern India, or Kerala and Karnataka; or the study tour may focus on a different sort of place such as the Sinai desert or Oswiecim, the town near Auschwitz/Birkenau. These visits are intense, with a lot packed into a short time, and they may involve being in an unfamiliar culture. Often, on study tours, expectations are overturned and students are surprised by what they discover about religion and themselves.

So, what follows is about how to get the most out of group visits – a few hours, a day, or several days – and there is more detail in the next chapter on independent fieldwork.

Starting points

This is a summary of some key starting points to approach studying living religion on a group visit. There is a more extended theoretical discussion of these ideas in the earlier chapters:

- Don't view religions as monolithic. There is diversity within every religious tradition so be alert to the particular strand of the religion whose followers and places you are going to visit, for example Southern Baptist Christianity or Bengali Vaishnavism.
- As part of this particularity, find out about the cultural, geographic, political and linguistic specifics of the group you will visit, for example are there refugees or asylum seekers in this congregation?
- Remember that in some places of worship not everyone can go everywhere, so there may be an area you can't go in. For example, in the Church of Jesus Christ of Latter-Day Saints, popularly known as Mormons or abbreviated to LDS, visitors can go into what is known as the 'church' but not into the 'temple'.
- Be aware that the boundaries between traditions, especially Asian religions, are sometimes constructed or highlighted in the 'reported religion' of the textbook paradigm of 'World Religions' as clear and distinct identities. In reality things are more complicated, and exploring 'living religion' in the field means encountering traditions that are evolving and dynamic and which sometimes challenge these neat divisions. For example, understanding Hindu and Sikh traditions may be developed by a visit to a Valmiki or Ravidass temple (see Takhar and Jacobs, 2011).
- Remember that things don't always go to plan when you are in the field. Both authors have had the experience several times of arriving at a place of worship where a visit has been arranged and confirmed, only to discover that no one is expecting us. One of us has queued with students for several hours in Jerusalem to get up onto the *Haram al-Sharif* only to find the entry closed just as we got there. These things happen, and sometimes there is nothing that can be done.

These are all important points but don't overanalyse in advance. A group visit will get you out into the field where you can actually visit a place of worship such as a 'Christian church' or a 'Hindu temple' and you can begin your direct encounter with living religion. To get the most out of this, you do need to prepare.

Preparing for your group visit to a place of worship

The more you understand about something, the more you will see when you encounter it; you will have a more sophisticated vocabulary and will be aware of wider connections. So, generally, the more you know and understand about a religious group or place before your visit, the better. There is an exception to this, and it is worth thinking about, although it is not an excuse for not preparing for the visit. Going to a new place produces surprises, but very quickly people stop noticing things that they were really aware of at the beginning; the surprise, even the shock, wears off. First impressions are really useful so make it a part of your preparation to always be alert in the first few seconds and minutes of being in a new place.

Do some background research. Use print and online sources to develop your understanding of the religion(s) and the particular place(s) you are visiting. Check the local news media to see if there are any reports about what is happening in the area or articles about issues affecting the communities in question. Prepare questions to ask the people you meet on the visit. Make sure these are not just questions to which you could easily find answers on the Internet. You have a precious opportunity to ask questions of a real live human being who is a follower of a particular religious tradition so ask things *you* really want to know about. It may only be during the visit that something strikes you and you want to ask about it, but if you have been thinking about what you want to get out of the visit, you will be more alert to the learning opportunities that are there.

If the group visit is to be assessed in some way you may be asked to do a preliminary assignment based on some background reading and research. Perhaps you have been asked to read a particular book and comment on the ideas in it that most interest you, or to submit questions you want to ask a speaker. If there is an assignment based on the visit, make sure you know exactly what you have to do and keep it in mind during the visit.

Etiquette

This section will help you to dress and behave appropriately for different places of worship which you may visit in any kind of group fieldwork. You are guests and will often be treated as *honoured* guests. You should reflect on this aspect of your visit and include it when you write up your experiences. You may be offered refreshments and sometimes you will be invited to participate to some extent in the activities that are taking place. We will discuss the issues that this raises for some students. You need to be aware of the ways in which a particular tradition manages the roles of men and women within a place of worship. This is usually more important if you are attending a service of worship rather than an empty building. Similarly, social rules concerning speech, food, gifts or money often need to be navigated effectively so as not to offend or inconvenience hosts or other users of the sacred spaces who are not a part of your group.

Whenever you visit any place of worship, it is a good idea to dress smartly and modestly. Clothes also need to be loose enough to enable you to sit comfortably on the floor. Scruffy, skimpy or very tight-fitting clothes are not appropriate for men or women. You may need to take off your shoes, so as well as ensuring that they are comfortable, also make sure that they are not too difficult to get off and on. In many places women will need to cover their head, so it is a good idea for women to carry a scarf on field visits. Where men need to cover their head, such as in a synagogue or gurdwara, the appropriate covering will be provided.

Christian places of worship such as churches, chapels, cathedrals, abbeys, monasteries, convents, meeting houses and so on vary considerably. This diversity depends on the particular Christian traditions, with their key doctrinal differences as well as historical, geographical and cultural differences, so you need to be really clear that no single Christian place is typical. For a good introduction to studying churches see Cameron et al. (2005). In the past it was a Western custom for men to take their hat off when they went inside a church, or any building, and that is generally still the custom today at least amongst older people. Most women would have worn a hat in church, but that is no longer generally the case. Churches in some countries, including in Southern Europe and the Middle East, will require that people do not wear shorts and that they cover their shoulders. It is a generalisation, but in many black-led churches worshippers dress very smartly, and if you are attending a service there you might want to look smart too.

Just as the buildings differ, so do the services. Some are very formal, with a choir singing beautiful music and everything set out in a service book, some are very informal, with lots of participation from the congregation, and some, as in a Quaker service, are mainly in silence. A lot of the service will be in English in most Christian denominations in the English-speaking world, and you can choose how much you join in with songs and prayers. You should stand and sit when everyone else does. However, the part of many Christian services called the Communion is trickier. This is known by many different terms and is the focus of serious disagreement amongst Christians. The ritual will use some form of bread and wine or grape juice. This is distributed in different ways, but usually only to people who are full members of the church, so, unless you are, you should not receive Communion. In some churches people who don't receive Communion go for a blessing. You do not have to do this, but you could if you wanted. During the service there will probably be a collection when people give money which is used to run the church or to support charity work. If you are there as a group, you should not feel required to give anything as your institution will almost certainly make a donation.

In a **Muslim** *masjid* (mosque) modest dress is really important. You have to take your shoes off near the entrance and women must cover their head with a scarf. There will be a place for worshippers to wash which you should be able to visit if the mosque is quiet, and men and women will have separate areas for the prayer. Your group will probably all stay together if you are not attending the prayer. There are no chairs where people pray so you may well be asked to sit on the floor to listen to the imam or other speaker.

If you are attending a service you may be asked to go to the separate men's and women's areas, but you may all be able to be at the back of the men's area or watch from a balcony or side room. You will not be expected to join in the prayers which will take about fifteen minutes. The busiest and longest prayers take place on Friday lunchtime. They are called *jumma prayers* and include a sermon, but you may be asked not to come at that time because a group visit would add to the traffic problems that often arise near the mosque on a Friday. There is no collection of money, although you may see boxes where money is collected for charity.

Although it is easy to visit a mosque in the non-Muslim world, it is often impossible in the Muslim world to actually go into a mosque either to visit or to attend the prayers. There are some exceptions to this, and if you are on a study tour in Istanbul, it is easy to visit the Blue Mosque with the tourists and also possible to go at prayer times, while some very large and recently built mosques welcome visitors, in Abu Dhabi, Muscat in Oman, and Casablanca in Morocco, for example.

When you are visiting a **Hindu** ashram or *mandir* (temple), all your senses will be involved. There are different smells and sounds, and lots of images. You will be asked to remove your shoes and leave them by the door, maybe in a rack, and there are no seats so you may have to sit on the floor – some temples offer cushions. There will probably be worshippers coming in and out during your visit, and temples will vary by having both set services and drop-in access for personal devotion. You will notice that offerings are often made to the statues or depictions of deities – the *murtis* – and when you leave you may well be given a piece of fruit or sweets which have been offered in this way. This is called *prasad* or 'blessed', and often meals for worshippers and visitors will be made from food that has been blessed in the temple in a similar way. Some people may feel uncomfortable receiving something which has been offered to the deities. Only you can decide what is right for you, but it is a good idea to discuss this with your tutor before you go. It is really important for everyone to be aware of the beliefs and values that they bring to the study of religion. If you are joining in a meal, you should only take an amount that you can eat, as to leave food on your plate could be considered disrespectful.

There is a wide spectrum of approaches to money in different Hindu communities. Some temple visitors expect to give money as a part of their pilgrimage, or act of worship, but at the other end of the spectrum, there are temples which do not allow money on the premises (you can read more about this in the example below, when one of the authors inadvertently transgressed this particular issue of etiquette!). Time spent in a temple during worship will involve being offered *arti*. This uses the symbolism of light as another sign of blessing, and worshippers pull the light into their mind with their hands when it is offered to them. You can choose to participate in this. In India you will be able to visit many different temples, perhaps joining pilgrims at a shrine or sitting with the congregation while they sing *bhajans* (devotional songs).

A **Jewish** place of worship is usually called a synagogue although some Jewish communities, particularly in America, call their building a temple. In Hebrew there are three terms which reflect three different purposes played by a synagogue. A *bet knesset* is a house of assembly, which is what the word 'synagogue' actually means. In other words it is a place where Jews meet together. A *bet midrash* is a house of study, which reflects the importance of education within Judaism; study is a holy activity for Jews. The third term, *bet tefillah*, means a house of prayer.

If you are visiting on the Sabbath, for a service, you will not be able to take pictures in most synagogues, nor should you write anything. Men will need to cover their head. In Orthodox synagogues men and women sit separately for services At other times you will probably be able to take photographs, sit together and men may not need head covering. The person welcoming you to the synagogue will guide you.

If you attend a service, some, most or almost all will be in Hebrew. You will have a service book, probably with English translations, which will help you follow what is going on. You will also have a *Chumash*, which has the text of the *Torah* in Hebrew and English and also the linked readings from the *Neviim* or Prophets. You may or may not wish or be able to join in depending on how much is in Hebrew, but you should sit and stand when the rest of the congregation does. There will not be any collection of money during the service. Afterwards there may be food and drink for everyone which you will be invited to share and this is a good opportunity to talk to members of the congregation.

In a **Sikh** gurdwara visitors have to cover their head and take off their shoes. There will be racks to put your shoes on and scarves are available. Usually for men they are triangular and someone will help you to tie the scarf if necessary. Tobacco and alcohol are forbidden so you must not bring either into the gurdwara. In warmer countries (and in the Punjab itself) there are often shallow pools of water at the entrance to gurdwara complexes to symbolically cleanse your feet as you pass through. In the main worship space there may well be someone reading from the sacred text, the *Guru Granth Sahib*, during your visit, or musicians singing religious songs called *kirtans*. You will have to sit on the floor. Worshippers will come in and out all the time and go up to the Granth. They will prostrate, make an offering and then perhaps walk around the Guru Granth Sahib, which is kept under a canopy and is covered with a beautiful cloth when it is not being used. It is interesting to see how quite young children are taught how to offer respect to the scriptures. Worshippers may spend some time in the worship hall and as they leave someone near the door will offer them *kara prashad*. This is a mixture of semolina, clarified butter and sugar and is understood as food that has been blessed. If you receive it you should eat it respectfully, but you will not offend anyone if you don't want to receive it. If you do choose to take the *kara prashad*, cup both hands together, as it can be deemed 'offhand' or lacking in seriousness to just hold out one hand casually.

The kitchen or *langar* is a key part of the gurdwara where everyone is invited to have a vegetarian meal. It is deliberately vegetarian so anyone can eat it. There will be curry, chapatis, dhal and some milk pudding; it will be spicy but not very hot, and you can usually have water or tea to drink. You have to decide whether you want to eat this food, and should only take what you will eat. Most people will sit on the floor to eat, but there may be some high tables where you can stand to eat. When you have finished, take your tray to where the washing-up is done. Remember that everyone there is a volunteer and that everyone who comes will be fed. This is an important part of Sikh life – it is a practical way of performing *seva*, or service to humanity – so find out as much as possible about the *langar* while you are there. Gurdwaras will also have a variety of other ways in which they help the local and wider community.

In a **Buddhist** temple or *vihara* the person who meets you may be a monk in robes, but you may not meet either monks or nuns. You will need to take off your shoes and probably have to sit on the floor or on a cushion. You may be invited to participate in a short meditation during your visit, with your eyes closed and probably focusing on your breathing. There will be lots of elaborate things to look at in the shrine room, including statues of the Buddha, flowers, incense, pictures and other decorations. Everything is there for a reason so don't be afraid to ask what the significance is of what you can see. Buddhism is focused on the *dharma* or teaching of the Buddha and so your questions will be a useful trigger for the speaker to unpack a bit more of the *dharma* for you.

If you attend a service there will be chanting, probably not in English, although you will get a copy of the words and maybe a translation, there will be a talk about an aspect of Buddhism and maybe a longer period of meditation. You will probably see notices for classes in meditation and in Buddhist teaching. Buddhist temples in the West often attract both Buddhists who came originally from a Buddhist country in Asia and Westerners attracted to Buddhist ideas and practices. Similarly, if there are monks or nuns, they may be from traditional Buddhist countries or be Western converts.

New religious communities offer an enormous range of possibilities for the exploration of any local religious scene, and it is not possible to discuss all the different expectations and norms here. Be guided by your tutors as to what is appropriate. For example, dropping in to a New Age bookshop in Glastonbury that doubles as a hub for palmistry or aura photography requires little attention to dress, but attendance at an Aetherius Society meeting would require smart, even formal, clothes.

Of course there are also many other religious groups we have not included by name here, but the guidance we have given will help you make the most of the opportunities. There are no absolutely foolproof guidelines that will cover every possibility, but do not let that worry you. We have all made mistakes when encountering religious people and places with which we are not very familiar, and sometimes these occasions offer the greatest opportunities for learning. Indeed, one of the authors once made a faux pas when he handed cash to a Hindu swami who was running a half-marathon to raise money for a hospice. The problem was that, as part of their vows of poverty, the swamis in the community in question try to avoid touching money wherever possible. The swami was very good humoured, and was happy to make an exception as the donation was for his charitable work, but even small transgressions such as this one (and by a researcher who should have known better!) demonstrate the careful paths we have to walk when engaging with religious communities so as to be a good 'guest'.

Tricky issues

While it is the case that making honest mistakes is okay and you should not be afraid to engage fully with the places you are visiting, there are two issues which we are going to discuss here in a bit more detail because they may require decisions on your part about how fully you will participate in a visit to certain places. The first of these concerns rules about menstruation and food, and the second is about participation in religious activities with which you are uncomfortable.

Menstruation and food issues: Skanda Vale, in Wales, is a fascinating place visited by many groups for a day or perhaps longer. It describes itself as a multi-faith ashram (monastery) of men, and 'the Community of the Many Names of God'. It has some distinctive requirements for visitors. Firstly, people must not take leather jackets, belts or bags into any of the temples, and must leave their shoes outside; men and women sit separately. Also, they ask that for three days before the visit no one eats any meat, poultry or fish, and takes illegal drugs. If you do not do this, then you are asked to sit outside or at the back of a temple during the *puja* (worship) and so you are not fully participating. At Skanda Vale menstruating women are also asked to stay on the edge of what is happening. Any single woman planning to stay overnight must come with another female friend.

There are clearly issues here of ritual purity involving food, and also gender taboos which can be found in several religious traditions, although they are not usually raised during a group visit to a place of worship. See Guterman et al. (2007) for some discussion of menstrual taboos. At Skanda Vale you have to decide whether you will be vegetarian in the run-up to the visit, and women must decide whether they will distance themselves if they are menstruating. Everyone going on the visit will need to reflect on the issues and come to his or her own considered and argued view.

How far should you go? People will differ in their judgements but issues of participation will be much more of a concern for some people than others, and in some situations rather than others. For example, John is a minister in a Pentecostal church. He was concerned about going into a Hindu temple because he knew he would see people worshipping images of the deities, the *murtis*. He did not want to have anything to do with what he perceived as idolatry, the worship of idols or false gods even though he, himself, would not be actively involved. He did go into the building but was clearly uncomfortable during the visit. If you have concerns about idolatry, do you accept the banana or orange, for example, that is offered to you as *prasad* as you leave the Hindu temple? Do you take it, out of politeness, but not eat it (which may well lead to offense)? Or, in the case of Skanda Vale, do you eat lunch even though the food has been offered to the deities?

Similarly, participation in ritual can be divisive for students from a variety of backgrounds. Even when taking relatively small groups of students into the field, reactions can be polarised, and informative for other members of the group. One such example concerned a group of students partaking in *puja* at a Hindu temple – a simple procedure which involved sitting calmly through *bhajans* (songs), seeing food and donations being presented to *murtis* (statues) and then passing your hands over an *arti* flame and marking your forehead with *kumkum* powder. One student in the group, who was a Latter-Day Saint (Mormon), politely refused to participate in any of the activity as "Mormons can't do that" in a Hindu temple. Another member of the group, who also happened to be Mormon, happily partook of every aspect of the ritual. Such clear examples of difference in how religious people perform their religious lives and identities is a great reminder of the dangers of essentialising the responses one should expect from representatives of different traditions. These religious participants (who just happened to be students) clearly did not agree on 'what a Mormon should do' in such circumstances, and of course the same will apply to every occasion you visit a community or site; your experience will be moulded by your responses and the actions of your host and fellow participants.

Clearly these issues of participation do not involve a visit to an empty building, but refer to a group visit involving worship. What happens if you are an atheist who has rejected a Christian upbringing. Do you go with the group to a Christian service? What about attending a papal audience in Rome with thousands of other people who are on a pilgrimage? What about if you are a Jew and have a strongly monotheistic belief. How do you deal with Christian worship of Jesus Christ? Perhaps you are a Muslim who rejects the teachings of a newly emergent religion, such as Scientology – how would you respond to the sincere expression of a worldview that you may consider to be opposed to your own? There are no absolute answers here, and what is most important is that you take the time to reflect on these tricky issues before going on visits, although you can't predict all the possible scenarios you might encounter. What we explore next are the skills of participant observation, and the issues of participation in more detail.

Participant observation and data collection

At the heart of the ethnographic methods we use for studying living religion in the field is participant observation – spending time at a place, with people, at a ritual, on a journey and so on. You notice what it is like, watch what happens, listen to what is said, ask questions, and collect every impression and other data that you can. That begins to unpack what is meant by 'observation'. We will discuss this more fully first and then consider the 'participant' part. Finally there are some practical suggestions.

Observing

The ethnographic literature is full of discussion about the nature of 'observation'. John Van Maanen began his engagingly written book *Tales of the Field* with these words:

> It [the book] is about how one culture is portrayed in terms of another in an ethnography. It rests on the peculiar practice of representing the social reality of others through the analysis of one's own experience in the world of those others. Ethnography is, therefore, highly particular and hauntingly personal.
>
> (Van Maanen, 2011, xiii)

If you give a group of people sitting in the same room the following instruction: 'For the next five minutes I want you to observe and to write down what you observe. Don't talk!', I wonder what you think would happen. Well, usually a number of people look really puzzled. Often the instructions have to be repeated several times. Then, slowly, people begin to look around and perhaps to write something. At the end people can read out what they have written, and the first thing everyone notices is how different the written accounts are. One person has listed the objects on the table in front of them, another has minutely described the pattern on her skirt, a third has reflected on his own discomfort about not being sure exactly what was required of him by this task, a fourth has written, rather poetically, about the sunlight streaming into the room and the sound of birdsong outside on a beautiful spring day. And so it goes on; each individual has done something different and written about it differently. That is why 'observation' is not such a simple activity as it might seem at first glance. This section will explore some of the theoretical and practical aspects of observing in the field.

Curb your enthusiasm

One important factor in observing usefully is to be aware of the bias of our own observations, and to reflect upon the preconceptions we all bring to any fieldwork scenario, especially when critically analysing your observation notes.

In a recent study tour to New York City, a large group of students (forty-two) were taken to a wide variety of religious communities and met with an interesting diversity of religious hosts and voices. Two of these hosts were the Church of Scientology and an Orthodox synagogue. Both of the host voices at these religious communities spoke of their religious lives and the communities that used their services.

In the group discussion with tutors that followed the visits, every single student noted that Scientology charged members of its community to receive training and services – many noting how they felt uncomfortable with this. Only one solitary student, however, also noted that the synagogue charged families a $1,200 annual subscription as a membership fee.

Be careful with your preconceptions – they will affect what you observe and remember during site visits.

Tim Ingold, in a fascinating but difficult book, *Being Alive: Essays on Movement, Knowledge and Description*, says that "being observant means being alive *to* the world" (2011, xii). Each person will bring his ~ess, his or her life, to the moment in time and the place whe is happening, so inevitably each person will observe differe standard, ideal way to observe, but rather there are princip' will help. Religious teaching, for example from the Bud people to 'Wake Up!' and the overall advice about observation of living religion is to be as awake as possible, to notice as much as possible, to be as open as possible to what is happening and to its impact on you and others.

There is a theory that some people are mainly visual learners, some auditory learners and some kinaesthetic learners. It is useful if you know how comfortable and confident you are at each of these different ways of observing and try to ensure you use all five senses. Look, listen, sense with your body, smell and perhaps taste! One student commented about visiting a Hindu temple, "I understood that this was different because I could use all my senses to feel what it meant to be in a different tradition. It was incredibly motivating for me and I wanted to know more."

What do you look at or listen to? What are you trying to sense? How does smell fit in? What are you tasting? The course of study you are doing, what you have been told about the purposes for your visit, and the preparatory reading and thinking you have done will direct your attention in some but not other directions. This process of selection, and also interpretation, will continue through the analysis and the writing up. As long as you stay alert for the unexpected and the contradictory, it is actually helpful to have some focus. It is important in academic work to have theoretical perspectives, as we have seen, but it is also important to remember the singular nature of a particular place which cannot be fully known in advance. It is also important to remember that the presence of the researcher is likely to influence what happens in any particular situation.

Ways of seeing the world

Consider this quotation from Ian McGilchrist writing about the right and left hemispheres of the brain:

> the brain has to attend to the world in two completely different ways, and in so doing to bring two different worlds into being. In the one we *experience* – the live, complex, embodied, world of individual, always unique beings, forever in flux, a net of interdependencies, forming and reforming wholes, a world with which we are deeply connected. In the other, we 'experience' our experience in a special way: a re-presented version of it, containing now static, separable, bounded, but essentially fragmented entities, grouped into classes on which predictions can be based.
>
> (McGilchrist, 2009, 31)

It is his contention that this second way of observing the world became predominant in the Enlightenment and has badly limited our ability to understand ourselves, other people and our world in a fully human way. A similar point was made in the discussion on epistemology in chapter 2 where we saw how more engaged ways of knowing are generating much needed awareness and understanding.

What we want to do finally in this section on observation is to say a bit more about body knowing and also to encourage you to practise what is sometimes called heart knowing. Being an embodied knower means giving attention to what you are learning that you couldn't have from watching a film, because you are as fully *present* to the situation as you can be. Using the five senses is part of that. When we watch a film we only see what the director wants us to see. It is not the same as really being there. Anyone who has watched a news report of an event that they were part of realises how different the two experiences are. We sometimes talk about the 'atmosphere' of a place, and the body gives us lots of information that we put together to describe this. It might be hot or cold and we might be sweating or shivering; the place might be packed with people, bumping into us and pushing and shoving, or we might be the only ones there; we might be standing for a long time or sitting, perhaps uncomfortably, on the floor.

One very obvious aspect of embodied knowing in many places we might visit is walking. Obviously, thinking about engaging with living religion while you walk suggests a connection with the religious act of walking known as pilgrimage. We have discussed some ideas around pilgrimage, study and religious tourism in chapter 2. What follows describes walking as observation.

Walking into Bethlehem

Most people arrive in Bethlehem in an air-conditioned coach; we walked. It seemed very important that we did, meaning that we had to wait to go through the military checkpoint in the wall dividing Bethlehem from Jerusalem, and that we could also look carefully at the graffiti on the wall – a lot of it written in English and waiting to be seen by outsiders such as us. It is quite a long, uphill, busy road and in the hot sun it was a real effort. Arriving on foot into Manger Square felt like an achievement and in some ways a place we had earned a right to be, if only for a short while. Going into the Church of the Nativity involves entering through a very small door; one has to stoop to get in. When it is busy in the church there is a long wait in a line to go down the dark, uneven steps into the place where, as centuries of Christians have believed, God (too) was *incarnate*, or as we might want to say, 'embodied'.

Now, to consider a rather different aspect of embodied knowing – with the heart. Most of the time when we pay attention to something we do so in our head. But it is possible, and really useful, to pay attention with the heart by bringing the heart into electromagnetic resonance with the brain – what is called 'entrainment' or coherence. The Institute of HeartMath was founded in 1991 and a few years later Childre and Martin published *The HeartMath Solution* (1999). One of their claims is that entrainment reduces stress, improves health and performance and enhances perception and intuition (1999, 15–22). Although you probably do this already to some extent and in certain circumstances, we can train ourselves to be aware of what places, people or situations are 'telling us', and to find ways to express these insights. The following is a practice exercise which you could use. It is taken from Buhner (2004, 275–77).

Observing deeply – 'heart knowing'

Go to an area of shops you really like. Walk around letting yourself sink into the feeling of the place, become immersed in it, relax into its nature. Look around and go to the shop you feel most drawn to. Stand in front of it. Let yourself receive sensory impressions from it and allow them to grow strong in you. Notice the feelings you have and let yourself explore these, touch their edges and shapes. Give yourself permission to be slow with this exploration, and not to judge what arises. Pay attention to the doors and windows, to the colours, to the signs, to the display, to the area in front of the store – how does each part feel to you? Overall what is the primary feeling this shop communicates to you? Now, write everything down in your fieldwork journal. Then choose another store and repeat the process. Compare the two. What different kinds of feeling did they generate? Can you tell why? Can you put this into words?

You can practise this kind of heart knowing on people and the natural world, as well as places. Whenever you go into a religious place, or attend a ceremony, take the time to notice, in subtle emotions, what is being communicated to you. Just remember that you are not trying to *think* while you are doing this but to be receptive, to be *aware*. If you want to develop these skills of observation then have a look at *How to Be an Explorer of the World* and do some of the exercises it suggests (Smith, 2008).

Being a participant

The term '*participant* observation' suggests that you are observing something that is going on, and not just visiting an empty place. As we have seen, you will need to decide for yourself how much you actually participate in what you are observing. For example, one third-year student reflected, "The service at the synagogue was very powerful. At first I wasn't sure whether to participate but by the time we were half way through I was happily singing along and fully enjoying the experience." Sometimes people are concerned that by actually *doing something* during a ceremony they are compromising their own beliefs or values.

Let's take the example of visiting a *gurdwara*, a Sikh place of worship. As people arrive in the worship hall they go up to the scriptures, the *Guru Granth*

Sahib, put an offering in the box and prostrate – kneeling and putting their forehead on the ground. Should you do that too? As you leave the hall, you notice someone sitting with a covered bowl in front of them. People stop and are given a sweet, sticky food known as *karah prashad*. They eat it. Should you go up and receive some? Finally, you are invited into the *langar*, the kitchen, where everyone is invited to eat together, where the food is always vegetarian so anyone can eat it. Should you queue up, take your filled tray and eat it? We can't tell you but we can make two recommendations.

The first is that if you are making a fieldwork visit to a *gurdwara* (or anywhere else) you must make sure you research beforehand as much as possible so that you know what is likely to happen and what it signifies for the participants. Reflect on your own beliefs and values so that you know what you are comfortable with. Of course, the actual experience may make you change your mind and reflect differently – see the text box below – but you still need to be well prepared.

Being open to experience

One of Lynne's students, a Christian minister, wrote this after a guided visit to Jerusalem and the Galilee and considering what is said here might help you reflect on the attitudes we take into any participant observation. It is also a good example of reflexivity.

> Being in the Holy Land was a lifetime ambition fulfilled. My emotional expectation, heightened by a sense of unrealistic, fanciful notion of perhaps encountering 'Jesus' in some kind of spiritual experience, filled me with optimism and hope. Places like Calvary, Gethsemane, Mount of Olives, Bethlehem, and the Sea of Galilee are all places imprinted on my heart through scripture reading, study and active faith. To me the Holy Land was, of course, hot and everyone was supposed to be Holy.
>
> When I landed it was cold, and certainly not reverent, with no sense of being more spiritual than any place I had been before. However I left Jerusalem and the Galilee more knowledgeable, and better prepared with a kind of confusion that will bring revelation in its own time as I continue to grow.
>
> My main enjoyment was the shattering of my illusion that was a bubble created by ignorance through lack of experience. The bursting of that bubble was painful and took lots of adjusting during the nine day trip. It was ironic that a principle of learning taught two years ago by you Lynne (which I was not in favour of at the time) became the staff that steadied me in the process of change and learning. What was the principle: forget what you think you know and embrace what you are about to learn from the perspective of those you wish to learn from. I enjoyed the experience of re-evaluating everything in the light of fresh evidence and real experience that could not be denied.

The second recommendation is to always remember that you are a guest: "There are few shortcuts and no ways to learn one's way around an unfamiliar social world without being there and banking on the *kindness of strangers*" [our italics] (Van Maanen, 2011, 152). The example of the *langar* was chosen partly because *hospitality* is a key religious requirement for Sikhs. There are obligations on guests, and Graham Harvey has written about this aspect of fieldwork which he calls 'methodological guesthood' in his chapter in *The Routledge Handbook of Research Methods in the Study of Religion* (2011, 227). Guest researchers bring their hosts gifts – their presence contributes to what is happening and their interest and perspectives give the hosts new ways of understanding the significance of what they are doing. Once strangers have become guests, they do not have to agree with everything the host says and does, but by "sharing the concrete bodily experiences of the people being studied researchers are likely to gain richer understanding of the embodied, sensual performances of vernacular and quotidian religion" (2011, 226).

There does still seem to be an idea around that a religious studies researcher mustn't *be* religious – whatever that means exactly. Consider this short quotation from a very long poem by the very 'religious' poet T.S. Eliot in his *Four Quartets*:

You are not here to verify,
Instruct yourself, or inform curiosity
Or carry report. You are here to kneel
Where prayer has been valid.

(Little Gidding, 1)

It may be that, in order to do fully embodied fieldwork, you do participate in ways you may not have foreseen. In Nigeria, Harvey says that "I have seen deities in their homes. I have learnt how to prostrate in the presence of deities. I have learnt how to offer things when seeking guidance from deities" (Harvey, 2013, 140). A few pages later he explains how he decided to draw the line in his participation. He wanted to take a photograph and the shrine guardian agreed but said that first they needed to sacrifice a goat. Harvey writes, "I decided that a goat's life was more valuable than a photo, and that sacrifices should be for more important matters than photography" (2013, 150).

Practical suggestions and issues for your group visit

Here are some suggestions for what you can do during any visit:

- be aware of the wider context of the place, especially if you arrive by coach;
- look at any notice boards both inside and outside the building. See how the place of worship talks about itself, and what activities are going on and what organisations are related to the place;

- be aware of who is there, and how they are using the various areas in the building;
- identify the main focal point in the worship space and make sure you understand how it functions;
- notice the congregational areas and those to which only some people are admitted;
- really look around at the objects in the space, note what they are like and think about how they function;
- notice the decoration, if there is any, and the impact that it has;
- notice what you are drawn to, what catches your attention;
- be aware of what surprises you, that you hadn't expected;
- quietly, by yourself, sit or stand where a worshipper would be and become aware of the atmosphere, what you particularly notice, and the overall sense that you get of the place.

Fieldwork journal and making notes

It is obviously important that you use your journal, whatever form it takes, to keep notes about what happens in the field. Take the time to put down everything you can think of: words, descriptions, ideas, connections, information, feelings, reactions. Don't censor anything, or worry about spelling, grammar and punctuation at this stage, just write! We recommended practising 'observing' before you go into the field for the first time, and it is worth practising making notes too.

There is a real art to making field notes, and you need to be very clear what and who you are making notes for. That, of course, depends on what you are being expected to learn from the visit. You may have a talk from someone within the community and that is a great opportunity to hear an insider voice. Remember, though, that if the person only gives you basic information about the religion, you do not need to scribble everything down. You can get this sort of information from lots of different sources. Try, instead, to think about how this information is being put across, what ideas about the tradition are being stressed and what isn't being said. Try to get more personal reflection from the speaker; for example, you could ask what he or she most values about coming to this place of worship, or how it differs from other places of worship in the same tradition, what makes it particular and distinctive. Remember to ask the questions you prepared in advance. Perhaps have them written down in your fieldwork notebook.

Also make notes of what particularly strikes you about the place, note down any questions you have, and any connections you can make with wider issues to do with the religion and the study of religion. Reflect on the whole experience of being there, of the impact on you of the building and the community. Even if you can't make notes during a visit, make them as soon as possible afterwards.

When you get home review your notes, check any assignment you have to do, based on the visit, and note how you are going to tackle this.

Some people like to record what is said by a speaker or guide and this can be useful although you have to be clear about what you will do with the recording. Listening to it can take a lot of time, but it does free you to really concentrate on what is being said and to notice your responses. You might want to use a recorder to make a note of your experiences on a visit and your immediate reflections. Memory is faulty, and recording reflections, observations, perceived connections and questions in real time immediately after an event strengthens the link between the lived reality of the religion you are encountering, your analysis and reflection upon this, and the formal written assessment that your tutors will often require.

Collecting *stuff* is really useful. There might be written material you can take away, such as a newsletter from a place of worship, you might be given a candle as part of a ritual or you could choose a stone or a leaf from a site. There will sometimes be opportunities to buy postcards, books or other souvenirs and artefacts. When you are back at the computer writing up the observation, this stuff can re-evoke the sense of the place and the experience.

Technology in the field

If possible, it is a good idea to take photographs so take along some form of camera. Let's say you are going to a ceremony somewhere, you can have a record of the outside of the place, the inside before the ceremony begins, and perhaps of some of the people. If there are notice boards, inside or out, photograph them. Generally you should not take photos during religious rituals, and should not photograph people without their agreement. You can use the photos in a number of ways. Firstly, they will remind you, days or weeks later, of what it was like and what happened. When you are writing up your fieldwork, you can use the photos to help you to get plenty of descriptive detail into your account. You might, depending on the nature of the assignment, include some photos in your final work. If you look at examples of published fieldwork you will see that some of them have pictures. They have been carefully chosen to complement the text, and there is always a statement about what the picture shows. They are not there to make the work look pretty, so make sure that if you use them in your assessed work they are to support your text, and not just to please the eye.

Obviously there are issues about photographs. If you are attending a ceremony or meeting someone for an interview in a place of worship, check with the person who has agreed to your visit whether you can take photos and what, if anything, you shouldn't photograph. There are some occasions which, for reasons connected to the religious ceremony itself, you cannot photograph. For example, if you are attending an Orthodox Jewish Sabbath service you cannot use any sort of electrical equipment because it would break the religious rules (the *halakah*) about Sabbath. Do not try to take covert photographs. It is dishonest and unethical. We are going to discuss the ethics of fieldwork fully in the next chapter, and you will see that sometimes it is important not to disclose the actual identity of the site of your fieldwork. In that case, don't include any photo, or physical description, that would pinpoint the place. Finally, there is another issue about cameras. It is ironic in a way, but a camera may stop you looking. As we have seen, it is really important that you are as present as possible to what is going on and a camera distances you, it gets between you and the action. Use them thoughtfully and sparingly.

Assessment for group fieldwork

There are a number of examples of assessment for independent fieldwork in the next chapter which would be worth having a look at now. Assessments for group fieldwork vary a lot, and so we are only highlighting here some suggestions about how to approach whatever assignment you have been given. The main point to stress is that you need to make clear what *you* have *learned from being in the field*. From a tutor's point of view it is really frustrating when students produce work, supposedly based on fieldwork, that could have been done by simply going to the library or looking on the Internet. It misses the point entirely and betrays a lack of understanding about engaging with living religion.

In the previous paragraph we have highlighted the two key aspects of group fieldwork. The work you produce needs to make connections between your fieldwork and what you have learned about a particular aspect of the study of religion. It must also reflect the fact that only *you* could have done the work in the way you did because you bring your unique perspectives to your study. This is the case whatever you have to produce: a PowerPoint presentation, a fieldwork journal, an essay, a portfolio or a poster presentation.

Chapter summary

This chapter has focused on doing group fieldwork and picks up the theoretical ideas in the earlier chapters to inform the practicalities discussed here. Most students value the group visits they do a lot because of the opportunities they offer and, as with everything, the more you put into the visits, the more you will get out. Sometimes, as a result of short group visits, students are keen to do longer ones in their own country and abroad. Some students also want to begin to do independent fieldwork and that is the subject of the next chapter.

Further reading

Read chapter 9, 'Fieldwork in the Study of Religion', in Chryssides and Geaves (2013, 241–74). This is a straightforward textbook discussion of group fieldwork written by two scholars who have often taken their students into the field. There are lots of practical examples here and some reference to issues to consider.

To whet your appetite further for the study of living religion in the field, read Meredith McGuire's book, *Lived Religion* (2008). This is a very clearly written discussion of what can be explored through fieldwork and includes a very wide range of examples and ideas to consider.

Questions for consideration

1 Reflecting on your own beliefs and values, are there any aspects of engaging with living religion during a group visit that you are not comfortable with?
2 When you have a group visit as part of your course think about the following:

   • what am I most looking forward to on this visit?
   • what do I want to get out of this visit?
   • what are my anxieties about this visit?
   • what do I need to do to prepare as well as possible for the visit?

3 How will going with other people on a group visit enhance your learning about living religion?

Bibliography

This list includes all the texts referred to in the chapter and other recommended reading.

Buhner, S.H. 2004, *The Secret Teaching of Plants: The Intelligence of the Heart in the Direct Perception of Nature*, Rochester, VT: Bear and Company.
Cameron, H., Richter, P., Davis, D. and Ward, F. (eds) 2005, *Studying Local Churches*, London: SCM Press.
Childre, D. and Martin, H. 1999, *The HeartMath Solution*, New York: HarperCollins.
Chryssides, G.D. and Geaves, R. 2013 (2nd edn), *The Study of Religion: An Introduction to Key Ideas and Methods*, London: Continuum.
Guterman, M., Mehta, P. and Gibbs, M. 2007, 'Menstrual Taboos among Major Religions' in *The Internet Journal of World Health and Societal Politics*, 5(2).
Harvey, G. 2013, *Food, Sex & Strangers: Understanding Religion as Everyday Life*, Durham: Acumen.
——2011, 'Field Research: Participant Observation' in Stausberg, M. and Engler, S. (eds) *The Routledge Handbook of Research Methods in the Study of Religion*, London: Routledge, 217–44.
Ingold, T. 2011, *Being Alive: Essays on Movement, Knowledge and Description*, London: Routledge.
McGilchrist, I. 2009, *The Master and His Emissary*, New Haven, CT: Yale University Press.
McGuire, M.B. 2008, *Lived Religion*, Oxford: Oxford University Press.
Smith, K. 2008, *How to Be an Explorer of the World*, London: Penguin Books.
Takhar, O.K. and Jacobs, S. 2011, 'Confusing the Issue: Field Visits as a Strategy for Deconstructing Religious Boundaries' in *Discourse*, 10(2).
Van Maanen, J. 2011 (2nd edn), *Tales of the Field*, Chicago: University of Chicago Press.

5 Independent fieldwork

Reflexivity, case studies, interviews and writing up

Introduction

This chapter is about doing fieldwork on your own. Maybe you have to do a study as part of a taught module, such as one about contemporary religion, or perhaps you have to design and carry out some research during a field study tour abroad. Fieldwork may be a part of your dissertation research or you might be doing a placement where you stay with a religious community for a few days or weeks. In all these situations you will be using and developing skills, and ways of thinking, that are similar to the ones we have been discussing so far in this book. The difference in this chapter is that we will explore in more detail the ethnographic methods you might want to use, and will refer you to examples of extended studies of religious individuals and groups, where you can get inspiration, practical ideas and plenty of interesting discussion about studying religion in the field. This chapter will be more practical than chapter 2, where we covered the more theoretical aspects, and you will get lots of concrete suggestions and examples about how to approach your individual fieldwork.

Most student fieldwork will not be full-blown ethnography: you aren't going to spend months or years in the field studying a particular culture, tradition or person. You probably aren't doing anthropology for your degree – although some of you reading this may be – and the most you may have done is a lecture or a module on the anthropology of religion. Nevertheless, if you are going to study religion in the field you are going to be using ethnographic methods. To do that well means being able to reflect on the process, so this chapter begins with the topic of reflexivity.

Reflexivity

Reflexivity means being able "to reflect-in- and -on-action, engage with feelings, and be able to make informed and committed judgements" (Smith, 2005). You have to reflect on the nature of what you are doing, on what you bring to the processes, on what happens in the field, on how you will write up your findings and on the meaning or significance of what you have found. To put it very simply, the idea is that the more you understand yourself and how you operate, the more chance you have of understanding somebody else. The work you do will impact on other people and it will also have an impact on you. Being as aware as possible of what is going on is what reflexivity is about.

Lots of writers have discussed the need for reflexivity in the workplace, in education and in qualitative research, and feminist writers have been particularly insistent on its importance (see, for example, Schon, 1990; Spickard et al., 2002; Linden, 1993; Behar and Gordon, 1995). There are plenty of definitions and explanations of reflexivity, but one way to get an idea of what is involved is to read examples of people doing it. Reading any of the books listed at the end of this chapter as examples of good fieldwork-based research into religion will give you plenty of insight into the importance, difficulties and achievements of reflective practice. One of the most interesting discussions of the impact of doing research on the researcher is *Making Stories, Making Selves* (Linden, 1993), in which the author explains how the interviews she did with Holocaust survivors profoundly influenced her own Jewish identity. This book is also very useful for its highly reflexive and creative approaches to writing up fieldwork in ways in which the constructed nature of the text is clear.

Thinking about reflexivity

Here are two different examples of statements about reflexivity. The first is a definition of reflexivity and participation in religious practice:

> A development of participant observation in which researchers devote time and effort to considering the experience of being involved in religious acts. The more participatory phases of fieldwork might provide researchers with a sense of 'what it is like' to be a full participant or 'insider'. Reflecting on this provides an additional way of analyzing data and enriches the published result by enhancing description and argument.
>
> (Harvey, 2011, 244)

The second example contrasts the importance of reflexivity in two very different contexts:

> By becoming self-reflexive about my own 'sacred' spaces and practices, I was better able to see the many symbolic practices by which my respondents are comforted ... *Tradition*, in contrast, focused on women who had made major life choices that were the opposite of mine ... Here I found that although my emotions did not provide me with access to others' similar feelings, sometimes they actually afforded me insights into how my very different stance might be impeding my full understanding.
>
> (Davidman, 2002, 21; 23–24)

So, reflexivity demands awareness and imagination about yourself and others. You must have a notebook to write in – we can call it a fieldwork journal or a logbook. This book is 'for your eyes only' but you will certainly refer to what is in it in the final writing-up stage in a number of ways. There are some practical suggestions here for using your fieldwork journal in your individual research work. Use the notebook to help you keep a focus on reflexivity, with a record of your responses, ideas, concerns, insights, reflections and so on. It is a good idea to:

- choose a notebook that is pleasing to use and easy to carry around;
- write down everything that comes to mind;
- *make sure you have at least one reflective entry every time you do some work on your project* and this may be in the field, reading a book or using the Internet;
- next time you do something read what you wrote last time;
- include jobs to be done, bibliographical information of books or articles you want to read;
- try out writing a sentence or paragraph about something which you have been thinking about;
- date your entries.

Of course, you may well prefer to do this in electronic form. Just make sure that it is easy to access wherever you happen to be.

It will help you to be reflexive if you keep alert for the intersubjective relationship between you and the material. Whether you are out in the field or reflecting on your experiences while you are in the library or working at home, consider answering some of the following questions as you carry out your work. It will be a good idea to write down responses to these questions in your fieldwork journal, but also to notice responses to these aspects of the research while you are in the process of observing a ritual or listening to a response to an interview question.

Here are the questions:

- What excites and interests you (most) about the work you are doing, the people you are meeting, the places you are going?
- What disturbs or troubles you?
- What challenges you?
- What seems familiar or comfortable to you?
- What seems strange to you?

In reflecting about these questions, it helps to identify the things in your own experience, in your life and relationships, beliefs and values, that mean that these things resonate with you.

Then there are two rather different reflexive questions:

- How does what is happening relate to your *understanding* of this person or group of people?
- How does what is happening relate to your *wider understanding of religion*?

These last two questions reflect the fact that work on living religion in the field is designed to generate knowledge and understanding – and so reflexivity also has to concern epistemology. Re-read the section in chapter 2 which covers epistemological issues in fieldwork. You have to reflect on your own understanding of the ways in which religion can be known and understood, and you have to communicate this when you write up your fieldwork. Since it is YOU, the researcher, who generates the knowledge and understanding, it is clear why you have to be reflective about the whole process.

Theory in fieldwork

Theory in fieldwork is important because it shapes every aspect of the process. It may be that the research is planned to generate or develop theoretical aspects of the study of religion, although it is unlikely that, if you are doing this, you are really a neophyte researcher! Much more likely, you will be working within theoretical frameworks about religion, or about a particular religion. It is important to recognise the theoretical lenses you bring to the field. For example, in this book we have suggested thinking about reported, represented and lived religion. Depending on which of these you wanted to explore, you would construct your fieldwork in different ways.

As we have seen, twentieth-century Western researchers in religion often assumed that religion is really about belief and/or institutional practice. Meredith McGuire argues that this is a result of what is known as the 'Long Reformation' – the whole period of change in what counted as legitimate religion in Europe and the Americas. It was both a Protestant and a Catholic process, reshaping and reforming what was to be understood as Christian faith and practice. As she writes:

> During the Long Reformation, both Catholic and Protestant reformers attempted to purify religion and refocus its rituals away from the (presumably baser) material concerns and towards spiritual concerns. Thus the religious practices people had previously used to address their own and their community's everyday material concerns were defined as marginal and inferior at best or as completely out of bounds, sinful and punishable at worst.
>
> (McGuire, 2008, 55)

She is interested in studying these forgotten aspects of religion, which do not fit into neat categories of belief and practice.

More generally, as we have seen, it is now taken for granted by many scholars that the definition of religion as essentially about beliefs, founders and texts owes its origins to the Protestant Christian perspective on religion as belief in God and concern with salvation. Just as the Western Protestant countries had economic and military power over much of the world, so Protestant Christian ideas had a kind of universal hegemony or power. They came to be seen as *true*. We have discussed colonial or imperial practices and ideas in chapter 2, and this is just to remind you that what religious people do, ways of studying this, and ideas about what counts as religion are interconnected.

So far, you have read some explanations and ideas about two key general issues for individual fieldwork: reflexivity and theory. What follows now explores the practical side of planning, carrying out and writing up fieldwork.

Planning your fieldwork

What shall I study?

Firstly, you have to decide what and where to study. There is a tendency for students to choose to research something novel, something new, that they don't know much about. Maybe this is partly because anthropology and ethnography is still often seen to be the study of the exotic. However, choosing the unfamiliar or the strange is not really a good idea; it is always better to *build on what you already know* when you are doing fieldwork for the first time. The issues, methods and processes are complex, as you will have learned from reading this far in the book, so it makes sense to choose somewhere or something where it is as easy as possible to generate the data that you need, and where you already have an understanding of some of the wider issues and theoretical aspects from the study you have already done.

Secondly, while individual fieldwork often ignores particular examples of mainstream religion that would be easy to do and generate lots of interesting material, sometimes students make the opposite mistake of thinking that studying their own religious tradition, and perhaps even their own particular community, if they have one, would be the easiest option. They are wrong! Using ethnographic methods is much less complicated if you are not a member of the group you are studying. Re-read the section in chapter 2 for the theoretical discussion about insider/outsider approaches to the study of religion. Of course, as we have seen, as a researcher in the field you need to be very aware of what you bring to the research. You may have very legitimate and strong personal reasons for choosing a particular project, but there are a number of problems that arise if you are also fully an insider.

Firstly, you will take too much for granted and not give attention to what is obvious to you either during the fieldwork or in writing up what you find. That means that you, and the reader of your work, will miss out on key aspects of what is going on that are necessary to develop some understanding of the significance of the findings. Secondly, even if you are highly reflexive and can take steps to try to ensure that you don't miss these key aspects, you still have to juggle two distinct roles – one as a member of the group being studied, and the other as the researcher. Other members of the group will have different expectations about you than about an unknown researcher. For example, they may assume that you will always portray the group in a positive light.

Let's just consider one final problem: that your relationship with the group precedes the research and will continue beyond it. If fieldwork generates knowledge and understanding – which is why we do it – then it is important to be very clear how we know what we claim we know. We will give much more attention to the practicalities of this later in the chapter, but the point here is that inevitably a lot of what you know about your group would not have been learned during the fieldwork and you would find it very hard to be clear about this. Ironically, this is the reason some students see this as the best option. They think it would be easy because they wouldn't have to do much work; they already know and understand a lot. However, the point of doing fieldwork is to *learn*. And those students trying to find what seems like the easiest option are right about the work that does need to be done for good independent fieldwork. That is why it is a good idea to build on what you already know something about, because you have to understand as much as possible *before* you start the fieldwork. You have to develop your understanding about the tradition you are exploring.

How do I get started?

When you are planning your research, write a proposal setting out:

- where your fieldwork will be;
- why you have chosen this;
- your initial ideas about the kinds of things you are especially interested in;
- these same ideas expressed as questions;
- your ideas about how you will generate the data that will address or help to answer these questions;
- a short bibliography of six recent books and articles that relate directly to your chosen place or community and your areas of interest. You do not have to have already read these for this to be useful – but at this point you must do some research to see what you need to read before you go much further.

It is a good idea to keep this proposal short – about one side of A4 – and sharp. Put in detail and keep things as tightly focused as possible; ideally what you have chosen should be easy to do, especially if this is your first attempt at independent fieldwork. This kind of work generates data very quickly and can be time consuming to analyse. Keep in mind the number of hours you have available for the project, the word limit for the written work and the nature of the actual assignment you have been set. In other words *be realistic*.

What sort of assignment might I be doing?

Here are a range of different assignments that undergraduate students have actually tackled using independent fieldwork. They are different in length, level and details. You might already have been asked to do something else, but these examples will help you to understand various ways in which independent fieldwork can be used in formal assessment.

- Students are asked to attend worship in two different traditions within a religion, such as at an Orthodox and a Liberal synagogue, and to explain the ways in which what they experienced relate to different understandings of being a member of that religion.
- Students visit an art gallery, select one or more items seen there, and discuss the ways in which a religious narrative or belief is expressed by this.
- A 2,000-word exploration of a particular place of worship comparing its online and offline presence.
- Students are asked to read a section in a textbook about Hinduism and identify three aspects to discuss with informants at two different *mandirs*. The written task was to compare the responses from the informants with the textbook.
- A PowerPoint presentation about an aspect of Muslim identity in Britain based on two interviews with British Muslims. The issue of identity is an important one in understanding living religion.
- A 3,000-word report of a study of a worshipping community which requires participant observation at worship, an interview with a member of the community and the analysis of various publications and other materials produced there.
- A student who visited Nepal with a university group chose to extend his time there and base an assignment for a module on religion and culture on research he did while in the field. The 4,000-word essay explored the therapeutic efficacy of shamanistic healing rituals and practices in Nepal.
- A study for a 10,000-word, final-year undergraduate dissertation based on interviewing local Christian ministers, exploring their views about why church attendance has declined and what they are doing to encourage people to attend. This was a very interesting study because the student discovered that in most of these churches attendance was actually *increasing*.

It is worth saying again here that anything that you write for an assignment like the above should be directly related to your experience in the field, and it needs to be informed by the theoretical, social, historical and political context.

Most importantly it must be something you could not have produced only by visiting the library or going online.

Carrying out fieldwork

The case study

A case study involves studying one particular place in some depth. This might be a particular religious community or a small geographical area, like a particular road, or one particular group of devotees or something that is happening at a particular time. It is a very flexible method because it can easily be planned to suit the things you are most interested in; you can choose something that is easy for you to access, and the scale of the project can range from a very short case study to something much more detailed. The case study also enables you to combine different methods of exploration. It is not really a method in itself; rather, it is the choice of what is to be studied. The assignment of a study of a worshipping community, listed above, was based on a small case study. This section will help you understand just what a case study is, and involves, and what its strengths and weaknesses are. Then there is some material about student placements which are really a particular and very rich form of case study. Chapter 4 discussed participant observation and the following sections will deal in more detail with interviews, questionnaires and the ethical issues raised in all such research, and then will cover the analysis of the data produced and ideas and examples about writing up the research. Using online methods of research such as an email interview is discussed in the next chapter as part of a full consideration about going online to study living religion.

As a neophyte researcher using a case study, you are employing ethnographic methods but are not engaged in a full-blown ethnographic study. You are not going to spend months or even years living in a strange culture, learning the language, participating in most of the activities and really getting to know some, at least, of the people. Nor are you going to arrive in some exotic, far-away place, like Bruce Parry in the BBC TV series *Tribe* (2008), where you are going to be the centre of attention and take part in rituals designed for the people who belong in that place.

What you *are* going to do in a case study is explore the particular, the singular. You are studying *this* street, *this* place of worship, *this* group. You might, once you have had some practice doing fieldwork, deliberately choose to focus on *two* distinct places or groups in order to draw out what they have in common and how they differ, but you must also do justice to each one in its own right in order to try to understand the actual lived experiences of the people in *this* context and not just use the data for some purpose of your own. You will also find that while every case is singular, it is also complex and not everything can be studied. Choices have to be made about what to focus on and what methods to use. Methodology needs to be considered in the light of two other 'ologies': ontology and epistemology. We discussed these in detail in chapter 2 so this is just a summary here. Ontology raises basic questions about reality, of what *is*, of what reality is like. Epistemology is about what can be known, about what it means to know something, and about the relationship between the knower, or would-be knower, and what can be known. Methodology is concerned with the *how* of knowing. How can you, as a researcher, go about finding out what you think is there to be known?

Basically, the answer to that question is that you turn up, having prepared as much as possible in advance, and observe, collect evidence and listen to what is happening, what people are doing, saying or maybe singing. You aim to *notice* a lot and not prejudge. You spend time trying to figure out what is going on, and you do that partly by asking people about what you have seen, read and heard. You use all your senses, you try to be aware of your own responses to what is happening, you reflect a lot afterwards and you write. There is much more detail about all this in the sections that follow.

These are the methods and the great advantage of a case study is that it is rich in detail, strong in description and in potential for interpretation and further questioning. Although what you are studying is a bounded system, a *case*, the boundaries are not impermeable and so the case study can provide insight into an issue or illustration of a theory. Case studies can also help to generate theory as you reflect on the significance of what you have discovered is going on, but they are not useful for testing theories where quantitative research is needed. Case studies are always concerned primarily with the particular and not with generalisation. You cannot assume that what happens in your chosen situation happens more generally, or that what the people you speak to say about the significance of their religion for them is typical of other members of the same group or of other groups of a similar tradition.

The Community Religions Project

Since 1976, the Community Religions Project at Leeds University in the UK has conducted fieldwork research on religion and religions 'near at hand' in the cities of Leeds and Bradford and beyond (see website list). A group of final-year undergraduate students carry out a detailed study of a chosen neighbourhood in Leeds, which is called the 'Religious Mapping of Leeds Project'. A particularly interesting project in 2011 returned to an area previously 'mapped' in 1994/5 and so could explore changes taking place. Although working as a group and not as individuals, this is independent fieldwork. Preparation for this begins in the first year at Leeds with a study of a place of worship and the taking of oral histories. Some of the results of this fieldwork are available on the website, and provide invaluable examples of student work.

Mapping activities, such as the ones described in the text box above, are an example of an extensive case study. It would be possible to do a similar thing on a smaller scale such as mapping just one street. We have briefly discussed in chapter 3 how potentially rich maps are in the study of living religion. Just walking along a street and noticing all the different 'signs' of religious activity is informal fieldwork. Noting carefully each one, photographing it and marking it on a street map, begins to build this into a case study. Reflecting on your reactions to walking there, to what you find, and talking to people on the street about their perceptions would add more data. This material could be presented in many ways, including a poster, electronic media, a portfolio of different material or a written report of some sort. Obviously some streets will be much more rewarding for this sort of study than others, so, as in all fieldwork, *choosing* the case is really important.

Southall

In the UK, students from many parts of the country go to Southall in West London to visit places of worship and often to carry out some independent work in the streets, to browse and buy in the many fascinating shops, and to eat in one of the cafes or restaurants. Daniel Faivre, one of the people who really began to get to know the religious diversity of this small area and to introduce it to others, often claimed that it had more places of worship per square mile than anywhere else in the world. It is also rather convenient that there is an extensive published ethnography of Southall called *Contesting Culture: Discourses of Identity in Multi-Ethnic London* (Baumann, 1996), which includes lots of data and some very interesting theoretical reflections about two words which are often (over)used in discussing living religion. These are 'culture' and 'community'. As the title suggests, there is also plenty of material about 'identity'. One student said after a visit to Southall that it had changed her whole understanding of religion – she realised how limited her own upbringing had been, which never gave her the chance to meet and interact with a diverse range of people. She went home (to Ireland) enriched with new experiences and ideas, and a large number of artefacts and clothes representative of the cultures she had met in Southall.

We have discussed already some of the issues of choosing what and where to study when doing independent fieldwork. It is worth adding something here about choosing a case. Do not spend ages trying to get the perfect case. As a neophyte researcher you must look at the practicalities and keep it as simple as possible. Here are some things to consider:

- Is the place, and the times you would need to go, realistic for you? That is to do with distance, transport, your other commitments and so on.
- Is it easy to contact the place and arrange to visit? Often there will be someone who is referred to in some ethnographic literature as the

'gatekeeper'. This person, because of his or her role, will be able to provide access to (some of) what is going on and you need to identify him or her as soon as possible.

- Will this place give you the kind of data you need for your assignment?
- Are you comfortable and open minded about going there? This is trickier but important.

You may be doing independent research for the first time so you won't be as confident as an experienced researcher. We have discussed the fact that there are aspects of religion we may not like or find difficult in previous chapters. There is no point in choosing a case which you are frightened of, expect to hate or which you hope will confirm all your prejudices about something. For example, if you know that you get easily embarrassed by intense emotional worship, don't choose a charismatic prayer group where they speak in tongues and are 'slain in the spirit'.

Wherever you go you will find interesting data and even when you don't find something you expect to find, that is interesting and useful in itself. The case has to be 'good enough' to meet the requirements of the task. Complete the planning sheet we discussed above and discuss these issues fully with your tutor.

Student placements

Some students will have the opportunity to spend longer with a particular religious community, sometimes actually living with the people involved or in a guest house. Look at *Living Religion* at Bath Spa University for examples of undergraduate work of this kind (see website list). Spending a few days somewhere allows you to live the life of the members, at least to some extent. You can go deeper into what is happening and probe different understandings amongst the various members of the community so that you have a more nuanced understanding. It allows you to develop and practice many of the skills we are discussing in this chapter and also the kinds of interpersonal skills that are useful in any workplace.

It would be a good idea at this point to refer back to the sections in chapter 4 about participant observation, and the practical suggestions about going into the field; these are also important and useful when researching independently. In the rest of the chapter we move on to consider some of the other methods available to you, such as interviews and questionnaires, the ethics of research, analysis of data and writing up your work.

Interviews

If you want to know what something means to someone, the best way to find out is to ask them about it. Essentially that is what an interview is, and it is a very valuable tool for engaging with living religion. You might use an interview on its own or it might be part of a larger case study. In this section there are some ideas and issues to consider about interviews in order to use them well and also practical advice we can give you.

Interviews are time consuming, as we shall see, but they do yield rich detail and they give people an opportunity to explain, in their own terms, 'what is going on'. So, you are not just getting an *emic* perspective, you are also getting it in what Clifford Geertz termed 'experience-near concepts' – that is:

> one that someone – a patient, subject, in our case an informant – might himself [*sic*] naturally and effortlessly use to define what he or his fellows see, feel, think, imagine, and so on, and which he would readily understand when similarly applied by others.
>
> (Geertz, 1983, 57)

Interviewees are often called 'informants' in the literature because they provide the researcher with key information about a situation or a group.

Just like all aspects of research, conducting interviews is not particularly easy or straightforward and there are some important questions to consider. How do you know that the interviewee is telling the truth? How should you phrase your questions to make sure you get the kind of data you are interested in? Should you interview people on their own or do a group interview? How do the complex power relations between the interviewer and interviewee affect the outcome? Sometimes interviews are more like conversations and you may get people telling you things without your asking them anything. Some interviews are very informal and others follow a rigid structure. You have to choose what suits your research best.

There are three main types of interview which can be usefully referred to as 'structured', 'semi-structured' and 'unstructured'. The *structured* interview is usually part of a survey of a number of people, and the questions and possible answers are all established beforehand. Each interview needs to be conducted in the same way – so it is rather like a verbal questionnaire. This may be quite a useful method, for example, if you want to carry out phone interviews. At the other end of the spectrum are *unstructured* or *non-directive* interviews; there is no set pattern to them so they are open ended and the control of the interview is much more in the hands of the interviewee. 'So, what is going on for you at the moment?' might be a typical opening for this type of interview. For a neophyte researcher, with limited time, this is probably not the most useful type of interview for you, although in some circumstances it really allows the researcher to begin to perceive or understand things he or she hadn't been aware of at all.

Probably most useful in many ways for engaging with living religion is the *semi-structured* interview. A number of questions are decided on in advance and written on a prompt sheet, there is scope to respond to what the interviewee says, ask supplementary questions, and vary the order of the questions, but where several people are being interviewed for the same purpose, the same set of questions is used. Questions can elicit information, judgements and reflective comments. Often it is interesting to ask respondents to make a choice about something and explain what led them to choose as they did. So, for example, you could ask, 'If someone was making a film about ... [whatever it is that you are researching – the community, a ritual, a place of worship and so on], what would you want to include in the film?'

There is definitely an art to framing the questions you use. These can be either 'open' or 'closed' and generally you should avoid too many closed questions. These have only one, usually right or wrong, answer and although they elicit information, they don't help the interviewee to relax and begin to speak more freely. You might want to know the age of the person, what his or her occupation is, how long he or she has been involved in whatever you are researching, or other factual matters. It is probably a good idea to get this sort of material dealt with early on and then move to open questions where there are various ways of responding. For example, you could follow up the closed question of 'How long have you been a member of ... ?' with 'Can you tell me how you got involved in the first place?' Hopefully, then, the interviewee will begin to tell a bit of his or her story. If you listen carefully to the response you could then ask a follow-up question, such as 'So, since you were initially attracted by the friendly warm welcome [for example], what is it that keeps you still coming to ... ?' Generally, it is more helpful not to ask 'why?' but, as in the examples, ask 'how?' or 'what?' The reason for this is that 'why?' is often heard as a negative judgement – and so may lead the interviewee to feel they have to justify themselves and make you sound hostile. For example, the question above, 'What is it that still keeps you coming to ... ?' feels rather different from 'Why do you still keep coming to ... ?' Keep thinking about how to phrase open questions that you think will lead the interviewee to tell you what you want to know! Generally it is better if the interviewee does not know exactly what you are going to ask because it allows for a more spontaneous response. If possible, resist requests to see the questions, but you may decide that if this is the only way to get an interview you really want, it is worth it, and you can always ask follow-up questions in the actual interview.

It is always a good idea to 'pilot' your interview questions. You try out what you have decided on, with someone who is a bit like the people you actually want to interview, see what happens, and also get his or her feedback about what 'worked' or 'didn't work'. Then you can adjust your questions or your approach. You can also test out the practicalities of your recording equipment – more on this below – and get some practice in interviewing. Everyone will tell you that the more interviewing you do, the better you get at it. It is also a very good idea to watch or listen to interviews on radio, podcast or television, and concentrate on how they get the interviewee to open up about the things that matter to them. An interesting website with lots of interviews is the American site *On Being* with Krista Tippett (see website list). You will find lots of useful material there about religion, spirituality and contemporary culture as well as being able to listen to unedited examples of an excellent interviewer at work.

Both you and the interviewee will probably be a bit nervous although neither of you may be aware of how the other is really feeling. It is your job to put the interviewee at ease as much as possible so that you get full answers to your questions. Here are some of the practicalities of this. Make clear how long the interview will take and make sure the person you are interviewing knows your name and understands about your research, what you are expecting and what you will do with what he or she tells you. It is important that you are honest about your research and realistic about your levels of knowledge and ignorance. We will give some specific guidance on this in the section on ethics, but you must make sure that you have what is called 'informed consent', including about the recording of the interview.

Consider how to build 'rapport'. Sit at an angle to one another, not directly face to face which can be more intimidating. You can match your body movements to the interviewee's, and show, by nodding or smiling, that you are listening carefully and that the person is giving you what you want. You also show this by building on what he or she has said in your next question, or by saying back to him or her what you have heard to check you have got it right. But don't agree with the interviewee, or disagree, or bring in your own experience. An interview is not the place for you to talk about your views, and it is not a conversation. You *can* show your real interest in what you are being told. Start questions with phrases such as, 'I was wondering whether you ever ... ?' or 'You mentioned ... , can you say a bit more about that?' or 'I'd be really interested to know ... ?' or 'I don't quite understand ... , can you explain ... ?' This is active listening which will encourage the interviewee to feel heard, to relax and to trust you. If possible, while you are listening, pay attention to anything that you are *not* being told, and phrase a question to probe this. Keep an eye on the time and towards the end it is always useful to ask whether there is anything else the person thinks you should know, or wants to add, to what he or she has said. Make sure it is clear when the interview is finished.

You can only give this kind of attention to what the person is saying to you if you do not have to take notes. This is one reason why it is a very good idea to record the interview with a small digital recorder. The technological aspects of this are continually improving and you should find out what is easily available to you that will work well. You do not want to get home only to find that someone's voice is too quiet to be heard properly. Practise with the recorder in different settings and find out how to operate it most effectively. You will be able to download the recording to a computer and listen to it as often as you want, and this is the other reason it is useful to have a recording.

The other main practical issue is about where to hold an interview. Sometimes you will seize an unexpected opportunity to record a conversation with someone, but if you are arranging an interview, there are a few things to consider. It needs to be somewhere quiet enough for the recording to be clear. You don't want to be disturbed in the middle of the interview and you definitely don't want to be somewhere you feel uncomfortable. In many religious places there will be offices or meeting rooms and this will be ideal. You can interview in a quiet cafe or similar public place. Do not go to someone's home and do not invite anyone to your home. This is a basic matter of safety. As with any visit as part of your fieldwork, it is always a good idea to tell someone where you are going.

Now some of those other issues about interviewing. Who do you interview? How do you know they are telling the truth and what about the power issues? Choosing whom to interview obviously depends on what you are hoping to get from the interview. Group interviews are useful when you want people to respond to each other and not only to you. You might present them with something to respond to – photos, words, a video clip – and ask what it makes them think of or give them a task where they have to choose, from what you provide, the item that best represents their understanding of something. You could have a ranking task where explanations of something need to be put in order and the group can then discuss with you, and one another, the reasons for their choices. Record the comments in the usual way. This sort of interview is very open ended, but it will generate lots of ideas that you might not have thought of and so some researchers use a group interview before they design individual interviews. It is also the case that this sort of group interview gives the participants the opportunity for expressing and listening to views and ideas that they probably wouldn't otherwise have had a chance to do. Your research is then significantly changing the experience for the 'locals'.

In an individual interview, if you talk to the person responsible for a particular place of worship or ritual event you will obviously get a different perspective than if you interview someone who just happens to turn up. Younger people might see things differently from older people. What about gender differences or the varying experiences of people from different classes, races or ethnicities? As a neophyte researcher you will not be working in a context where people do not speak any English, but it is worth making sure you and the interviewee can communicate clearly. It is also a good idea at this level NOT to interview children and young people as the ethical and practical issues involved make for some complications. So, consider who you actually *can* interview. As with the case study you may not end up with what you consider ideal for your research, but you do have to do the best with what is realistic – take what you can get and make the most of it! You don't want too many interviews either because they generate a lot of data very quickly and you need to *use* the interview data well – see the section below on analysis. You will need to explain in your written account how you selected your interviewees.

It should be obvious from the last paragraph that people are in different power relationships both to you and to each other. A lot has been written about power relationships in interviews because they are going to affect the interview in a number of ways and they also relate to the issue of how far you can trust that what you are told is true. We live in an unequal society, so an interviewer who comes from a more powerful section of society may not be able to get an open and trusting response from an interviewee who feels consciously or unconsciously inferior. A worker being interviewed by a boss will probably be careful not to say anything that might upset the boss. A man interviewing a woman may ask questions that do not relate to a woman's experience. A white person interviewing a black person or an older person interviewing someone in his or her early twenties are two other obvious situations of unequal power relations and experiences which will, inevitably, affect the interview. As always, reflexivity is essential, and the specific details in any particular piece of research need to be discussed in the report.

A rather different and perhaps more common power difference for the neophyte researcher is that you will be very aware that your research depends on getting good interview data so you *need* the interviewees in ways that they certainly don't need you. At the same time, the formalities of the interview mean that you control a lot of what is happening and the interviewees may feel apprehensive at the start, perhaps just because they want to be helpful to you and are not sure they will be able to tell you what they think you want to hear. It is encouraging that, after an interview, interviewees may comment that they have found the experience interesting, enjoyable or worthwhile, and you will hopefully feel that you have heard things that are genuinely interesting for you and useful for your research.

However, it is important that you remember that in an interview you will nearly always be getting 'represented' religion – people are telling you what they want you to hear about something and so they will tend to put it in a good light, and they may want to please you with what they say, so leave out more uncomfortable aspects. This does not mean that your interviewees will deliberately set out to lie, although there are topics for interviews where one might expect that interviewees would exaggerate or deny their behaviour – sexual or violent behaviour would be examples of this – but these subjects are not what your interviews are likely to be about. In a British law court a witness swears to tell 'the truth, the whole truth, and nothing but the truth'. However, this is impossible – How can one know the 'whole truth' about something? Philosophers have wrestled for centuries with the question Pilate asks Jesus in John 18:38: "What is truth?"

You are not going to solve the issue of validity completely. Of course, you can always check on the facticity of information you are given and you can always ask different people for their version of something. Sometimes the process of *triangulation* is useful, where you use different methods or approaches to your topic and see if the different data converge around a common understanding. You might look at documents, observe rituals and interview some people. If there is coherence between the data from each, then this strengthens your claims that your conclusions are valid. As far as the interviews go, to be able to claim the trustworthiness of your data, you do need to have confidence that the interviewees are genuinely sharing their perspectives on things, using their own language and experiences. If you sense that they are telling you an 'official version' in a rather rehearsed way, rather than reflecting on their own understanding, you might want to ask for examples, or ask how they would explain this to someone who didn't quite understand. You will always get partial answers to questions and the things that are uppermost in someone's mind at the time, but you can always lead the interviewee to reflect more fully.

It would be worthwhile here to distinguish briefly between *validity* and *reliability*, although these terms relate much more to testing than to qualitative methods. The last few paragraphs have considered validity – does the interview really generate the data it sets out to find? Reliability is about getting consistent results. If you interviewed the same person on another day, would you get the same answers? If another person asked your interview questions, would they get the same answers? The answer is probably not. The advantage and disadvantage of an interview is its subject-subject nature which provides a detailed, in-depth and sometimes very personal response but which is not repeatable.

This section has explored details of the theoretical and practical aspects of an interview, and we might sum up by suggesting that what really matters overall is that you show yourself to be receptive, reflective, open and trustworthy. This is also important in those more informal conversations that arise in fieldwork, over the washing-up or walking with someone. Sometimes you will gain real insight from these occasions so it is useful to be sociable and ready to engage with people in different ways.

Questionnaires

Questionnaires are best used to collect quantitative data in answer to closed questions or preselected responses, although they can include more open questions to elicit description, explanation or judgement. They are not easy to word successfully, require a certain level of literacy on the part of the respondents, and often the return rate is very low so deciding to use a questionnaire must be because it really is the best way to get the data required to answer a well-chosen research question; a questionnaire is never an easy option.

However they are fairly quick, can generate interesting data and sometimes enable comparison with existing wider research findings. For example, looking at a site like *British Religion in Numbers* in the UK or *PewResearch* in the US you might identify an existing piece of research which has used a survey or questionnaire to establish its findings, and you could use or adapt this to replicate the research in your particular context. Attitudes to Muslim women wearing a face veil is a fairly hot topic in a number of countries, and you could look at a national survey such as the one conducted by YouGov in 2013. You could use the same questions – one about wearing the *niqab* in court and one about a general ban – as part of a questionnaire/survey amongst fellow students. If you include questions about age, gender, religious affiliation, social class and voting habits, you could correlate your findings with the wider research. You could get students to complete a written questionnaire in class – and so get a very good return rate – or you could ask people on campus the same questions orally – a structured interview – and continue until you get as many responses as you want.

If you want to design your own questionnaire, you would need to read more specifically about how to do this and you would need to pilot your questions carefully. They need to be unambiguous and very clearly worded, and can include a sliding (Likert) scale such as one including 'strongly agree, agree, not sure, disagree, strongly disagree' in response to a statement. If your pilot guinea pigs struggle to respond, or say things like 'well, it depends what you mean by ... ' or 'this doesn't apply to me', then you know you have to go back to the drawing board.

Professionally developed large-scale questionnaires are mainly used to generate statistical data. They may have somewhere between 1,000 and 2,000 responses which can then be generalised to the whole population. Sophisticated statistical analysis produces percentages and correlates responses to different questions to see if there are positive or negative links. Sometimes students use very small numbers of responses to a questionnaire to produce tables, graphs, pie diagrams, bar charts and all manner of other supposedly impressive statistical data. Don't do it! If you have twenty completed questionnaires, then don't say '5 per cent said this' or '20 per cent said that'. Use the actual numbers – 'one person responded ... ' or 'just over half said ... '. Your sample is not representative and so cannot be used to generalise. You can correlate responses to different items, and there are computer packages that can be used in student questionnaire-based research. What a small-scale questionnaire can also do is to get some interesting qualitative data – you can ask people to write brief or even quite lengthy responses to questions or other triggers.

Designing questions, developing rapport

Have you ever been aware of, or influenced by, a presence or a power, whether you call it 'God' or not, which is different from your everyday self?

The above quotation, known as 'Hardy's question', because it was developed and used by Alister Hardy in the 1970s, breaks all the rules of question design and has also played a central role in research in Britain and elsewhere into religious experience (see, for example, Hardy, 1979; Hay, 2007). It is possible to use questions in a questionnaire which explore intensely personal and inner experience and to get detailed descriptions and reflections in response. However, this is only likely to be successful where there is some rapport between the researcher and the respondents. That could be built up in person using a structured interview, or it could be developed where the response is in writing, and questions gradually become more personal and intimate. For her master's degree Lynne used a written questionnaire with questions taken from three published sources and included Hardy's question (Scholefield, 1988).

The early questions such as 'What was your first proud achievement?' and 'Which of your personal characteristics would you most like to change?' encouraged the respondents to reflect on their lives and share experiences and thoughts that perhaps they had never spoken or written about before.

Use this example to take time to reflect upon how the development of rapport between you and your subject may affect the outcomes of your research.

One very useful aspect of a questionnaire in qualitative research into religion can be to identify good potential interview subjects. In that case you would include a question about whether the respondent would participate in a follow-up interview. This could be useful whether or not you know the people completing the questionnaire but if you want to use it in this way, the responses cannot be anonymous. We will have more to say about confidentiality and anonymity in the next section on ethics, but you need to be clear about whether offering anonymity is an important part of your questionnaire design.

Ethics

The ethics of research is quite complicated because it can involve so many different aspects, but the most important thing is that you give careful consideration to the fact that you are working with living people. What you do or don't do could affect someone in a negative way, so you have to make every effort to see that this doesn't happen. We are aiming for 'ethical integrity'. There are no generally accepted standards or guidelines for fieldwork in religion, nor any established code of ethics, and every university will have its own guidelines that must be followed. There are lots of sources to help you think this through. Several books on the study of religion have good chapters on ethics, for example Bird and Lamoureux Scholes (2011) and Chryssides and Geaves (2013). Eileen Fry has written brief but quite useful online guidelines for qualitative research in religion, which she categorises as competence, consent, confidentiality, conduct and care (n.d.). We have already referred to some of these aspects and what follows sets out the main issues to consider. Perhaps this can be summarised by saying that it is really important that you do not put either yourself or your informants at risk, and that includes risk to their reputation.

'Informed consent' is a key concept in qualitative research, so you must make sure you understand its ethical importance and ways to achieve it as fully as possible. The practicalities usually used in student work are an information sheet and a consent form. The information tells the potential informants about your work and what you are hoping they will provide for you. It also makes clear that they can withdraw from the research at any time. The information includes details of the kind of data you will collect, how you will store this securely, who will have access to it and how you will use it in any finished work. You will need to consider how much control you want to give your informants over the data you have collected and the finished product. You may want to check back later that you have understood things correctly and got things accurate, so you might include something about a possible second contact. It should also make clear how you will approach the issue of confidentiality and anonymity. There is more about this aspect coming up later. Two copies of the consent form need to be signed by the informants and you after they have had a chance to read the information sheet. They keep one copy and you keep the other. This may seem rather formal especially if your project is a very small one but it is helpful in a number of ways. Preparing your information sheet forces you to be very clear about your work and what you are hoping to get from the informants. Having to sign the consent form means that the informants have actively agreed to help you in ways that have been clearly stated. However, it would be naive to think that all informants fully understand what they are consenting to. Obviously the process just set out requires good levels of literacy, and the information sheet, however carefully prepared, may still not really convey what the experience will be like for the informant.

We have briefly discussed power issues and if someone is pressured into participating then, even if they sign a form, they are not genuinely consenting. With some groups of people this will be a more serious issue and that is partly why we advise you, as neophyte researchers, not to involve children. If your research *must* involve other vulnerable groups, such as those with mental disabilities or trauma victims, then the ethical issues of informed consent become even trickier, and you will have to give very special attention to this aspect of your planning and practice. Occasionally in the past, research has been carried out 'undercover' without disclosing the true identity of the researcher or the fact that research is being done. A published example of early undercover research is by Leo Festinger et al. (1956). There are different views about the ethical issues raised by this practice, but we consider that as a neophyte researcher you should plan research that is both practically and ethically straightforward.

Confidentiality may appear to be a more straightforward issue than consent. It is common practice in qualitative research to disguise the identity of places and people so that they cannot be identified. Pseudonyms are used and distinguishing characteristics are avoided without losing the rich 'thick description' that gives ethnographic writing its power. Sometimes it can be useful to agree the pseudonym with the informant, and details about a person or place can be changed without losing the reality of the living religion being studied. However, there are two issues that arise – one practical and the other much more interesting and worth some careful thought. If you carry out research in a small place, then people there who read your work are likely to know who you are referring to, and who is saying what. It may also be the case that where you interview someone occupying a particular role, it is impossible to disguise that role and still use what he or she has told you. In these cases there is not complete anonymity, although people outside the place where you did the research will not know the actual location or identity of the participants. In your information sheet you can state that you will use different names to disguise the person and the place, and you can guarantee that only you will listen to any tape recording that is made and that the data will be securely stored.

In some ways, confidentiality is a convention rather than an ethical imperative! Ruth Linden, who studied Holocaust survivors, reminds us that anonymity is not the only way of reporting research but a "representational strategy with political, historical, as well as psychological consequences for our respondents and us alike" (1993, 107). If these people survived Nazi attempts to dehumanise them, to replace their names with numbers and ultimately to destroy them completely, then their real names are highly significant. The Holocaust museum in Jerusalem is called *Yad Vashem* – a place and a name – taken from Isaiah 56:4–5, and the Hebrew word often used for God is *ha Shem* – the Name. In many religions names are important – they signify meaning at many levels. So, there may be ethical and religious reasons not to mask the identity of your informants. Whatever you decide to do, make sure that you explain your understanding of the issues and the reasons for the choices you have made.

As well as respecting the dignity and perhaps also the privacy of our subjects in the field, there are also ethical requirements to reference our sources of information properly in sharing what we have discovered with our subjects or in writing up the findings. Throughout the process of research it is important to act responsibly and to communicate as clearly as possible the basis on which we have made particular judgements. One final point: do not post comments about your research on sites such as Facebook or Twitter!

Analysing the data

Doing fieldwork generates data quickly, so you may find yourself with more than you expected and the first task is to sort it out. As you go, keep alert for any patterns that are emerging, for material that gives you varied perspectives on a particular issue, and for things that don't seem to fit. Re-read your fieldwork journal and look at any photographs to remind you of what the experience was like, and keep adding thoughts to your journal. As you read or explore other relevant sources such as books, articles or material online, make notes of any connections you see, of relevant theoretical ideas, and of any useful quotations. Some researchers use large sheets of paper for 'mind maps' of all the linked material. You need to highlight the data that will enable you to write rich description, and you need to identify what will help you to both explain and interpret your chosen 'snapshot' of living religion.

If you have done an interview, it is worth listening to it several times. Sometimes you will need to make a full transcript for a 'perspective' rather than an 'information' or 'ideas' analysis. If you are interested, for example, in the language people use to talk about their experience of power in a ritual, a form of discourse analysis, you need to be able to identify and analyse in detail the exact words they used. Having a full written version on the computer also allows you to use computer software to search for patterns. However, transcribing an interview is very time consuming and often you do not need this level of detail to make use of what your interviewee has told you. In that case, as you listen to the interview, make a note of each question you ask and the main points in the reply, and only record verbatim particularly vivid and distinctive comments. You can use these in your written work to convey the characteristic perspectives of each interviewee. Once you have a written record of some sort, listen to the interview again and notice anything of interest which is not in the *content* of what is said. Are some questions difficult to answer? Are some responses full of energy and enthusiasm? Is there anything the interviewee seems to be avoiding? What is not said?

Keep notes of all of this, add relevant material to your mind map, and begin to highlight the key themes that are emerging and the connections you are beginning to be aware of. If you have a questionnaire, either written or oral, then begin to make a simple record of the number of particular answers to each of the questions. Where you have asked for fuller details, begin to list these, note if there are several similar responses, and if there are particularly striking responses. See below for an example of the kind of record you need for each of your questions:

Displaying results

The following are the responses to Hardy's question – see the earlier text box – from 114 school students aged 14 or 15. There were sixty-seven girls and forty-seven boys.

Have you ever been aware of, or influenced by, a presence or power, whether you call it 'God' or not, which is different from your every-day self?

	OFTEN	*SOMETIMES*	*ONCE OR TWICE*	*NEVER*
Girls	5	13	24	25
Boys	3	10	15	19
Total	8	23	39	44

The data could be presented like this in your finished work or the actual numbers could be given as percentages if you have a fairly large number of responses. Or a summary could be written, for example '61 per cent of the students answered "yes" to Hardy's question'. In practice it is worth using a range of different ways of communicating the results so as to make for a 'good read'. What you don't want to do, as we said earlier, is to try to make the results look more statistically significant than they are.

With a questionnaire you can correlate the responses to different questions, or compare different groups of respondents. For example, in the research reported above it was possible to explore whether girls responded differently to boys. They did, with girls responding more positively to many of the questions. What the questionnaire won't tell you is what the reasons might be for these findings, so you have to refer to other relevant literature which might discuss the issues, and you have to develop your own possible explanations and justify them. Be careful not to assume that because two aspects of your data are connected, there is necessarily cause and effect; it may be that both are caused by a third factor, or that what you have seen as a connection is actually a coincidence. In large-scale questionnaire research the statistical analysis can be very sophisticated. If you are using a questionnaire as part of your independent research into an aspect of living religion, the analysis will be much simpler, but because of the small-scale, mainly qualitative nature of your research, you will be able to describe what you find very vividly and interpret its significance in detail.

This is what 'analysis' involves. You work on the data you have collected to see what it shows, then you separate out different aspects of what you have found and explore the possible meanings and significances for the bit of living religion you have studied. You also make connections with other reading and research, theoretical ideas, wider aspects of a particular religious tradition and your own growing understanding of the study of religion and of research. All of this analysis requires writing in different ways – you definitely don't do it all in your head! In fact, the sooner you start to write, the better, as we will see in the next section.

Writing up

There has perhaps been more interesting discussion about 'writing up' in ethnography than about other aspects of the methods – see, for example, Behar and Gordon, 1995; Clifford and Marcus, 1985; Van Maanen, 2011; Wolf, 1992. Writing is, itself, a way of knowing; often we don't know what we know until we try to articulate it. It is also our way of communicating what we know and understand to somebody else, and for students it is (usually) the means by which their independent fieldwork is assessed. Of course a presentation is delivered orally but it still requires a 'script' with evidence, examples and argument. The exact nature of the writing will depend on the task set, but in every case you will have creatively 'constructed' the finished piece of work. It is the constructed nature of the text which needs some exploration, and this section will include some discussion of this as well as practical advice and examples taken from students' work.

One of the ethnographers who has reflected and written about these issues is Clifford Geertz. His writing – both about the cultures he studied and his reflections on the processes involved – has been criticised, but the following quotation sums up a number of the issues we will be discussing here:

To grasp concepts that, for other people, are experience-near, and to do so well enough to place them in illuminating connection with experience-distant concepts theorists have fashioned to capture the general features of social life, is clearly a task at least as delicate, if a bit less magical, as putting oneself into someone else's skin. ... The trick is to figure out what the devil they think they are up to.

(Geertz, 1983, 58)

And then to communicate that to the reader. Eisner talks about 'criticism' as the process needed for writing up research (1985). Just as when an art critic writes about a painting or sculpture, the reader begins to see more, to see something of what the critic has seen. This is a 'maieutic' process: birthing new perception in the reader. This approach is 'interpretive', and in order to interpret an aspect of living religion, both field notes and the final text need 'thick description'. It is also a creative process and involves writing 'tales' of the particular situation which has been explored. As Van Maanen has written about what he calls 'impressionist tales':

Their materials are words, metaphors, phrasings, imagery, and most critically, the expansive recall of fieldwork experience. When these are put together and told in the first person as a tightly focused, vibrant, exact, but necessarily imaginative rendering of fieldwork, an impressionist tale of the field results ... [It] is a representational means of cracking open the culture, and the fieldworker's way of knowing it so that both can be jointly examined. ... Transparency and concreteness give the impressionist tale an absorbing character, as does the use of a maximally evocative language.

(Van Maanen, 2011, 102–3)

The following text box is an attempt at an impressionist tale by a third-year undergraduate student which is an extract from an assignment based on a study visit to Rome. It is called 'Women Who Scream' and it illustrates some of the theoretical points made in this section.

'Women Who Scream'

The bus judders again and I am pressed into the body of a stranger. I hope that you are worth it, Teresa. Teresa, tucked out of the way, in a grimy stained building on a junction corner. I push through the door of the church and there is darkness inside. I wait for my pupils to dilate. There is a rattle of coins being dropped into a donation box, and another candle is added to the flickering twilight of the church. The quiet hums happily to me; I am happy. This is what I came for.

I come to the side chapel and stand square in front of the Ecstasy of St Teresa, turn my body to face this softly sighing woman, who looks like she could be singing or sleeping. She is dishevelled, her clothes in disarray. The teasing angel, who smiles on her with a gentle upturned mouth, tugs at her dress, fingers holding an arrow delicately like a pen or a witch's wand. I move as close as I can and rest my hands on the balustrade that circles off the altar, try to imagine the breathy whisper from her parted mouth; she is so very nearly real. Later I try to imagine what her laughter would have sounded like.

As I stand in Santa Maria della Vittoria, the afternoon sun illuminates the sculpture for a second, and for a moment she is golden. This is life broken wide open. She is not the 'woman who screamed' of my title as I imagined her to be. I do not hear her crying out in pain or pleasure, but quietly filled up with an other worldly ecstasy altogether transcending human feeling. But there is something quite inexplicable about this sculpture that screams to me, something that stirs and stills me equally.

This text is clearly constructed, subjective, creative and interpretive. There is no doubt that the student was there in the church, and the 'thick descriptions', although not extensive, convey a particular time and place, sense impressions and the responses of the writer. It is obvious that what has been learned here, has been learned by reflection on experience, as well as wider reading and research. There is real engagement with a piece of 'religious art' and an expression of mystical experience, both significant aspects of the study of religion. Of course, this is not the whole written assignment, but the connections, judgements and interpretations that follow are drawn out from this 'tale' and their credibility is, at least partly, justified by their resonance with it.

This approach to writing up fieldwork does not attempt to generalise, but focuses on the detailed and particular circumstances of the situation and the experiences of those involved – both researcher and researched. The autobiographical elements provide insight into the perspective of the writer. The writing is both richly descriptive and analytical because it selects and highlights what are understood by the writer to be the significant elements. Where it is done well, the reader can see and understand them too. Of course, not all good writing about fieldwork in the study of religion is so highly personal as the example of 'Women Who Scream'. The following textbox comes from the introduction to a fairly recent textbook for the study of religion that brings together scholars approaching lived religion in different parts of the world.

Living vignettes

every chapter begins with some kind of snapshot, illustration, evocation, or vignette of a real or typical event. This is a further strategy that we have employed to keep the lived reality of living religions in view. These vignettes are not all of the same length or kind. Some

form brief introductions to a chapter ... some are about public ceremonies, other are about activities in people's homes. Some are about
what religious people do when they visit a sacred site, others
about what it is like for students or visitors to observe other people
doing their religions. Some imagine the inner thoughts of someone
caught in a moment of decision, others attend to everyday acts. ...
Vignettes can be defined as brief, elegant but open ended narratives
or word-pictures ... not complete in themselves; they lead to further
discussion.

(Harvey, 2009, 3–4)

Here are some practical questions to consider when you are writing up your
fieldwork:

- What exactly is the task that you have been set? What kind of finished product
  will best accomplish this?
- Is it obvious that what you have learned is 'experiential knowledge'?
  In other words, have you made it clear what you learned in the field?
- Is the writing reflexive? Are *you* in there?
- Is the descriptive writing 'thick'? Do you convey a vivid sense of what was
  happening in a specific place and time, and the experiences of the people
  involved?
- Is the writing imaginative? Do you use 'maximally evocative' language?
- Is the writing interpretive? Do you discuss the meanings of what you studied
  in the field?
- Is the writing analytic? Does it clearly show what you understand as the
  significant aspects of the living religion you have studied?
- Have you enabled the reader to 'see what you see'? Remember they were not
  present, as you were.
- Is the writing open ended? Does it engage the reader and suggest further
  possibilities?

If you are going to produce good-quality writing, you have to think about
'how' you write as well as 'what' you write. You need to work from different
sources – photographs, field notes, items you collected, questions and ideas
raised at the time, later reflections and so on. You will need to draft and redraft
your writing, trying different ways of setting out the same material. One of the
best ways of learning to write well is to read good examples of other people's
writing. There are lots of published examples of interesting fieldwork in the
study of religion. The ones we have chosen below illustrate a range of what is
possible in large-scale research. They come from different parts of the world
and span the last thirty years. As a neophyte researcher your work will be very
small scale, but reading some of these might inspire you, give you ideas about
religion and help you to see how to write well about your fieldwork.

Recommended fieldwork accounts

- Eileen Barker (1984) *The Making of a Moonie: Brainwashing or Choice?* is a classic work from a leading authority on new religious movements. By actually engaging with the living reality of the Moonies, Eileen Barker was able to show how misguided some of the reported material about the Moonies actually was.
- Lynn Davidman (1991) *Tradition in a Rootless World: Women Turn to Orthodox Judaism* is a rich ethnographic study of modern, secular but disillusioned American women choosing to explore, and perhaps join, strictly observant Jewish communities, which themselves are also, at the same time, struggling with aspects of secularism.
- Abby Day (2011) *Believing in Belonging* brings new perspectives on theories in the sociology of religion by examining what is often dismissed as 'nominal' Christianity. This is shown to be a factor in many people's cultural identity.
- Hanifa Deen (2003) *Caravanserai: Journey among Australian Muslims* explores the experiences of Muslims in Australia by journeying to meet them and by retelling their stories in a vividly written narrative. Her commentary and interpretation casts quite a harsh light on the wider Australian society in which they live.
- Lynn Foulston (2002) *At the Feet of the Goddess: The Divine Feminine in Hindu Local Religion* is based on extensive ethnographic work and explores the local details and differences between individual Indian goddesses, their stories and rituals, and their presence and power in people's lives.
- Paul Heelas and Linda Woodhead (2004) *The Spiritual Revolution: Why Religion is Giving Way to Spirituality* is based on a very detailed empirical study of one northern town in England. Researchers counted the numbers of people attending Christian worship and interviewed a large number of people in the town about their involvement in practices that could be termed 'spiritual'. A theoretical model is suggested that makes sense of their data.
- Ruth Linden (1993) *Making Stories, Making Selves* is an extended reflexive exploration of learning about a particular group of Holocaust survivors. The impact of the research on both the researcher and the researched comes through vividly.
- Saba Mahmood (2005) *Politics of Piety: The Islamic Revival and the Feminist Subject* was written before the 'Arab Spring'. This ethnography of a grassroots women's piety movement in the mosques of Cairo, Egypt, explores connections between ethics and politics, and embodiment and gender.
- Karen McCarthy Brown (2011) 3rd edition, *Mama Lola* is an early feminist study of Vodou in New York. It is based on the very close relationship that developed between the author and the Vodou

priestess in Brooklyn, and is written using photos and vivid narrative accounts of rituals and events.

- Alex Norman (2011) *Spiritual Tourism: Travel and Religious Practice in Western Society* focuses in rich detail on the town of Rishikesh in India, which he describes as a 'spiritual marketplace', and the popular Christian pilgrimage in Spain, the Camino de Santiago de Compostela, to advance the case for the idea of the 'spiritual tourist'.
- Robert Orsi (2005) *Between Heaven and Earth: The Religious Worlds People Make and the Scholars Who Study Them* is located between religious studies and theology. Orsi reflects deeply on the relationship between his own American Catholic upbringing and family, and the scholarly study of 'devotion' to the Virgin Mary and the saints.
- Susan Palmer (2010) *The Nuwaubian Nation* is written by a white Mormon woman exploring an African-American patriarchal, racialist new religious movement. Almost inevitably, therefore, it has a fascinating introduction about reflexivity and studying religion in tricky situations.
- Robert Putnam and David E. Campbell (2010) *American Grace: How Religion Divides and Unites Us* is based on a two-part interview survey of more than 3,000 respondents to explore changes in religion in America. They chart both growing polarisation and also more interfaith activity. The book has some interesting vignettes of different communities.

Chapter summary

This chapter has considered in some detail the major elements of the ethnographic study of religion. Ideas about doing fieldwork have been combined with practical advice and examples. Having read it all through early in the preparation for your own independent study of living religion, it is a good idea to refer back to the separate sections as you carry out the various parts of the work.

Further reading

Graham Harvey has written a very helpful chapter on 'Field Research: Participant Observation' in *The Routledge Handbook of Research Methods in the Study of Religion* (Stausberg and Engler, 2011, 217–44). He has useful things to say about various aspects of conducting fieldwork, and is especially good on the need for us, as researchers, to *respect* the people we are studying.

Personal Knowledge and Beyond (Spickard et al., 2002) is a very accessible book containing lots of short, interesting chapters about ethnology and the study of religion. It will help you think through, in more detail, a lot of the issues raised in this chapter. There are also plenty of examples of published work for further research.

Questions for consideration

1   What aspects of living religion most interest you? What made you choose them? How could you research this in the field?
2   How can you incorporate independent fieldwork study of living religion into an assignment you have to do?
3   What is the best thing you have read about living religion? What is it that you particularly like? How was it researched? How was it written? How could you use some of these approaches in your own work?
4   What are the ethical guidelines for qualitative research at your institution? How will these impact on your independent research?

Bibliography

This list includes all the texts referred to in the chapter and other recommended reading. All websites accessed on 31.10.14.

Barker, E. 1984, *The Making of a Moonie: Brainwashing or Choice?*, Oxford: Basil Blackwell.

Baumann, G. 1996, *Contesting Culture: Discourses of Identity in Multi-Ethnic London*, Cambridge: Cambridge University Press.

Behar, R. and Gordon, D.A. 1995, *Women Writing Culture*, Berkeley: University of California Press.

Bird, F. and Lamoureux Scholes, L. 2011, 'Research Ethics' in Stausberg, M. and Engler, S. (eds) *The Routledge Handbook of Research Methods in the Study of Religion*, London: Routledge, 81–106.

Chryssides, G.D. and Geaves, R. 2013 (2nd edn), *The Study of Religion: An Introduction to Key Ideas and Methods*, London: Continuum.

Clifford, J. and Marcus, G.E. (eds) 1985, *Writing Culture: The Poetics and Politics of Ethnography*, Berkeley, CA: University of California Press.

Davidman, L. 2002, 'Truth, Subjectivity and Ethnographic Research' in Spickard, J.V. et al. (eds) *Personal Knowledge and Beyond: Reshaping the Ethnography of Religion*, New York: New York University Press, 17–26.

——1991, *Tradition in a Rootless World: Women Turn to Orthodox Judaism*, Berkeley and Los Angeles: University of California Press.

Davidson Bremborg, A. 2011, 'Interviewing' in Stausberg, M. and Engler, S. (eds) *The Routledge Handbook of Research Methods in the Study of Religion*, London: Routledge, 310–22.

Day, A. 2011, *Believing in Belonging*, Oxford: Oxford University Press.

Deen, H. 2003, *Caravanserai: Journey among Australian Muslims*, Freemantle, WA: Freemantle Arts Centre Press.

Eisner, E. 1985, *The Educational Imagination*, London: Collier Macmillan.

Festinger, L., Riecken, H.W. and Schachter, S. 1956, *When Prophecy Fails*, Minneapolis, MN: University of Minnesota Press.

Flanagan, K. 2001, 'Reflexivity, Ethics and the Teaching of the Sociology of Religion' in *Sociology*, 35(1), 1–19.

Foulston, L. 2002, *At the Feet of the Goddess: The Divine Feminine in Hindu Local Religion*, Eastbourne: Sussex Academic Press.

Fry, E. n.d., 'Ethics and the Qualitative Study of Religion' accessed online at www2. derby.ac.uk/multifaith-new/images/content/seminarpapers/EthicsandtheQualitativeStudy ofReligion.htm

Geertz, C. 1983, *Local Knowledge: Further Essays in Interpretive Anthropology*, New York: Basic Books.

Gobo, G. 2008 [trans. A. Belton], *Doing Ethnography*, London: Sage.

Hardy, A. 1979, *The Spiritual Nature of Man*, Oxford: Oxford University Press.

Harvey, G. 2011, 'Field Research: Participant Observation' in Stausberg, M. and Engler, S. (eds) *The Routledge Handbook of Research Methods in the Study of Religion*, London: Routledge, 217–44.

——(ed.) 2009, *Religions in Focus*, London: Equinox.

——2003, 'Guesthood as Ethical Decolonising Research Method', *Numen*, 50(2), 125–46.

Hay, D. 2007, *Why Spirituality is Difficult for Westerners*, Exeter: Societas Imprint Academic.

Heelas, P. and Woodhead, L. 2004, *The Spiritual Revolution: Why Religion is Giving Way to Spirituality*, Oxford: Wiley-Blackwell.

Hesse-Biber, S.N. and Leavy, P.L. (eds) 2006, *Emergent Methods in Social Research*, Thousand Oaks, CA: Sage Publications.

Hume, L. and Mulcock, J. (eds) 2005, *Anthropologists in the Field: Cases in Participant Observation*, New York: Columbia University Press.

Leavy, P. (ed.) 2014, *The Oxford Handbook of Qualitative Research*, Oxford: Oxford University Press.

Linden, R. 1993, *Making Stories, Making Selves*, Columbus, OH: Ohio State University Press.

Mahmood, S. 2005, *Politics of Piety: The Islamic Revival and the Feminist Subject*, Princeton, NJ: Princeton University Press.

McCarthy Brown, K. 2011 (3rd edn), *Mama Lola*, Berkeley and Los Angeles: University of California Press.

McGuire, M.B. 2008, *Lived Religion*, Oxford: Oxford University Press.

Norman, A. 2011, *Spiritual Tourism: Travel and Religious Practice in Western Society*, London: Continuum.

Orsi, R.A. 2005, *Between Heaven and Earth*, Princeton, NJ: Princeton University Press.

Palmer, S. 2010, *The Nuwaubian Nation*, Farnham, Surrey: Ashgate.

Parry, B. 2008, *Tribe*, London: Penguin.

Putnam, R. and Campbell, D.E. 2010, *American Grace: How Religion Divides and Unites Us*, New York: Simon & Schuster.

Sargisson, L. and Sargent, L.T. 2004, *Living in Utopia: New Zealand's Intentional Communities*, Farnham, Surrey: Ashgate.

Scholefield, L. 2009, 'Memories and Translations in the Stories Told by Converts to Catholicism and Islam' in *DISKUS*, Vol. 10.

——1988, *Spirituality and Values*, unpublished MEd dissertation, Exeter: University of Exeter, 14–16.

Schon, D.A. 1990, *Educating the Reflective Practitioner*, Oxford: Josey Bass Inc.

Smith, M.K. 2005, 'Elliot W. Eisner, Connoisseurship, Criticism and the Art of Education', *The Encyclopaedia of Informal Education* accessed online at www.infed.org/thinkers/eisner.htm

Spickard, J.V., Landres, J.S. and McGuire, M.B. (eds) 2002, *Personal Knowledge and Beyond: Reshaping the Ethnography of Religion*, New York: New York University Press.

Stausberg, M. and Engler, S. (eds) 2011, *The Routledge Handbook of Research Methods in the Study of Religion*, London: Routledge.

Van Maanen, J. 2011 (2nd edn), *Tales of the Field*, Chicago: University of Chicago Press.

Wolcott, H.F. 2001, *The Art of Fieldwork*, New York: AltaMira Press.

Wolf, M. 1992, *A Thrice Told Tale: Feminism, Postmodernism and Ethnographic Responsibility*, Stanford, CA: Stanford University Press.

Websites

This annotated list includes all the online sources we have referred to in the chapter as well as some recommended sites. We have given the URLs (web addresses) accessed on 31.10.14, but these do change so for ease of use we have listed them by the name of the organisation in alphabetical order.

British Religion in Numbers. This major British resource has both data and written guides to understanding religious data. www.brin.ac.uk/

Community Religions Project. Since 1976, the Community Religions Project at Leeds University in the UK has conducted fieldwork research on religion and religions 'near at hand' in the cities of Leeds and Bradford and beyond. http://arts.leeds.ac.uk/crp/

Diasporas, Migration and Identities was a major funded project led by Professor Kim Knott. Many of the research projects are closely connected to the study of living religion, and the website has a range of useful materials such as podcasts, link websites and material to be downloaded. www.diasporas.ac.uk/index.htm

Living Religion website at Bath Spa University has lots of useful information about possible places to visit, examples of student research work carried out while staying with a religious community, and some resources. www.livingreligion.co.uk/

On Being is an American public broadcasting site with long weekly interviews relating to religion, spirituality and contemporary culture. The website also has links to some excellent material related to the weekly topic. www.onbeing.org/

PewResearch – Religion and Public Life Project has extensive data and analysis about many topics related to religion and society, including religious affiliation, and religious belief and practice in America. http://religions.pewforum.org/

The Pluralism Project at Harvard University has been running since 1991, charting the changing religious landscape of the United States within a global context. There are a number of case studies included as a means of teaching theology and religious studies. www.pluralism.org/

Religion and Society. A rich source of data about religion in Britain, including videos of debates, podcasts, reports of research findings and much more. www.religionandsociety.org.uk/

Religion Bulletin is the blog site of the *Bulletin for the Study of Religion* published by Equinox where contributors discuss issues in the study of religion. www.equinoxpub.com/blog/

Religious Diversity in New Zealand. These are extracts from the Human Rights Commission's Annual Race Relations Reports 2004–10. www.hrc.co.nz/race-relations/annual-review-of-race-relations/religious-diversity-in-new-zealand

The Religious Studies Project. A really good link to scholarly approaches to religious studies. www.religiousstudiesproject.com/

Research Methods for the Study of Religion: University of Kent. This is probably the best website for excellent articles and select bibliographies about a whole range of different ways of studying living religion. www.kent.ac.uk/religionmethods/index.html

6 Virtual fieldwork
Engaging with religions with new (and old) media

Introduction

Many books on the study of religion aimed at students have, in recent years, included chapters on the Internet. The problem is, they are almost invariably out of date as soon as they are published. Descriptions of the rise in usage of the Internet by religious groups, or repositories of useful materials and guides to help students approach the study of religion(s), are helpful, but static, ways of communicating emergent information. This chapter aims to be different, in that the focus will not be on how religious communities and the new media co-exist (although this is interesting and will be touched upon), but will instead be on how individual religious practitioners use online media; and also how student researchers can think and reflect on the ways in which they can interact with the rapidly changing landscape of online communication, including social media as well as more established media, as a part of engagement with living religions. To do this, we need to explore not just the fact that religions do use online media, but why they do so, and to understand what opportunities this offers the student in engagement with living religion.

This chapter will not be deeply theoretical – there are others who have helpfully discussed this before, and their texts are highlighted at the end of the chapter – but will address issues and ask questions about which and upon which students need to reflect if they are to use new media critically and academically in relation to religion in the non-meat world.

Religion and the Internet: starting points and recent developments

One important issue to be clear about at the start is the scholarly conversation regarding 'religion online' and 'online religion'. These terms are now common in the study of religions, but were first critically used by Helland (2000) and Hadden and Cowen (2000). Based upon research in the late 1990s, when the Web was a very different place to now, these scholars distinguished between religion online, which offered *information* about religion, and online religion, which offered opportunities for *participation* in religious activities. Subsequent to this, Young has critiqued these terms further to differentiate between two types of relationship: (a) information versus participation and (b) primary reference to offline religious materials versus primary reference to religious activities that take place online (2004, 94).

Since these important foundational works on religion's relationship with the Internet, our understanding and use of online, networked or cloud technologies have changed almost beyond recognition. The move from Web 1.0, which was used essentially as a passive information portal, to Web 2.0, which offers sites and portals that are better designed for interaction and active participation, means that it is increasingly difficult to differentiate between different forms of media – smart TVs, tablets and phones now have access to entire back catalogues of TV networks' outputs, which means that there is no longer a clear divide between online media and traditional media – newspapers have websites, TV is streamed online, and websites and social media interfaces are no longer computer dependent, but are mediated through phones, the new generation of smart watches, and even in devices such as Kindles, which are predominantly designed for reading digital texts, but also have basic browsing functions. Even textbooks now often have companion websites (although they are often passive content in a textbook format which simply uses web pages instead of printed pages), so we will address media which include an online presence even if they are not traditionally web based. In short, we have moved from a 'cloud of unknowing' to a cloud of connection.

This huge rise in online media provides a world of opportunities for students, but having the skills to critically engage with the material is quite another matter. For instance, any modern student can find an online video within seconds, using popular search engines and video-streaming sites, and this has the huge advantage of *seeing* rather than simply reading about a performative aspect of religion. Such media give life to subjects – for example, to see a West African Yoruba dance, you do not need to travel thousands of miles as previous generations of scholars would have needed to do, but can instead view a video of the performance on your phone anywhere in the world with a Wi-Fi or 3G signal. However, although such an opportunity provides a myriad of benefits to the student, it also raises new and interesting questions. How does viewing a video compare to being physically present at a religious ceremony or performance? Can you be a participant observer with an online community of religious practitioners, and what does it mean for a religious ceremony, such as a Christian Eucharist, which is normally conducted in person, to be conducted virtually?

'Represented Religion'

Religion online, as first described by Helland and referred to above, is a focus in the later parts of this chapter, but investigating represented religion online is an important first step in engagement with living religion online. Religion is represented online in many ways and for many reasons – we will explore some in the paragraphs below – but perhaps the most important function of represented religion online is the sharing of information and the subsequent projection of religious identity for the relevant groups or communities. Often the ways in which information is offered online make it a different learning experience for students from simply reading information in a textbook.

Using a variety of old and new media to engage with represented religion is important as they offer information about traditions, which may or may not differ from textbook accounts, and also offer excellent emic voices and primary sources. This can be from something as simple as an organisation's homepage – perhaps the Vatican's website – or a more particular projection of information, such as an online interview with Tariq Ramadan on European Islam (2007). Each of these types of very simple online forms of communication provides key information which can be used as background research to then engage further with *living* forms of the religious traditions in question. There is also an important epistemic and experiential aspect to using online information to do simple research. Whilst we would never advocate *just* using online sources – the effective use of academic textbooks, journals and monographs is an essential skill for any university student – there is no doubt that online resources offer a different route into learning, and can facilitate a different learning experience for the researcher. This is particularly the case when it comes to the project of religious identities. *Hearing* someone deliver a lecture, or reading from a sacred text, or watching a debate offers a different learning experience to reading an essay or philosophical dialogue – and we shouldn't forget that the over-whelming majority of texts in religious history, be they sermons, cosmological stories or philosophical dialogues, were intended to be read aloud by their original authors.

Misrepresented religion online

One of the dangers of using the Internet during your studies is the amount of misinformation online. Sometimes this can be useful, if carefully contextualised as we outline below, but often it is simply unhelpful and academically dubious. Of course, part of the necessary learning is about how to distinguish between information which is robust and academically useful, and information which should not be considered helpful or authoritative.

The prevalence of misinformation

The Internet is essentially a forum for self-publishing. Anyone can write a blog, design a website, or upload a lecture or video to the Web. Increasingly, through the use of social media, opinions and commentaries on events are disseminated with enormous speed, often 'going viral' within minutes or hours, meaning that amongst much useful information, there will also be accidental or deliberate misinformation.

Recognising misinformation

A good way to judge the value of information online is to use the same criteria that you would use for standard published works. When looking at a website, is the design professional, does it tell you who the publisher of the site is, and the specific author of the text you are reading? If it does give a name, check what else the person has written – does the author hold an academic position or does the person perform a role relevant to the subject he or she is writing on? What are the author's credentials, and what references does he or she give to other scholars or relevant information? If the website or blog gives an opinion or judgement on a subject you are studying, check this in relation to the thoughts of other scholars and writers – it is all too easy to put forward a position promoted from just one source as authoritative, but it may well be that the majority of scholars do not agree with such a position. Cross-referencing between web sources, as you would with books in a library, is a good way to ensure you do not present a minority view as if it were widely accepted. By treating websites to the same standard of scrutiny that you would any academic source, you will easily begin to spot 'commentary' as opposed to 'opinion'.

Using misinformation

Sometimes, misinformation can actually be very useful to scholars, once you have identified material as such. Perhaps you are researching how the media treat new religious movements, or how Islamophobia has risen in Europe in recent decades; such subjects would necessitate exploring, perhaps, what far-right political groups write about Islam, or evangelical Christian views of pagan communities. Such sites might not pass the 'academic credibility' test, but they would be excellent primary sources to engage with how the communities in question view the 'religious other', and thus could be used, if contextualised properly, even though they may not represent mainstream academic opinion or may not even be wholly accurate. Similarly, information which is not necessarily misinformation, but is perhaps contested information, is also very useful. Examples such as apostate testimony – that is, narratives from people who have left religious communities – are potentially very valuable sources of rich material, but they need to be contextualised as contested; not everything an apostate says may be true, and the community the person has left may well have their own narrative of events to contest the leaver's story.

Religion is represented online for a variety of reasons. Often, it is with regard to evangelism – particularly with a focus on engaging with younger people who may now be moving away from traditional forms of weekly religious attendance. A high-profile example of this is the Jehovah's Witnesses, whose homepage is available in over 300 languages, from Abaknon to Zande, and which receives over a million unique site visits every day. This evangelism is inextricably linked with more traditional forms of outreach, such as door-to-door witnessing and the distribution of leaflets and magazines in public places like train and bus stations across the world. By visiting and researching sites such as JW.org, you can amass a wealth of literature and contextualising information, which you can then utilise to understand (*verstehen*) Witnesses when you meet with them and engage with them about their practices, beliefs and writings. Often religions also utilise the Web as a form of corrective, for example to address criticism that may be aimed at them, or to promote their own understanding of events to counter what they perceive as unfair media treatment. Perhaps the best known use of such a tactic is by the Church of Scientology which, for a number of years, had perhaps the most efficient web presence of any growing religious movement, and effectively uses this to promote its own worldview against that of its critics' (mis)understanding of Scientology.

By accessing such simple sites and utilising them as repositories of information, you can do far more than simply 'learn about' different religious traditions. By utilising a 'presearch' methodological approach to the sites you visit (see textbox below), you can use *represented* religion as a means of preparing the way for deeper engagement with lived religious traditions. Put simply, research-ing online does not stop you physically visiting places – it is not a question of 'either or', but rather 'both and'. One such example is with regard to visiting sites that have limited access. On a recent study tour to Jerusalem, we took students up to the *Haram al-Sharif*, knowing in advance that only our Muslim students would be allowed into the al-Aqsa mosque or the Dome of Rock. As the majority of the group were Christian or non-religious, only a minority of the group entered the actual buildings. However, by accessing presearch information online, students who were not able to enter the buildings were able to contextualise their knowledge of photographs and videos from inside the Dome of the Rock and al-Aqsa with their experience of the whole space that is the *Haram al-Sharif* and the various activities taking place there. In this way, the Internet acts as a *narthical* space for student learning – a space in which the student moves from the outside world into interaction and engagement with a religious place, community or idea. What is learned in this way can then also facilitate a closer encounter during actual embodied experiential learning.

One further issue needs to be raised in this introductory section on repre-sented religion online – and that is the simple fact that *all* media, old and new, goes through an editorial process before it is released into the public domain. This may be as personal as an individual's blog reflecting his or her worldview, or the official declarations of a religious movement being written online concerning major moral issues. The examples don't matter, but what does matter is to always remember that everything you see or read online (and indeed offline) has an editorial bias or angle behind its message. Of course, this does not automatically devalue the information you are accessing; indeed it is often what makes the information interesting and helpful for scholars. What is important is that you *contextualise* any information you use from online sources.

Wikipedia is not the Devil – 'presearch' and the world's sixth most popular website

One significant source of information for many students (whether tutors like it or not) is *Wikipedia*, the world's largest online encyclopaedia. An oft-demonised website, *Wikipedia* is the community-edited project founded by Jimmy Wales and Larry Sanger in 2001. It now boasts over 30 million entries in nearly 290 languages, of which around 2 per cent – or 600,000 articles – are written on religion and religions.

A central tranche of *Wikipedia*'s identity as an open-access community resource is that anyone, as long as they register on the site, can act as an editor or contributor for entries. This is, at the same time, the website's greatest strength and the reason why it receives so much criticism amongst academics. One outspoken critic was Michael Gorman, previously president of the American Library Association, who criticised *Wikipedia*'s reliability and accuracy by stating that academics who recommended the site for their students' use were "the intellectual equivalent of a dietitian who recommends a steady diet of Big Macs with everything" (Stothart, 2007).

We disagree slightly (and not just because the occasional Big Mac never hurt anyone) because *Wikipedia* can be an excellent resource for *pre-*search.

Now – let us be clear – we do not recommend that our students use *Wikipedia* as an academic source, and we do not allow them to quote or reference from it; there are far better textbooks, monographs, journals and academic encyclopaedias from which they should be working and quoting. However, sometimes we are all inevitably asked to research areas that are totally new to us, or for which we might not know where to find the best resources. In such instances, accessing *Wikipedia* provides a route into *pre*search – where you can read articles on subjects to introduce you to a topic so that you can then yourself access the primary and secondary sources that they cite. In so doing, you are not using *Wikipedia* itself as the source, but as a conduit to find original sources, which you can then use as a springboard to locate mainstream scholarship. Of course, as a part of this exercise you can yourself judge the quality of the original *Wikipedia* article, and this will be a useful skill to learn, as you weigh different academic writing and viewpoints against each other in the course of your studies.

And finally, a quick word on the 'problem' of *Wikipedia*'s volunteer editors, researchers and contributors. It is not alone in such a methodology.

In 1857 something called the *Reading Programme* was instituted to facilitate a group of volunteers to collate English words and to categorise their usage. The system for the volunteers working together was haphazard, based on a paper filing system, and often led to lost documentation and multiple errors in the data that was subsequently published. Undeterred, the volunteers pressed on with their knowledge accumulation project and, in 1879, *An Appeal to the English-speaking and English-reading Public* was launched to gather more accurate information on the everyday usage of words. Over 1,300 further volunteers replied from across the UK and the USA, providing over 1 million quotations and word usages. In 1928 the first full accumulation of an alphabetical list of their findings was published in the first edition of the *Oxford English Dictionary* – now the most authoritative guide to the English language for the world's 1.2 billion English speakers.

Engaging with 'Living Religion' online (or 'fieldwork without the field')

When we move from Helland's notion of 'religion online' to 'online religion' (even if we critique such categories), we move towards what Stout has called "full-experience occasions" rather than simple "social network occasions" (Stout, 2012, 79–80). In short, we move towards the actual practice and performance of religion in a networked and virtual world. In so doing, we must remember that "the Internet is not a monolithic or placeless 'cyberspace'; rather, it is numerous new technologies, used by diverse people, in diverse real-world locations" (Miller and Slater, 2000, 1). As such, there are many ways in which religious practices are undertaken and performed 'without a field', and below we discuss a few of these and reflect upon how neophyte researchers may engage with them in their studies.

One important development when engaging with fieldwork without a field is the practice of virtual pilgrimages and cyberpilgrimages, which are now common in many traditions and communities. To begin with it is necessary to explain the differences between virtual pilgrimages and cyberpilgrimages, and for this Hill-Smith (2011) has written a particularly helpful article which is very accessible and understandable for neophyte researchers. In short, "the term 'virtual pilgrimage' incorporates non-computer-based pilgrimage forms such as storytelling or physically enacting pilgrimage rituals from afar", whereas cyberpilgrimage is specifically used for "pilgrimages performed online" (2011, 236). One example of a virtual pilgrimage is one run by Our Lady of Lourdes Hospitality North American Volunteers, which offers North American Catholics who are unable to travel to France a pilgrimage experience which includes multimedia presentations of the sights of Lourdes, music of a similar type played at Lourdes, physical contact with a piece of the Grotto rock, and the chance to wash in water brought over from Lourdes especially for this purpose. In so doing, the organisation provides a service which they believe is "like an actual pilgrimage to Lourdes ... our Virtual Pilgrimage is a holy encounter with God under the watchful care of Our Lady" (Lourdes Volunteers, 2014).

Two recent examples of cyberpilgrimage, which also enable participants to perform pilgrimage without physical relocation, but with the specific use of Internet technologies, are the UK-based 2009 Christian Aid-sponsored Israel-Palestine pilgrimage, and the USA-based 2011 Cyber Pilgrimage to Santiago by congregants from the First United Methodist Church of Seattle. Each of these initiatives facilitated individual and communal religious participation in prayer, ritual, visual imagery, sound, cultural context and, in the case of the Seattle pilgrimage, very real physical engagement, as the participants' footsteps in the Greater Seattle area were recorded and mapped across the cyber-route to Santiago. Of course, such activities raise a myriad of questions – can a cyber-pilgrimage replace a traditional pilgrimage? Is a traditional pilgrimage some-how more 'authentic'? One scholar who suggests that virtual/cyberpilgrimage creates problems of authenticity argues that virtual pilgrimage moves the focus of the pilgrimage from 'body and place' to the 'mind in space' (MacMillan, 2011, 1).

However, as Hill-Smith notes:

> it is not uncommon for cyberpilgrimage sites to urge visitors to undertake ritual-reflecting activities at home, such as removing shoes, lighting candles or walking in nature. This incitement to *physicalisation* is clearly intended to mitigate, at least somewhat, this disembodiment, by generating a real-life physical relationship to activities being undertaken virtually.
>
> (Hill-Smith, 2011, 241)

This is a crucial point, and one we agree with, and indeed would take further. If we are to understand religion as an everyday performative act, we must realise that we are corporeal all the time – we do not go outside our bodies to engage in online pilgrimages or rituals, and we are still occupying a performative space; it is simply that this space has changed from physical transportation to a networked transformation of meaningful networked and relational religious performance.

One particularly interesting area – a full study of which would be a book of its own – is the use of avatars or online personas in communities and realms beyond the meat world. Popularised by the website Second Life (Barrett, 2010), religious communities which entirely exist in cyberspace critique and challenge many accepted understandings of what religion is and what religious people do. One early example of this was the Church of Fools, which was established in 2004 and supported by the Methodist Church of England. The initiative was an attempt to create a "dedicated church environment in shockwave rather than adding something to an existing online world" in which people could create avatars who had a "variety of hair and skin colours and dressed in different clothes styles" (Jenkins, 2008, 100–104). Individual congregants of the Church of Fools, which operated standard Sunday morning services, were able to control their avatars, including the performance of bending, praying, signing the cross and raising the arms in celebration. The Church of Fools ran as a three-month experiment, but paved the way for subsequent online churches and ritual activity within a cyber realm (Gelfgren, 2010).

Of particular interest is how, in the Christian context currently being discussed, the sacrament of the Eucharist relates to conceptions of 'authority' and 'authenticity'. Quite simply, is it possible for a Eucharist to be conducted virtually? Of course, there will be theological debate over this, but even from a study of religion approach, this question is interesting as it explores issues about embodiment and communality across a cyber-gap between the online community and individual practitioners at home (or on the bus, or wherever they may be accessing the Web nowadays).

Helland has previously asked: "What action or online activity can be considered a genuine religious action? How is it possible to determine if the people practicing forms of online religion are in fact conducting actual religious activities and having genuine religious experiences?" (2005, 6). We would argue that it is problematic to use the phrase 'genuine religious experiences' which betrays an essentialism about 'what religion is'. If religion is changing, and our under-standing of religion as an everyday performative act is changing, then why should online religious experiences not be authentic? As Hill-Smith has noted, with regard to the performance of sung ritual:

> People singing along at home as a website transmits live hymn music *are* still singing along, but they are not *among* the physical throng of singers – their singing is *co-located*, both with the church-based congregation and with other worshippers singing along in their homes. Their experience is not *unreal* just because their bodies are in their homes and not in the church.
>
> (Hill-Smith, 2011, 241–42)

Similarly, online prayer groups and scriptural reading groups now pro-liferate, and Helland asks "is reading scripture from a website an enactment of an online religious practice?" (Helland, 2005, 5) One answer to this is – yes – reading online is different to reading the same text in a book. The online text is likely to be hyperlinked and offers a variety of experiences; whilst sitting with a biblical concordance allows you to look at parallel texts, translations and commentaries on select New Testament passages for example, using an online hyperlinked text allows you to view film and television enactments of the pas-sages, watch lectures delivered on the teachings found in the text, locate news stories about different communities' interpretations of the text which may affect contemporary social issues, navigate discussion forums on the passage, and contextualise the chosen writing with teachings, commentaries and social actions of mainstream and minority churches.

Finally in this short section of examples of religious performance in cyber or virtual realities, it is interesting to note the proliferation of religion online linked with new or emergent religious traditions. Carole M. Cusack (2010) has previously explored the rise of Matrixism, Jediism and the Church of the Flying Spaghetti Monster, each of which has created distinct and coherent online communities in a phenomenon linked to Campbell's (2011) conception of 'networked religion', and further highlights the networked reality of our permeable and liminal online/offline contemporary lived reality. Jediism in particular is a helpful example for our current discussion on the conflation of online and offline media and everyday religious lives, as it was originally conceptualised around a product of old media (film), developed within the contextualisation of wider cultural capital on religion (particularly the Chinese concept of a life force, or Chi) and is popularly performed through online media such as chatrooms and web forums, in addition to the provision of online training courses and online scripture readings. This provision of online training is also prevalent in New Age spiritualities (see the section on Glastonbury in chapter 3); and services such as correspondence courses in Karmic Astrology and Tarot readings by Skype are now increasingly common, along with interactive TV channels and websites offering psychic mediumship and one-to-one readings without the person being present in a room with the practitioner.

Of course, such online training courses and distance-delivered religious services are not just ways to facilitate lived religious experiences, but are also very strong examples of the projection of religious identities by practitioners, in a form of represented religion we have discussed previously. To finish this section, we will look at another example of how represented religion using visual media can facilitate everyday lived performative religious practices, which can in turn be studied by neophyte researchers.

Film as *darshan* – everyday media and everyday religion

Describing a generation before DVDs and the Internet, Marie Gillespie has written a fascinating account of the lived experience of a British Hindu family, with particular focus upon their interaction with film and TV. Below is an excerpt from her study, which focuses on the mother of the family:

> The mother is the keenest viewer of religious videos and will stay up, accompanied by her children, until the early hours of the morning watching them. There is a tone of guilty pleasure in her voice when she admits to having hired five videos at the weekend and watched them all … .
>
> […]
>
> For her, religious films provide comfort and solace from life's everyday anxieties. When she or a member of her family is ill or when she is worried, she will view them compulsively. But they also function as

part of her and her family's religious practice itself. Such viewing is a form of religious ritual. Incense is lit at the start of the film and a salutation to God is made. Often a puja will be performed before or during viewing. Once a 'god' film is put on, it must be viewed until the end. No food is allowed to be eaten whilst viewing, except prasad (or holy food) and if, for example, Krishna appears on screen, the mother encourages her children to sit upright with toes pointing towards the screen and to join hands, as in acts of worship at the temple.

In fact, the viewing of 'god films' is regarded, by the mother especially, as an act of pleasurable devotion in itself. The appearance on screen of favourite gods such as Krishna, in close-up, gazing direct to camera, with eyes seemingly penetrating the viewer's inner core, is for them like a divine apparition in itself. It is as if the gods speak directly to the viewer. Such viewing is considered to 'bring the gods into you' and if, after watching, 'you can bring the gods into your dreams', then it is considered to be a divine visitation whereby blessings are bestowed and favours may be requested.

(Gillespie, 1993, 51, 54)

We highlight the case study of everyday lived religious performance in the textbox above, even if it is from a previous generation of technology, because the observation and engagement with everyday details that Gillespie undertook for her study serves as a useful example as to how we should approach visual media and religious practice. Whilst there is much good material available which looks at religious motifs in films, or engages with critical ways to analyse narrative, imagery and metaphor in films about religion (see, for example, Mitchell and Plate, 2007; Wright, 2007), there is little material focused on how these films influence and stimulate everyday lived religion. Of course, there are further examples of this that could be explored. Muslim TV channels and streaming video websites broadcast the call to prayer, sermons and live footage of pilgrims on hajj; and likewise a proliferation of Sikh television channels and websites broadcast live from the Punjab each morning and evening. Similarly, the Pope's Christmas and Easter message '*Urbi et Orbi*' is simulcast live on TV and the Web where Christians are encouraged to join in prayer with a leader and crowd that may be thousands of miles from them. Each of these examples shows simple ways in which engagement with visual media can impact upon performative everyday religious rites or actions, without the necessity of being in the physical places occupied by those presenting the message, or entreating a sense of community for devotees.

Ethical issues

Participating in fieldwork without the field may be a relatively new approach to studying religious communities, but we would do well to remember that many of the ethical issues surrounding traditional fieldwork also apply to this new methodology. Rather than repeat what has been written before, we recommend that you look at the relevant section of chapter 5, and apply this advice to any work you undertake using virtual or cyber technologies; but in the following few paragraphs, we highlight some of the particular ethical issues which may arise from engaging with living religion in online spaces.

The first issue to highlight is that there is, of course, a 'Dark Side' of the Web. Although the Internet is arguably the single greatest advance in technology for education since the invention of the printing press, like all advances it creates new problems. One such problem is how to engage with controversial subjects. Access to the Web forces individual users to make choices about what they consider to be acceptable areas of research. Of course, many such choices are already controlled, or constrained, by the laws of your country (and also by firewall and security settings on university computer networks), but there are a myriad of grey areas between the black and white of simple legality or university regulations. Whilst, for example, hard-core pornography may be illegal in your country, or blocked by your university's network, many religious groups utilise forms of sexual or embodied ritual as a part of their worldview. Some groups even utilise very public forms of sexualised or naked protest to argue against what they perceive to be social injustices (Gregg, 2014b).

Sites selling or providing information on illegal drugs are also best avoided, but again in many cultures throughout history, and certainly in many contemporary shamanistic or shaman-related traditions, the use of hallucinogenic substances is essential for communication with 'other worlds' or non-human persons such as animals, ancestors or spirits. Further examples of complex areas include religious groups or individuals with extremist or exclusivist views. High-profile examples in Europe include the mass-murderer Anders Brevik and the rise of far-right nationalist organisations in the European parliament elections. Similarly, America has organisations such as the Westboro Baptist Church and Australia has the Exclusive Brethren (Doherty, 2013), each of which has caused high-profile media controversies in recent years. Finally, moral campaigners with religious worldviews will also utilise images that many people may find disturbing – from anti-abortion campaigners displaying photographs of aborted foetuses to anti-death penalty campaigners showing photographs of public hangings.

Responding to such controversial topics of study, and the online media which are relevant to them, is not easy; but when considering the ethical implications of such studies, you should always seek advice from your tutor, and ensure that any research topic will not counter any policy of your institution. One sensible 'middle way' that we have encountered is for students to negotiate with their tutor and computer services administrator the use of a non-networked computer when they need to visit websites that may cause controversy – for example the Westboro Baptist Church's 'God Hates Fags' or 'Priests Rape Boys' protest websites. In this way, web searches that would otherwise create problems are logged and accountable as a part of your research, but are not accessed in public areas and do not cause subsequent problems for you as a student at your institution.

Ethical issues are not just about the legality or morality of controversial subjects and their online presence, however, but are also raised by the problem of the sheer quantity of information and our seemingly 'access-all-areas' culture where all information is shared through social media within moments, and replicated (mirrored) on websites or social media accounts worldwide at enormous speed. Such a scenario means that much data online may not be illegal, but may raise questions as to whether or not the religious communities in question approve of the information that is 'out there' in the public domain, and which we as scholars can access. In short, the Internet allows us to walk where we may be barred, to read what may be considered secret, and to see what (in the view of the religion) should only be seen by select individuals or communities of devotees. Examples of this include the publishing of Free-masonry rites, traditionally held as appropriately shared only between initiated members, and mobile phone video footage of the inside of the Kaaba at Mecca, which is traditionally only viewable by special guests (and of course Mecca itself is only accessible for Muslims).

Perhaps, though, one of the most interesting ethical quandaries facing researchers is when confidential documents are leaked online. This is an issue that Mikael Rothstein has helpfully written about regarding the leaking online of confidential scriptures of the Church of Scientology. This is a complex issue, with a history covering several decades and multiple court cases, but Rothstein's helpful conclusion is that:

> with the breakthrough of the Internet an entirely new situation has been created. The texts are now, to a large extent, made available on many different home pages, and the ethical considerations on the part of the scholars should change accordingly. Pretending the texts are *not* there is ridiculous, and acting as if anyone with potential interest in the subject is unaware of this material equally meaningless. The texts are there, almost waiting for scholarly inspection and analysis.
>
> (2009, 368)

It is this last point which is relevant to the proliferation of religious information (some of it esoteric) which is online. Quite simply, just because something is available does not mean that you have carte blanche. As Rothstein points out, to pretend such information is not available makes no sense, but equally, the ethical consideration of the scholar must remain a priority in *how we approach and treat such information* so as to minimise the risk of discomfort or harm to the members of religious communities with which we are working.

Of course, how we treat people, as well as the texts which may impact emotionally upon religious people, should also be considered in a subtly differ-ent way when we conduct our research online rather than in muddy fields. One such issue is the concept of covert and overt research. Covert research means to conduct research when your informants and participants do not know that you are studying them, and in traditional fieldwork, this is frowned upon – indeed such a methodology "would make most modern University ethics committees run screaming to the hills" (Gregg, 2014a, 26). However, whilst it may be clear that to engage with, say, a local Hindu community as a covert researcher when visiting their ashram is clearly unacceptable, what if you were contacting Hindus in an Internet chatroom, or through a social media site? Often people use usernames that do not instantly suggest they are scholars performing research. If, therefore, a researcher reads postings in chatrooms or web forums, is it meaningful to understand this as a form of covert research? How does one perform fieldwork when there is no physical 'field'? Even if you 'out' your Second Life avatar as a researcher, there is a spatial and experiential distance created which radically alters how a generation of scholars brought up on physical engagement, embodied learning and participant observation relate to (and with) their subjects (2014a, 28).

Indeed, this spatial and experiential distance between researchers and the community that they are researching can create different responses and attitudes. Quite simply, many people behave differently online than they do in offline environments. Acting in virtual realms can create an epistemic distance between individuals and their subject, or fellow Internet users, which may mean that people act in ways that they couldn't or wouldn't do in their offline everyday life. Issues such as Internet 'trolling', a form of online bullying, sit at one end of this behaviour spectrum, but at the other end, there are multiple examples of individuals being radicalised through extremist websites, as they access communities and people they would not necessarily come into contact with in their offline communities (Stevens and Neumann, 2009). Of course, we are not suggesting that any conscientious scholar of religion, even a neophyte researcher, would consciously choose to act in such ways, but even in less extreme encounters we must always reflect upon our choice of words, tone of language, line of questioning and empathy with our informants, which can be particularly challenging if the views of our research communities clash with our own values and ethics. As with offline research, the key to an ethical approach to online research is to consistently seek to reduce discomfort or harm to our participants and partners, to critically reflect upon our own conduct and approach to the project, and to empathise using *verstehen* so as to contextualise our findings appropriately.

Chapter summary

This chapter has demonstrated that networked, online, virtual and cyber media help us to understand religion as an 'everyday' activity in the modern world – an activity which critiques notions of sacred and profane, religious action and everyday action. In the same way, we need to look beyond simple binaries of online and offline living, and the distinctions between online religion and offline religion. In a networked world with always-on broadband, 4G and public Wi-Fi, where we are more likely to read newspapers on tablets or phones than on stretched-thin pulped tree products, it no longer makes sense to differentiate between types of religion as online or offline, but instead to seek to explore the relational continuum between the ways in which people use a variety of technologies to perform their everyday religious lives.

Attending a physical church Eucharist requires the technologies of architecture, engineering, artistry, fermentation (for Communion wine), fashion (for priestly garments) and usually the technology of the internal combustion engine to ferry congregants to such places. The use of new technology, which has always been a dynamic of human existence and religious performance, simply asks new questions as to *how* people engage in everyday religious activities. This may challenge accepted notions of embodiment or community, but in so doing, the use of new media in relation to religion reminds us that "for those people who practice online religion, the Internet is not some place 'other' but recognized as a part of their everyday life and they are merely extending their religious meaning and activity into this environment" (Helland, 2005, 12). It seems highly likely that a large part of the future performance of everyday living religion will be facilitated through the Internet and our increasingly networked society.

Further reading

Helland, C. (2005) 'Online Religion as Lived Religion: Methodological Issues in the Study of Religious Participation on the Internet' in *Heidelberg Journal of Religions on the Internet*, 1(1) 1–16.
Stout, D.A. (2012) *Media and Religion: Foundations of an Emerging Field*, New York: Routledge.

Questions for consideration

1 To what extent can religious ritual online be 'authentic'? Argue both for and against the legitimacy and meaning of such acts, giving specific examples in your argument.
2 What are the ethical considerations you must reflect upon when conducting research in chatrooms and via email?
3 How can you best be sure that information you find online is academically robust and useful? List five criteria you could check such information against.
4 Discuss the ways in which you can effectively observe or participate in online religious communities. Critique how this may be different from your engagement with 'real-world' communities and practices.

Bibliography

This list includes all the texts referred to in the chapter and other recommended reading. All websites accessed on 31.10.14.

Barrett, J. 2010, 'Religion in New Places: Rhetoric of the Holy in the Online Virtual Environment of Second Life' in Changing Societies – Values, Religions and Education – Working Papers in Teacher Education No. 7, 19–23.

Campbell, H.A. (ed.) 2013, *Digital Religion: Understanding Religious Practice in New Media Worlds*, Abingdon: Routledge.

——2011, 'Understanding the Relationship between Religion Online and Offline in a Networked Society' in *Journal of the American Academy of Religion*, 80(1), 64–93.

Cusack, C.M. 2010, *Invented Religions: Imagination, Fiction and Faith*, Farnham, Surrey: Ashgate.

Doherty, B. 2013, 'The "Brethren Cult Controversy": Dissecting a Contemporary Australian "Social Problem"' in *Alternative Spirituality and Religion Review*, 4(1), 25–48.

Gelfgren, S. 2010, 'Virtual Churches: Transforming Religious Values and Practices' in Changing Societies – Values, Religions and Education – Working Papers in Teacher Education No. 7, 43–50.

Gillespie, M. 1993, 'The *Mahabharata*: From Sanskrit to Sacred Soap. A case study of the reception of two contemporary televisual versions' in Buckingham, D. (ed.) *Reading Audiences: Young People and the Media*, Manchester: Manchester University Press, 48–73.

Gregg, S.E. 2014a, 'Fieldwork' in Chryssides, G.D. and Zeller, B.E. (eds) *The Bloomsbury Companion to New Religious Movements*, London: Bloomsbury, 25–28.

——2014b, '"Queer Jesus, Straight Angels": Complicating "Religion" and "Sexuality" in the International Raelian Movement' in *Sexualities*, 17(5–6), 565–82.

Hadden, J.K. and Cowan, D.E. 2000, 'The Promised Land or Electronic Chaos? Toward Understanding Religion on the Internet' in Hadden, J.K. and Cowan, D.E. (eds) *Religion on the Internet: Research Prospects and Promises* (Religion and Social Order 8), London: JAI Press/Elsevier Science, 3–24.

Helland, C. 2005, 'Online Religion as Lived Religion: Methodological Issues in the Study of Religious Participation on the Internet' in *Heidelberg Journal of Religions on the Internet*, 1(1), 1–16.

——2000, 'Religion Online/Online Religion and Virtual Communitas' in Hadden, J.K. and Cowan, D.E. (eds) *Religion on the Internet: Research Prospects and Promises* (Religion and Social Order 8), London: JAI Press/Elsevier Science, 205–24.

Hill-Smith, C. 2011, 'Cyberpilgrimage: The (Virtual) Reality of Online Pilgrimage Experience' in *Religion Compass* 5(6), 236–46.

Jenkins, S. 2008, 'Rituals and Pixels: Experiments in Online Church' in *Heidelberg Journal of Religions on the Internet*, 3(1), 95–115.

Lourdes Volunteers, 2014, accessed online at www.lourdesvolunteers.org/virtual_pilgrimage/arrange.html

MacMillan, S. 2011, 'The Virtual Pilgrimage: The Disappearing Body from Place to Space' in *Journal of Religion and Society*, Vol. 13.

Miller, D. and Slater, D. 2000, *The Internet: An Ethnographic Approach*, Oxford: Berg.

Mitchell, J. and Plate, S.B. (eds) 2007, *The Religion and Film Reader*, London: Routledge.

Ramadan, T. 2007, 'Islam is a European Religion' *Salzburg Global Seminar*, accessed online at www.youtube.com/watch?v=lxjL3CIs0xw#t = 115

Rothstein, M. 2009, '"His Name Was Xenu, He Used Renegades ... ": Aspects of Scientology's Founding Myth' in Lewis, J. (ed.) *Scientology*, Oxford: Oxford University Press, 365–88.

Stevens, T. and Neumann, P.R. 2009, *Countering Online Radicalisation: A Strategy for Action*, London: International Centre for the Study of Radicalisation and Political

Violence. Accessible at http://icsr.info/wp-content/uploads/2012/10/1236768491ICSR OnlineRadicalisationReport.pdf

Stothart, C. 2007, 'Web Threatens Learning Ethos' in *Times Higher Education* 22 June. Accessed online at www.timeshighereducation.co.uk/209408.article

Stout, D.A. 2012, *Media and Religion: Foundations of an Emerging Field*, New York: Routledge.

Wright, M. 2007, *Religion and Film: An Introduction*, London: I.B. Taurus.

Young, G. 2004, 'Reading and Praying Online: The Continuity of Religion Online and Online Religion in Internet Christianity' in Dawson, L.L. and Cowan, D.E. (eds) *Religion Online: Finding Faith on the Internet*, New York: Routledge, 93–106.

Websites

This annotated list includes all the online sources we have referred to in the chapter as well as some recommended sites. We have given the URLs (web addresses) accessed on 31.10.14 but these do change so for ease of use we have listed them by the name of the organisation in alphabetical order.

Alpha Church – an example of cyber Eucharist – www.alphachurch.org/holycomm.htm

Church of Jediism – www.churchofjediism.org.uk/index1.html

Church of Scientology – www.scientology.org/ and www.scientologynews.org/

First United Methodist Church of Seattle – an example of cyberpilgrimage – http://cyberpilgrims.blogspot.co.uk/

Jehovah's Witnesses – www.jw.org/en/

The Methodist Church in Britain – an example of an online scripture-reading course – www.methodist.org.uk/prayer-and-worship/a-word-in-time

Our Lady of Lourdes Hospitality – an example of virtual pilgrimage – www.lourdesvolunteers.org/virtual_pilgrimage/arrange.html

The Prayer Group – an example of an international prayer community – www.theprayergroup.org/

Second Life – http://secondlife.com/

Sunflower Healing – an example of cyber-delivered religious services – www.sunflowerhealing.co.uk/

The Vatican – http://w2.vatican.va/content/vatican/en.html

Westboro Baptist Church – www.godhatesfags.com

7 Deepening and widening engagement with Living Religion

Introduction

So far this book has offered wide-ranging material to support neophyte researchers, probably undergraduates, exploring religion outside the lecture theatre. In this final chapter we are widening considerably the groups of people who we hope might be interested in engaging with living religion and the opportunities to explore living religion in more depth than is usually possible during an undergraduate degree. We also address university lecturers who are teaching undergraduate courses in the study of religion to offer some advice about how best to manage student learning in the field.

Postgraduate research

Postgraduate researchers at masters and doctoral level have the opportunity for much more extended, in-depth study, sometimes abroad, collecting data that will be analysed for a thesis. The principles, ideas, examples and suggestions in chapter 5 about independent research would still be a good starting point for postgraduate students. However, at this level it becomes so much more important that appropriate methodologies are chosen to produce the kind of data that will help to address the chosen research questions. Setting out the rationale for the details of the approaches used in the field becomes critical, and a dissertation may pass or fail as a result of the quality of what is often referred to as the 'methods chapter'. The earlier chapters of this book will help a postgraduate researcher to realise the range of possibilities that there are for engaging with living religion and also the need not to limit ideas of what counts as 'religion'.

Postgraduate research will engage with theory much more extensively than undergraduate work and connect at depth with other scholarly work. The suggestions for further reading below are classic and recent works which are particularly challenging and stimulating. Students will also be working to develop *new* knowledge and understanding of some aspect of religion, so will need to think very creatively about the topic. Fieldwork enables a postgraduate student to generate distinctive data whether the work is done near to home, in a distant country or somewhere in-between. Particularly in the early stages of planning it is really useful to read about the exploration of living religion that other people have already done. There is a very useful short podcast about PhD and post-doctoral fieldwork research by Bettina Schmidt as part of *The Religious Studies Project*. The other website that will be particularly useful is *Research Methods for the Study of Religion*. See the list of websites at the end of the chapter for full details.

Academic conferences

One important approach at postgraduate level is participation in academic conferences. This will involve you in listening to papers by scholars and other postgraduate students. Often these are works in progress, and feedback and discussion during the conference enable authors to refine and develop their work. As you progress in your research you will write and deliver papers. If you want to see what conference papers in the study of religion look like once they are developed as articles we recommend *DISKUS*. This is an online, peer-reviewed journal and we have suggested a paper from a recent conference in the further reading section in chapter 1. Now you might like to look at all the volumes to see the range of work, methodologies, theoretical discussions and ways of writing. Perhaps start with Volume 10 (2009). The papers in this volume show the importance of engaging with living religion for breaking new ground in the study of religion – see websites at the end of the chapter. Another key publication is the journal *Fieldwork in Religion* published by Equinox.

Further reading

The following are scholarly texts that we think will be particularly interesting to postgraduate students:

Bowman, M. 2012, *Vernacular Religion in Everyday Life: Expressions of Belief*, Durham: Acumen Publishing Ltd.

Day, A., Vincett, G. and Cotter, C.R. (eds) 2013, *Social Identities between the Sacred and the Secular*, Farnham, Surrey: Ashgate.

Geertz, C. 1973, *The Interpretation of Cultures*, New York: Basic Books.

Hervieu-Leger, D. 2000 [trans. Simon Lee], *Religion as a Chain of Memory*, Cambridge: Polity Press.

Ingold, T. 2011, *Being Alive: Essays on Movement, Knowledge and Description*, London: Routledge.

Knott, K. and McLaughlin, S. (eds) 2010, *Diasporas: Concepts, Intersections, Identities*, London: Zed Books Ltd.

Orsi, R.A. (ed.) 2012, *The Cambridge Companion to Religious Studies*, Cambridge: Cambridge University Press.

Stringer, M.D. 2011, *Contemporary Western Ethnography and the Definition of Religion*, London: Continuum.
Sutcliffe, S.J. and Gilhus, I.S. (eds) 2013, *New Age Spirituality: Rethinking Religion*, Durham: Acumen.

Teachers and trainee teachers

Engaging with living religion is important for teachers and educators in two ways. Firstly, as we have shown in this book, it is one of the best ways in which teachers and trainee teachers can learn about religion. Visiting places of worship and other sites of religion makes it easy to get really good photos, artefacts and other materials all of which can be used in the classroom. How much better for teachers to use real resources which they can contextualise in different ways and to be able to refer to their own experiences. This begins to focus on pedagogical approaches which are appropriate to the religious material being studied and to ways of enabling students to engage. For trainee teachers their school experience is also a kind of fieldwork which can be used to explore alternative pedagogies.

Just as we have learned so much from our fieldwork and so wanted to write this book to encourage other people to get the most out of doing this themselves, so teachers who are excited by their experiential learning will want to take this engagement with living religions into their classrooms. Many religious places will be delighted to welcome school groups and some have very well-organised programmes for pupils of different ages. It is also worth inviting religious people into the classroom as visitors. Engaging with living religion in these ways breaks down some of the limited factual approaches of an outdated World Religions paradigm, providing opportunities for students to engage with particular religious people and practice, with their own stories, beliefs and values. Various approaches to religious education over the years have encouraged teachers to take their students into the field, and the work of Robert Jackson has been especially helpful in bringing the results of ethnographic research into the classroom.

Warwick Religions and Education Research Unit

RE in state-funded schools in England and Wales should enable students to learn *about* religion and also to, reflectively, learn *from* religion. In the Warwick projects led by Bob Jackson and Eleanor Nesbitt, the interpretive approach has three elements: representation, interpretation and reflexivity. From early on they have taken the approach that religions are diverse, and that the best way to approach 'real' religion is through the lives of religious people. A number of excellent research projects have explored, in the field, the experiences of children and young people being brought up within a particular religious tradition. This ethnographic material is then used to develop classroom resources for religious education. Jackson has also linked this approach with ideas about dialogue – see Jackson (2012) and the section on interfaith dialogue below. The website details for the site are given below and see also Miller et al. (2013).

Inspired by the ethnographic work at Warwick, *Living Faiths* is a recently published series (Oxford University Press) for secondary schools which uses case studies, shown through film and print, of young people and their families in the UK who describe how their faith affects the way they live and the moral and ethical decisions they make. The emphasis is on the personal significance of religious faith, exploring the question: What does it *mean* to be a Buddhist, Christian, Hindu, Jew, Muslim or Sikh?

Pastoral workers

There are a number of professions where it is increasingly important that people understand the complex religious identities and practices of the individuals and groups with whom they work. As we have discussed throughout this book, understanding the religious realities of local and wider society develops best when people actually engage with living religion, and we would hope that reading this book will encourage those who haven't already done so to explore this multireligious world. In this section we highlight some of the particular possibilities for those working in chaplaincy, youth work and other forms of pastoral ministry.

In some countries there are chaplains working in hospitals, hospices and prisons as well as airports, schools and the armed forces. In most cases these chaplains are, themselves, members of a particular religious tradition, although they are often supporting people of other faiths and none. Sometimes chaplains are part of a multi-faith team. As chaplains develop their understanding of the diversity of religious faith and practice, they become resources for other staff working within their institutions. Some of the issues that will arise concern religious practices around food, attitudes and practices concerning the body, illness, death and dying, and issues of identity. These are not topics that are particularly addressed in the earlier chapters of this book, but the many examples of living religion that we have referred to, and the engagement with religious people that we are encouraging, will help provide a much more nuanced approach.

Chaplains who develop their understanding in these issues will be able to contribute in significant ways to the wider planning and organisation of their work places. For example, it is becoming a serious concern, at least in the UK, that the percentage of Muslim prisoners far exceeds the percentage of Muslims in the country at large. Why are Muslims so over represented amongst prisoners? How can these prisoners best be supported whilst they are in prison? How can they best be helped not to reoffend? Engagement with diverse Muslim groups in the area, with the lived religion of these prisoners, may help significantly in finding answers to these questions.

How about youth workers? When some Roman Catholic young people working in retreat centres in the UK met with Jewish and Muslim youth workers in Central London, it challenged their thinking in several ways. They were surprised to find that many of the issues they were grappling with were shared across the religions. The common factors enabled them to share experiences and ideas at quite a deep level and also made them aware of the diversity within both Judaism and Islam. This was their first opportunity to meet and talk at length with Jews and Muslims, and it impacted on both their understanding of two religions in Britain and their reflections on their own faith and practice. This very particular form of fieldwork was, in some ways, a form of interreligious dialogue and further discussion of that is the next topic.

Interfaith practice

In many parts of the world, dialogue between religions has developed significantly in recent years. The attitudes to 'other' religions within any particular tradition is, of course, an interesting topic of study in its own right and would be something worth asking about on any visit. Sometimes dialogue is on an international scale with leaders of religions meeting together, being photographed together, to pray for peace or to advance some other cooperation. There are also national and international dialogue conferences that some undergraduate and graduate students could be encouraged to attend.

This is not the place to go into detail about theories of interfaith dialogue; but in many ways what we have been arguing for in this book, as part of the study of religion, has some of the characteristics of dialogue. Although not everyone is religious, we all have beliefs and values and, on some occasions in the field, we may engage in dialogue with the people we meet. In the process we will learn more about them and about ourselves because that is what happens in dialogue. We can also deliberately seek out alternative, less-often-heard voices to dialogue with – see Fry et al. (2005).

There are also local dialogue groups with people from different religious traditions, which some students may be interested in getting actively involved in. Sometimes there are organised visits to the places of worship of the members of the group, occasionally taking the form of a day's pilgrimage visiting several different places. On an occasion like this there are plenty of opportunities for informal conversation with members of various traditions. A journey like this prioritises the local and so sometimes gives attention to voices that might not normally be heard. Organisations such as Cambridge University's Inter-Faith Programme provide excellent resources for groups, especially those developing shared textual reading. Interesting programmes and resources are also available from the Runnymede Trust, and St Ethelburga's Centre for Reconciliation and Peace. This centre is housed in a church in East London which was rebuilt after being bombed by the IRA, and there is also a tent for meetings, woven in Saudi Arabia and circular in shape. See the end of the chapter for the website details.

University faculty

This final section is addressed to staff who are teaching courses in the study of religion, using fieldwork and this book with their students. Our aim is to discuss a number of ideas which have informed the thinking behind what we have written and issues which, from our experience and that of other colleagues with whom we have discussed fieldwork, impact on the success or otherwise of such learning. We undertook a Higher Education Academy funded research project in the UK, which enabled us to consult a large number of staff engaged in fieldwork with students. We are very grateful for their support and encouragement, for sharing with us their experiences and for helping us to develop our thinking. We have named these people in the acknowledgements at the beginning of the book.

This book is written from a religious studies viewpoint, but we hope will be helpful and timely for students who approach the study of religion through a variety of learning methods – sociology, anthropology and theology in particular. Theology maintains an important role in how religion is studied within many universities and, as lecturers, we are both sensitive to the challenges that are faced when using categories or terms across nations. Within the UK, religious studies/study of religion has often become a counter narrative to theology, with its approaches to religion based on social scientific methodologies, although there are many departments within the UK which still teach theology and religious studies degree programmes as interrelated disciplines and several well-respected departments are still labelled 'divinity' departments due to historic church roots. In the Research Excellence Framework exercise, which judges the quality of academics' research publications, the subjects are held together in the same inspection panel, together with biblical studies.

Within the US, especially when it comes to the descriptions of faculty roles, religious studies is often used to describe subjects that in other countries, such as the UK, Australia and New Zealand, would be considered theology. US institutions will often refer to religious studies when talking of areas such as Catholic catechism or biblical studies, and again this is often linked with academic programmes that are run from institutions with church foundations. Of course, we are not here going to argue that just one of these approaches to the study of religion is correct, or enter a long debate about the relationship between theology and religious studies, but wish to highlight the simple fact that the approach that is taken by lecturers and tutors will radically affect the learning outcomes and experiences for the students.

Perhaps even more relevant to a discussion of student fieldwork is that, in mixed groups of students who may be taking courses on religion within degree programmes as wide as theology, religious studies, education, social policy, anthropology, history and many others, there will be a myriad of expectations and approaches which both tutors and students need to negotiate. Indeed, when we have taken students into the field, it has often been mixed groups of theology and religious studies students, and this will be the experience of many tutors and students, so it is important to address the practicalities, rather than just the methodological aspects, of this issue. Throughout the book, therefore, we have talked about the differing approaches and experiences of these diverse students, and here suggest ways in which tutors can manage these experiences, but first we will specifically address one or two recent developments in theological approaches to fieldwork.

There is increasing interest amongst Christian theologians about engaging with living religion within a theological framework. A very interesting book by Sarah Coakley brings together fieldwork research in two different church groups in England with theological exploration of the doctrine of the Trinity, sexuality and spirituality (2013). Other recent work brings together theological discourse about church and social science discourse about culture – see, for example, the series *Studies in Ecclesiology and Ethnography* (Scharen, 2012; Ward, 2012). This is a way of approaching theological understanding by paying careful attention to what people are actually doing – the living religion of practice in specific local contexts. For example, Scharen and Vigen (2011) argue that Christian ethics needs to be developed in conversation with the living presence of those people whom it concerns and not in some isolated academic office. They argue that this is a method that is very appropriate for Christians whose belief in the incarnation means that reality is expressed in concrete singularity.

The book *Practical Theology and Qualitative Research* (Swinton and Mowat, 2011) explores how the latest thinking in practical (or what is sometimes called pastoral) theology is about how to use theological learning in practical situations using the methodologies of the social sciences to enable the task of theological reflection. The authors take the reader through the actual process of developing and carrying out a research project, using some of their own research as examples. Case studies include: the rise in spirituality, the decline in church attendance, evidence-based medicine compared to needs-led assessments, the growth in chaplaincy, and how it is understood as separate from parish ministry.

Valuing first-hand student engagement with living religious traditions is essential to provide extended learning opportunities in addition to traditional book knowledge, which still represents the overwhelming majority of the student learning experience on undergraduate courses of religion. Of course, at the heart of this issue are the retention of robust academic standards and the systemisation of learning opportunities outside the lecture theatre.

This systematising must come through two major approaches: firstly, understanding field visits and study tours as 'embedded pedagogy' and, secondly, by connecting efficient curriculum progression and suitable non-traditional assessment. We use the term 'embedded pedagogy' to mean two main things. Firstly, that direct personal experience of interaction with living religion should be a formulated and structured part of the wider campus-based degree programme for undergraduate students. Field visits must be used to support and extend lecture theatre learning – they must not be seen merely as 'added value' or 'extension activities'; the first step should be to integrate field visits into the relevant areas of traditionally taught, campus-based modules, and the logical next step is to create modules focused upon experiential learning and field visits. Put simply, engaging with living religion should be at the heart of an undergraduate's experience of religious studies, not merely an adjunct. Secondly, by 'embedded pedagogy' we mean that the learning experience provided to students by field visits and study tours should be highlighted as an effective way of deepening engagement with the knowledge provided by standardised learning which occurs in traditional lecture theatre teaching.

Selecting locations

Whilst the practicalities of time and cost will always be uppermost in the mind of those planning fieldwork exercises for undergraduates, it is important to give due thought to the type of location that can serve as a focus for students. Simple steps, such as taking students to a variety of denominations when a group is studying Christianity, rather than just to the dominant denomination in your area, are of course achievable; but it is often even more interesting to look at communities which provide a counterpoint to narratives of the lecture theatre. For example, whilst a classroom session on Buddhism may focus on historical development and divisions between Mahayana and Theravada traditions, a visit to a local Buddhist centre in the UK could well be to a Triratna Centre (previously called the Friends of the Western Order of Buddhists). Triratna centres are highly welcoming and fascinating religious communities, but they are hardly representative of 'all Buddhism' and thus serve as an excellent way of deconstructing and contextualising textbook approaches within a local context. This is also an excellent way of challenging the definitions of 'religion' and 'new religious movements' as categories that are often (unhelpfully) used to differentiate communities.

Preference the local, or fairly local – even when on-campus courses veer towards topics such as the historical development of Yoruba traditions in Western Africa, or the origins of the Mormon Church in America. A field visit to a (semi) local West African or Mormon group could be used to prompt discussion of migration, hybridity, economic and social movement, schism, diaspora and a multitude of other angles that enrich historical or content-based lecture room sessions. Preferencing the local also provides students with invaluable possibilities to perform follow-up visits themselves. When leading group visits, you are opening up new opportunities for undergraduates who may well lack the confidence to visit unfamiliar groups without support, but initial class visits, often introducing students to gatekeepers and familiarity with community structures, do, in our experience, make students much more likely to deepen engagement on their own time. Clearly, performing initial visits locally allows students to do this more frequently.

One issue we would raise at this point, however, is to beware of unconscious exoticism. As we have previously noted, much of the work underpinning our approach to this book comes from a collaborative project with UK universities, who already undertake much excellent practice with students with regard to neophyte fieldwork. However, one tendency that we did note during this research was a propensity to direct students – especially students undertaking supported but individual visits, or those on placements – to a wide range of 'alternative' or 'minority' traditions and communities, at the expense of more established communities. In one case, spiritualist churches, Kingdom Halls, Humanist associations and other relatively recent communities were used as case studies to visit for students, but the local parish church was not. Now, of course, all of the chosen communities can serve as excellent foci for fieldwork, but it seems to us a missed opportunity if an approach to 'Lived Religion' centred upon undergraduate engagement beyond the lecture theatre does not also reinvigorate how we approach so-called majority traditions. If we take Primiano as our starting point, as we do in chapters 1 and 2, we must look for the vernacular performance of religion in the familiar and 'mainstream' as much as in the less familiar and 'alternative'.

Another issue which is often raised is the relationship a student has with a given community, or the wider tradition in which the community may fall. This has deep theoretical implications, which we discuss briefly in the insider/outsider section of chapter 2; but for tutors and lecturers, there is a simple logistical issue as to whether or not you allow your students to study a tradition of their own, if, indeed, they consider themselves to have one. Of course, there are different approaches to this, and we have encountered universities that do not allow any student to undertake a research project based on fieldwork with a tradition that is their own. Others have allowed a more subtle dynamic of not allowing students to study the specific branch, community or denomination that they may belong to, but are happy for them to study a community within the wider worldview. There is no right or wrong approach to this, but we raise the issue to ensure that tutors reflect on how such decisions will impact upon student expectations and learning outcomes – indeed, you may well decide that you want students to particularly act inside or outside the environment of a specific tradition, especially if they are utilising theological reflection in a comparative framework.

Of course, it is not possible, nor indeed desirable, to preference the local when it comes to residential study tours either to another town or city within the country or abroad. Although the same advice applies about preferencing a diversity of traditions and not seeking to exoticise your subjects of study, within relevant contexts local to your tour, there are several approaches which can be taken which are specific to residential-based group visits, and which may help you to plan when thinking about future ventures. One approach is to undertake a tour based on a specific tradition of study – for example, we have taken students to Turkey to view the diversity of modern Muslim movements in Istanbul, and into the interior of the country, with its small villages and towns which are radically different from a modern cultural capital such as Istanbul. Such a tour can prioritise understanding of the diversity within modern communities in the context of key historical buildings and locations. A further approach is to base your visit within a specific community – several institutions we have worked with utilise ashrams or artistic communities in India, who are used to welcoming students from a range of university disciplines, as a base for a wider interdisciplinary learning experience with the continuity of a host community.

Another approach is to choose a location rather than a tradition, and undertake a mapping exercise of a specific city. We have undertaken this in New York, where Manhattan was used as the focus, and this allowed investigation of the migratory history of New York, engagement with commercial and cultural (food, music and theatre) influences from religious communities, and visits to communities as diverse as Catholicism, Scientology, Judaism (Orthodox and Reform), Unification Church, Ramakrishna Mission and many others. The advantage of using location rather than tradition as the focus of a tour is that it invariably offers up unexpected opportunities to visit communities and places that may not be immediately obvious or even originally a part of a set itinerary, but which often turn out, for students, to be the most enriching parts of the tour.

Preparing students

It is well understood that student attitudes towards learning will impact upon their learning outcomes. This is perhaps never more relevant than in non-conventional learning environments, or non-standard assessment requirements. By taking students out of the comfort zone of the lecture theatre and the, perhaps, slightly less comfortable but still all-too-familiar zone of standard format essay writing, student expectations are necessarily challenged and need careful management to ensure effective engagement with the subject matter and satisfactory outcomes for the student learning experience.

Managing these student expectations begins with careful management of staff expectations. Indeed, although religious studies often successfully provides methodologies of practical engagement for fieldwork regarding individual student research or project work, whole-class or group engagement in the field somewhat lags behind. Whilst there are, of course, isolated pockets of excellent practice in our subject, too often learning outside the lecture theatre is dismissed by colleagues as 'academia-lite'. Field visits, and we should be very careful here to use the word 'visit' not 'trip', are extra-curricular events that are often primarily understood in terms of marketing exercises, student-bonding mechanisms in induction week, or other simplistic approaches. Whilst not denying the importance of the social experience for students on such visits – indeed, it is at the heart of their learning experience if managed effectively – and the importance of making courses attractive and exciting for students, there needs to be a pedagogic reassessment of the place of the field visit or study tour in the undergraduate engagement with diverse religious traditions and communities.

Of course, managing students on field visits and study tours requires careful prior management of expectations to ensure the students understand what is expected of them, and so that they may engage effectively in a contextualised learning experience that is embedded within their wider curriculum. Managing student expectations of unfamiliar religious or social contexts is vital to a successful learning outcome for a study tour. The provision of a seminar series prior to departure, where students can become familiarised with relevant cultural, political and historical contexts both for the religion or religions in question, and for the specific context of those religions in the country in question, has contributed greatly to supporting students. One way of achieving this effectively is in group book reviewing, where the students engage in group discussion and presentations focused upon directed reading tasks. It might be interesting to base this on a contemporary account of the country in question so as to provide a specific context – for example, on a recent visit to Turkey, a book by a BBC Turkey correspondent, which specifically examined the role of Islam in politics in contemporary Turkey, in addition to the role of Muslim minority groups in the country, was chosen by one of the authors in preference to a 'standard' textbook on Islam (Morris, 2005).

In current textbooks on studying religion in the field, there is a tendency to concentrate on the specific etiquette that is required when visiting places of worship and we have covered this in chapter 4. However, it is our view that students require much greater contextual detail so as to engage effectively with specific situations and sites, and focused seminars are one way of achieving this. They also promote a deeper level of understanding of the expectations we have for students. Treating the study tour as a part of the wider curriculum, rather than an additional extra, will also reinforce these academic expectations.

Finally in this section on preparing students, every opportunity should be taken to allow staff to reflect on their own experience of travel and interaction with religious people and places, even if they haven't got a background in formal fieldwork training, as this will support the development of this area of curriculum; if we are asking students to see the value in encountering religion in everyday environments and in valuing learning outside the lecture theatre, having your own examples will underpin effective dialogue with students.

Logistics

In this book, we have tried to link recent developments in theoretical approaches to the study of religion to a new pedagogy which privileges engagement with lived religions rather than textbook religions. As such, we hope that we have offered food for thought with regard to *why* tutors should encourage their students to undertake neophyte fieldwork, and *how* they may do this with regard to tutor-led group visits. Of course, none of this happens in a vacuum, and tutors are each restricted (and hopefully supported) by the practical everyday pressures of teaching and researching within their own workloads. Whilst this is not a 'how to' section with regard to planning undergraduate fieldwork opportunities, the following should, however, be useful in highlighting key issues that often need addressing.

Practical planning advice

- Always scout locations for group visits wherever possible.
- Always try to arrange a 'host voice' for your community – although he or she may give information that is very different from an academic voice, it is precisely this dissonance between the multiple layers of narrative that allows deep engagement and discussion with students afterwards.
- Carry out any necessary risk assessment and comply with first aid requirements, including having a contact sheet, with emergency contact numbers and medical details, for every student on the visit.
- Ensure that you get permission from students for the use of any photographs they may be in.
- Ensure that your institution's insurance policy covers your exact activity – this is particularly important for international visits, for example to the West Bank in Palestine.
- Cost the project early and clearly – apart from the few lucky staff who work in institutions that fund visits, most tutors will need to encourage students to attend tours, as they will need to fund visits themselves.
- Ensure that sufficient staff ratios are present – usually 1:10 is sensible, and tour operators will usually grant a concessionary staff place for every ten paid-for students.
- If students are going on individual residential placements, ensure that adequate facilities are available with regard to food and board.
- Ensure that students, individually or collectively, do not stop communities from offering their normal services to devotees – this is a fine balance, of course, as many communities are delighted to welcome you and see educational work as a core part of their mission or religious life.
- Discuss with your institution and the community a sensible donation in lieu of your partnership with the community – this must be negotiated on an individual basis, as we have experienced communities that refuse all donations to those that have taken to chasing finance departments for payments, but seek clarification so that goodwill is retained for future years.
- Ensure that you include your host communities in any process of ethical clearance regarding the use of photographs, other media or student work in marketing, website repositories or other public-facing portals.

Above all, develop a relationship with individuals in the communities to ensure an effective working relationship.

Assessing students

If fieldwork is only used as an illustration of material which has already been explored and learned in other ways, then it is not fully embedded in the curriculum; it is merely an add-on, used perhaps to increase motivation or help students to bond as a group. These are worthwhile objectives but do not enable students to learn how to use fieldwork to study religion. If students are expected to take fieldwork seriously then, we argue, it has to be assessed. Assessment is judgement based on evidence, and there are various ways in which students can produce evidence of their learning for tutors to judge. Although by no means exhaustive, the following discussion illustrates some of the creative ways in which field visits and study tours are being assessed. Some of these examples come from the shared best practice of the HEA project.

Common assessment types

- pre-visit book reviews
- student presentations
- field journals
- portfolios
- fieldwork reports/reflective essays

The 'Golden Rule' of fieldwork assessment is that it should not be an exercise that students could have completed by simply visiting your university library – it is essential to differentiate the learning experience with field visit-specific assessment tasks.

We will discuss five different forms of assessment, and the first is the book review. The previously given example of a suitable book for student review as a part of a study tour to Turkey noted the ways in which the book helped students to understand a number of aspects of religion in the country. This pre-visit reading introduced a number of theoretical ideas relevant to the place being studied and also historical, political and religious material. Obviously the success of this form of assessment depends to a large extent on the quality and relevance of the book chosen, and whilst there are a number that would be useful for a visit to Istanbul, New York or Jerusalem, there is, for example, no obvious choice to inform a visit to Rome.

Often students are asked to make oral presentations, perhaps with a Power-Point presentation or other form of visual material – for example highlighting material religion they have engaged with – to explain what they have learned from a particular visit. These may be individual or group presentations and are probably most useful if they are fairly tightly focused. The method requires students to be physically present, talking about what they learned, and thereby mirrors one of the factors of fieldwork itself – students are bodily engaged in their own learning, and they are the researchers, the instruments for generating knowledge and understanding.

Evidence of this engagement in the field is often assessed through the use of field notes, or logs, which are either submitted in their entirety or extracted and used in other forms. For example, the field notes might include vivid descriptions of a place of worship or a particular street. Students are encouraged to be reflective about their own role and responses to experience, and to interpret and analyse what they encounter in dialogue with theories and ideas as well as previous understandings. The fieldwork is likely to raise more questions than answers, and it is in responding to these issues that students convey some of the nuances and complexities that make studying religion in the field so worthwhile.

The fourth method to be discussed is the portfolio. This can take many forms, and is often a mixture of extracts from field notes, photos and other material evidence from the field, and extended reflection (a narrative). The advantage of this is that students have ownership of the writing process – they decide what information and reflection should be given precedence. There are, of course, many different ways of assessing this reflective work – one way we have encountered is to accept the journals as working field documents that reflect immediacy and informality, and another is to set the students the task of writing a critical reflection of their own portfolio to be submitted with the collection of work. One advantage of this process is that students engage with field writing as a primary source, and reflect upon events and responses that are only possible due to their physical presence in the field.

We are particularly keen to promote assessments such as the above as we have also encountered assessments which simply revert to bibliographic learning and fixed lecture theatre-style engagement with religious 'content' rather than lived religious communities. One study tour of which we are aware took students to a major European city – teeming with a diversity of living religious communities – only to set them the task of writing an essay on a painting of their choice in one of the city's many art galleries. For us, this was a huge missed opportunity, as the students could have completed the exercise on campus as easily as on the study visit. This does not mean that essays have no place in assessing field visits and study tours, though – it is that the topic of focus must be reflective of fieldwork and related to religion as a living phenomenon. One such example could be setting students a written essay to reflect upon a visit to a place of worship, asking them to critically analyse how the host voices challenged, contradicted or complemented their previous 'textbook' reading of the religion in question. Such an exercise, although still technically a traditional essay, would demonstrate an awareness of emic and etic perspectives and the ways in which experiences may shape an informant's responses. Utilising this exercise to compare and contrast multiple site visits, perhaps to linked traditions, would mean that students are not only working with the similarities of and differences between 'textbook' and 'lived' religion, but also exploring the diversities amongst and within different communities. Like most of the assessment methods discussed here, there is no way of knowing in advance exactly what students will learn. By embedding fieldwork in the curriculum and assessing appropriately, students are enabled to generate knowledge and understanding of living religion.

Chapter summary

This final chapter has done two things. Firstly, we have extended the ideas and practices of engaging with living religion to a wider range of people than university undergraduates. We have briefly explored possibilities for postgraduate students, religious education teachers and trainee teachers, pastoral workers and those interested in interfaith dialogue. These suggestions come out of the experience of work we have done in fieldwork study of living religion with these various groups. Secondly, and finally, we have addressed university faculty – those people who are teaching courses in the study of religion. We discuss a range of topics which are relevant to using fieldwork, and this book, successfully on undergraduate courses.

Bibliography

This list includes all the texts referred to in the chapter and other recommended reading.

Baumann, G. 1996, *Contesting Culture: Discourses of Identity in Multi-Ethnic London*, Cambridge: Cambridge University Press.

Bergland, J. 2014, 'An Ethnographic Eye on Religion in Everyday Life' in *British Journal of Religious Education*, 36(1), 39–52.

Coakley, S. 2013, *God, Sexuality and the Self*, Cambridge: Cambridge University Press.

Cush, D. and Robinson, C. 2014, 'Developments in Religious Studies: Towards a Dialogue with Religious Education' in *British Journal of Religious Education*, 36(1), 4–17.

Fry, H., Montagu, R. and Scholefield, L. (eds) 2005, *Women's Voices*, London: SCM Press.

Gregg, S.E. and Scholefield, L. 2011, 'The Student Learning Experience in Religious Studies Field Visits and Study Tours: Managing Expectations and Outcomes' in *Discourse*, 10(3).

Jackson, R. 2012, *Religion, Education, Dialogue and Conflict: Perspectives on Religious Education Research*, London: Routledge.

——1997, *Religious Education: An Interpretive Approach*, London: Hodder Education.

McClintock Fulkerson, M. 2007, *Places of Redemption: Theology for a Worldly Church*, Oxford: Oxford University Press.

Miller, J., O'Grady, K. and McKenna, U. (eds) 2013, *Religion in Education: Innovation in International Research*, London: Routledge.

Morris, C. 2005, *The New Turkey: The Quiet Revolution on the Edge of Europe*, London: Granta.

Nesbitt, E. 2004, *Intercultural Education: Ethnographic and Religious Approaches*, Eastbourne: Sussex Academic Press.

Scharen, C.B. 2012, *Explorations in Ecclesiology and Ethnography*, Grand Rapids, MI: Eerdmans.

——and Vigen, A.M. 2011, *Ethnography as Christian Theology*, London: Continuum.
Swinton, J. and Mowat, H. 2011, *Practical Theology and Qualitative Research*, London: SCM Press.
Ward, P. 2012, *Perspectives in Ecclesiology and Ethnography*, Grand Rapids, MI: Eerdmans.
Wolcott, H.F. 2001, *The Art of Fieldwork*, New York: AltaMira Press.

Websites

This annotated list includes all the online sources we have referred to in the chapter as well as some recommended sites. We have given the URLs (web addresses) accessed on 31.10.14 but these do change so for ease of use we have listed them by the name of the organisation in alphabetical order.

Cambridge Inter-Faith Programme at the University of Cambridge has excellent resources for anyone interested in interfaith dialogue and particularly scriptural reasoning. This specific web address is to a fascinating account by Prof. David Ford, the founder of this programme, of a recent journey to China to explore how this particular form of dialogue would work in that context. www.interfaith.cam.ac.uk/

The Council for Learning Outside the Classroom is the national voice for learning outside the classroom for 0–19 year olds. It is not specifically about the study of religion although it does have a small section on sacred spaces which would be very useful for any teacher or trainee teacher. www.lotc.org.uk/what-is-lotc/where-lotc/sacred-spaces/

DISKUS. This is the journal of the British Association for the Study of Religion (BASR). It is online and peer reviewed. There are articles about the theoretical aspects of the study of religions and examples of work done in the field. www.basr.ac.uk/

Education about Religions and Beliefs is a United Nations Alliance of Civilisations website, acting as a clearing house for discussion and debate related to teaching about religions. http://erb.unaoc.org

Fieldwork in Religion is an internationally peer-reviewed, interdisciplinary journal which publishes articles, review essays and book reviews relevant to the theoretical engagement with and practical undertaking of fieldwork in religion. www.equinoxpub.com/journals/index.php/FIR

Religion Bulletin is the blog site of the *Bulletin for the Study of Religion* published by Equinox where contributors discuss issues in the study of religion. www.equinoxpub.com/blog/

The Religious Studies Project. A really good link to scholarly approaches to religious studies. www.religiousstudiesproject.com/ For Bettina Schmidt's podcast see: www.religiousstudiesproject.com/podcast/podcast-bettina-schmidt-on-doing-anthropological-fieldwork/

RE-ONLINE is a good source of material and ideas for RE teachers and trainees. You can use it for some interactive things like 'email a believer'. www.reonline.org.uk

Research Methods for the Study of Religion: University of Kent. This is probably the best website for excellent articles and select bibliographies about a whole range of different ways of studying living religion. www.kent.ac.uk/religionmethods/index.html

RE Today Services is a resource for religious education that, interestingly, features pictures of students engaging with living religion on its home page. www.retoday.org.uk

Runnymede Trust is an independent race equality think tank in the UK. Although involved with wider issues of race and ethnicity, there have been several initiatives very relevant to the study of religion, including the recent New Muslims report which examines the diversities of British Muslim identity. www.runnymedetrust.org

St Ethelburga's Centre for Reconciliation and Peace has developed many interesting ways to bring people into dialogue and reconciliation and to build relationships across divisions of conflict, culture and religion. www.stethelburgas.org

Teaching Across Religions of South Asia is a website aimed at staff, not students, but it is very accessible and will help you to explore the ways in which people practice, think about and identify with religious traditions in South Asia and the South Asian diaspora which frequently cut across established boundaries of what constitutes 'religion'. http://tarosaproject.wordpress.com/

Warwick Religions and Education Research Unit is a long-running research unit with an international reputation and focus. Based on Robert Jackson's ideas about interpretive religious education, the unit has undertaken ethnographic work, curriculum and pedagogical development, and wider international research. www2.warwick.ac.uk/fac/soc/ces/research/wreru/

Index

174   *Index*

Gandhi, M.K. 32, 71
'gay-cure' theology 73
Geaves, R. 123
Geertz, Clifford 18, 19, 116, 127, 128
Gender Trouble (Butler) 25
Genesis 58
genocide museums 83
ghettos, Jewish 75, 83
Ghosts of Spain (Tremlett) 42–43
Gilhus, I.S. 14
Gillespie, Marie 146–47
Glastonbury, Southern England 60,
 77–80, 84, 86, 146; Chalice Well
 Gardens 78, 79; Goddess Temple 79,
 80, 84; High Street 78, 79; Thorn 77, 78
God 19, 58, 125; *see also murtis* (Hindu
 deities)
Goddess movement 3
Goddess Temple, Glastonbury 79, 80, 84
Goldberg, M. 11
Gorman, Michael 142
Gospels 61
graffiti 67
Gregg, S.E. 35
Ground Zero, New York 74, 76
group fieldwork 85–104; assessment 103;
 background research 88; difficult issues
 92–94; etiquette 88–92; journal/
 note-taking 101–2, 125; longer study
 visits 85; participant observation and
 data collection 94–101; preparing for
 visit to place of worship 87–88; short
 study visits 85; starting points 86–87;
 study tours 85; suggestions for group
 visit 100–101; technology 102–3;
 types 85
Guardian, The 72
Guest, M. 21
guests, group fieldwork 88
gurdwara (Sikh place of worship) 91,
 98–99; Gurdwara Sri Guru Singh
 Sabha, Sikh temple (Southall) 8, 57
Guru Granth Sahib (Sikh scriptures) 91,
 98–99
Guterman, M. 93

Hadden, J.K. 137
Hagia Sophia museum (Istanbul)
 56–57, 59
Haitian Vodou 3, 64
Hajj (pilgramage to Mecca) 44, 64
halakhic (Jewish religious) law 36
Halevi, Judah 47
Haram al-Sharif, Jerusalem 141

Haraway, Donna 24
Hardy, Alister 122, 126
Hare Krishna movement 9, 69
Harvey, Graham 2, 4, 15, 33, 34, 40, 66,
 100, 106, 130; *Food, Sex and Strangers*
 7; *Religions in Focus* 12
head covering 88
HeartMath Solution, The (Childre and
 Martin) 98
Hebrew language 90, 91
Hebrew Scriptures 32
Heelas, Paul 131
Helland, C. 137, 138, 143
Henderson, Bobby 33
Hesse-Biber, S.N. 16–17
'high culture' religious art 68
Hill-Smith, C. 144, 145
Hinduism 1, 2, 8, 111; and academic
 study of religion 14, 23, 31, 32, 36;
 ashrams 86, 90, 93, 150; group
 fieldwork 87, 90, 93; *murtis* (Hindu
 deities) 90, 93; places of worship 57,
 58; Vedas 31
Hiroshima, Japan 76
Hogarth, William 69
Holm, Jean 80
Holocaust museums 62, 74–75, 84, 125
horizontal learning 46
Hubbard, L. Ron (founder of
 Scientology) 61
Humanist associations 162

Ibn Battutah 47
Icelandic liberals 28–29
identity: communal 8, 29, 66, 69; cultural
 57, 131; English 77; ethical 71; group
 66; interrelated identities 2; as
 performance 25; religious *see* religious
 identity; self-identity 4, 29, 58; sense of
 9, 86; and worldview 28
image worship 32
Indigenous Religions 15
Industrial Revolution 78
informed consent 123, 124
Ingold, Tim 95
insideness/outsideness 29–30
Institute for Jewish Policy Research 27
Institute of HeartMath 97–98
institutions 3–4
interfaith practice 158–59
Inter-Faith Programme, Cambridge
 University 158, 169
International Association of
 Scientologists 35

'Women Who Scream' (impressionist
  tale) 128–29
Woodhead, Linda 36, 131
'Word' of God 31
World Religions paradigm 4, 14, 15,
  87, 156
World War I and II Graveyards 76
worship, places of *see* places of
  worship
writing: fieldwork, writing up 41,
  43, 88, 127–30; and reflection
  41–42

Yad Vashem (Holocaust museum,
  Jerusalem) 62, 74–75, 125
Yip, A.K.-T. 25
yoga 57
Young, G. 137–38
'Young Earth Creationist' Christians,
  US 31
youth workers 158

Zanzibar, Africa 75
Zine, J. 33
Zionism 11, 53